SEXUAL POLITICS AND THE MALE PLAYWRIGHT

SEXUAL POLITICS AND THE MALE PLAYWRIGHT

The Portrayal of Women in Ten Contemporary Plays

by GEETHA RAMANATHAN

McFarland & Company, Inc., Publishers
Jefferson, North Carolina, and London

Excerpts from the following plays are reproduced by permission:

Woyzeck by Georg Büchner, transl. Theodore Hoffman, in Eric Bentley, ed., *The Modern Theatre: 5 Plays* (Garden City, N.Y.: Doubleday, 1955). • *The Father* by August Strindberg, in Elizabeth Sprigge, transl., *Six Plays of Strindberg* (Garden City, N.Y.: Doubleday, 1955). Copyright 1955 by Elizabeth Sprigge; reprinted by permission of Curtis Brown, Ltd. • *Henry IV* by Luigi Pirandello, transl. Edward Storer, in Eric Bentley, ed., *Naked Masks: Five Plays* (New York: Dutton, 1952). Translation copyright 1922 by E.P. Dutton. Renewed 1950 in the names of Stefano, Fausto and Lietta Pirandello. Used by permission of Dutton Signet, a division of Penguin Books USA Inc. • *Marat/Sade* by Peter Weiss, in Günther Busch, ed., *Die Verfolgung und Ermordung Jean Paul Marats Dargestellt Durch Die Schauspielgruppe des Hospizes zu Charenton Unter Anleitung des Herrn de Sade* (Frankfurt am Main: Suhrkamp Verlag, 1964). Reprinted by permission of Suhrkamp Verlag. • *The Good Person of Szechwan* by Bertolt Brecht: copyright 1955 by Suhrkamp Verlag, Berlin; translation copyright 1985 by Stefan S. Brecht. Reprinted from *The Good Person of Szechwan* by Bertolt Brecht; translated from the German by John Willett; edited by John Willett and Ralph Mannheim. Published by Arcade Publishing, New York. • *The Physicists* by Friedrich Dürrenmatt, transl. James Kirkup (New York: Grove Press, 1964). Used by permission of Grove/Atlantic, Inc. • *Plenty* by David Hare (Garden City, N.Y.: Doubleday, 1978). Used by permission of Faber and Faber Ltd. • *The Ruling Class* by Peter Barnes, in *Collected Plays of Peter Barnes* (London: Heinemann, 1981). Reprinted by permission of Methuen London. • *The Hothouse* by Harold Pinter: excerpts are from *The Hothouse: A Play* (New York: Grove, 1980). Used by permission of Grove/Atlantic, Inc. • *What the Butler Saw* by Joe Orton, in *Joe Orton: The Complete Plays* (London: Grove Press, 1986). Used by permission of Grove/Atlantic, Inc.

British Library Cataloguing-in-Publication data are available

Library of Congress Cataloguing-in-Publication Data

Ramanathan, Geetha.
Sexual politics and the male playwright : the portrayal of women in ten contemporary plays / by Geetha Ramanathan.
p. cm.
Includes bibliographical references (p.) and index.
ISBN 0-7864-0063-3 (lib. bdg. : 50# alk. paper)
1. Drama—20th century—History and criticism. 2. Women in literature. 3. Sex role in literature. 4. Men dramatists—Political and social views. I. Title.
PN1650.W65R36 1996
809.2'9352042—dc20 95-45246
CIP

Manufactured in the United States of America

McFarland & Company, Inc., Publishers
Box 611, Jefferson, North Carolina 28640

For Usha and Vishu
Radha and K.V. R.

Contents

Preface

When I initially got involved with modernist dramatic texts, I was intrigued and moved by the male playwrights' intense commitment to vindicating the outsider. While I was fascinated by their indictment of society's fabrication of difference and marginality as insane and exterior to the self, I was deeply disturbed by the critical reception of the plays. Most readings of these canonical works seemed to me to be completely sympathetic to the motivations of the male characters, whose actions were often hostile and indeed violent to the female characters. I set out to discover why I could not conjure up the same sympathy that many of the authorized readers of the play expressed and about a year down the road discovered that it was quite simply because I was a female reader. Feminist criticism confirmed my visceral response to the plays.

The project became larger as I sought texts which did give pride of place to female characters. Was gender ideology substantially different in these plays because of the casting of the female as hero? In general I chose plays that I was taught as being representative of the great modernist tradition of innovation. I felt there was some value in rereading these texts from vantage points that were not exclusively formalist and universalist. At the very least, a feminist perspective would cast doubt on the unquestioning celebration of the male marginal as heroic and the playwrights as progressive.

I opted to open the texts by discussing the vitally important articulation between ideology and form. Such a move, I believed, would enable me to reread canonical texts. I chose to work with a set of plays that had intertextual connections and considered that the study would be more useful if I did not confine it to a very restricted period. Needless to say, my choices were impelled by my own personal engagement with these works and by my intuitive sense that the plays were marked by a certain ideological trauma regarding gender. Because I was concerned with exploring the relationship between marginality, sexuality, ideology and form I restricted myself to those canonical texts that explored these themes in dramatically progressive modes. I confined myself to a particular European theatrical cluster to lend focus to my study and set a cultural frame that would enable me to locate gendered subjectivities in sharper terms. I did not wish to collapse different theatrical traditions; nor did I want to merge very different cultural gender ideologies. While I was very interested in the work of female playwrights I felt that their versions of sexual politics were the subject of another book. After much soul searching, I finally settled on Büchner's *Woyzeck,* Strindberg's *The Father,* Pirandello's *Henry IV,* Weiss's *Marat/Sade,* Brecht's *Good Person of Szechwan,* Dürrenmatt's *The Physicists,* Hare's *Plenty,* Barnes's *The Ruling Class,* Pinter's *The Hothouse* and Orton's *What the Butler Saw.*

The advice and objections of professors Jim Hurt, Herbert Knust, Ruth Lorbe and Janet Smarr of the University of Illinois at Urbana–Champaign on reading very early versions of sections of the manuscript were useful. I appreciate their energy and time. I would also like to thank the University of Illinois' Unit for Criticism and Interpretive Theory for its colloquium series. Conversations I had following events in the colloquium inform my work in pervasive if intangible ways. The Academic Computer Staff at West Chester University have been unfailingly helpful. The College of Arts and Sciences at West Chester University kindly defrayed the costs of acquiring permissions from publishers to quote from texts. On a more personal note, I am grateful to Valerian De Sousa for his help throughout this project. Neus Bonet-Farran and Mona Fayad listened to my endless tales of difficulties associated with the project and asked me to shut up only once every ten times. I thank these three for helping me to keep my sanity.

Introduction

Traditional approaches to the study of drama have come under siege in the last thirty years. Semiotics, performance studies, poststructuralist approaches, Marxist readings, spectator analyses, feminist perspectives, to name a few, have altered the ways in which we read and view plays. Among the most compelling of these remappings of the field are the feminist interventions. Sue Ellen Case, in her pioneering *Feminism and Theatre,* discusses the complex articulation between the various kinds of feminism and forms of theatre within a materialist framework. She also deconstructs the classic male dramatic canon. She notes that early feminist work registered the invisibility of women as playwrights until the early seventeenth century (Case 1988, 7). Theatre historians are now publishing and distributing the works of women playwrights to make women's voices heard. Their efforts take the form of anthologies and critical texts on women playwrights. Helene Keyssar's *Feminist Theatre* (1985), Lynda Hart's collection *Making a Spectacle: Feminist Essays on Contemporary Women's Theatre* (1989), and Enoch Brater's collection *Feminine Focus: The New Women Playwrights* (1989) are a few of the critical texts that pay attention to women playwrights.

Feminist deconstructive readings of traditional texts are also being produced. In studying classical all-male productions, feminist critics have observed that the roles of women were cultural fabrications (Case 1988, 7). These classical plays did not represent women as they might have been historically, but constructed femininity. This is most clearly revealed in Aeschylus's *Oresteia,* where Athena casts her vote against the Furies in favor of Orestes, who has committed matricide. Radical feminist critic Mary Daly argues that the playwright establishes a patriarchal tradition that covers over a matrilineal heritage (Daly 1978). The exclusion of women is spelled out by Apollo's speech which splits the female body in an originary moment of violence that formulates the culture:

> The woman you call the mother of the child
> is not the parent, just a nurse to the seed,

> the new-sown seed that grows and swells inside her.
> The *man* is the source of life—the one who mounts
> ["The Eumenides," lines 665–70, *Oresteia*].

Among those feminist theatre historians who have ventured to reread the male canon is Michelene Wandor, who is also a pioneer in the work she has done to stage and publish women's plays. In *Look Back in Gender* (1987), Wandor turns to the modern British play. She maintains that the inclusion of gender as a category of analysis alters the way we perceive the text. She politicizes postwar British drama. Wandor's historical specificity makes it possible for her to suggest causes for male typologies of female characterization and also to draw conclusions about the relationships between men and women at the time the play was written/produced.

Attention has also been paid to the woman as spectator, notably by Jill Dolan in her foray into modern American theatre in *The Feminist Spectator as Critic* (1988). Her focus is on performance and spectacle. Dolan also has a reconstructive vision and offers examples of texts that do not objectify women. While much feminist work has been done to remedy the invisibility of women as actors, playwrights, and readers/viewers, much still remains to be done. Reading as a woman is still a fragile enterprise because it demands both unlearning and relearning.

Feminist research on women as viewers has been explored extensively by film scholars. Laura Mulvey in "Visual Pleasure and Narrative Cinema" argues that the congealment of the diegesis, the space of the narrative or the recounted story, was structurally endemic to classic Hollywood cinema because of the display of the female body. Using a politicized version of psychoanalysis, she observes that the pleasures of looking, voyeurism, and scopophilia accrued to the male in the diegesis and to the audience because the diegesis placed the woman as "to-be-looked-at." The woman became the object of the male gaze (Mulvey 1975, 6–18). Mulvey takes recourse to cinematic coding to demonstrate her thesis. Her view is that the female, if she identified with the passive female on-screen, would enjoy a very masochistic pleasure. Certainly, the male was the active player, and the female was the passive object in these texts.

B. Ruby Rich's rebuttal of Mulvey's argument is instructive. She frames the problem of the female viewer of male texts in general terms and concludes by conferring a certain power on the female viewer to produce meaning for herself, a meaning that may empower her rather than disempower her:

> For a woman's experience of culture under patriarchy is dialectical in a way that a man's can never be: our experience is like that of the exile, whom Brecht once singled out as ultimate dialectician for that daily working out

> of cultural oppositions within a single body. It is crucial to emphasize here the possibility for texts to be transformed at the level of reception and not to fall into a trap of condescension toward our own developed powers as active producers of meaning [Rich 1990, 278].

The feminist critic, by working dialectically—inside and outside the text—can both derive pleasure from the text and yet put male constructions of femininity under scrutiny. In so doing, she winds her way out of the masochistic position of identifying exclusively with the female character who may be the object of enunciation and who may also be visually shackled. The dialectical mode enables the female viewer to transform the meaning of the text without giving up pleasure.

In adopting a feminist framework to study modernist theatre, does the critic give up the pleasure of the text/performance because of the relentless sustained scrutiny of the female in the text, the positioning of the female reader/viewer outside the text? Does it take the fun away? Annette Kuhn's notion that such feminist strategies denaturalize or demystify what appears natural is accurate (Kuhn 1982, 3–21). Unearthing the hidden brings its own pleasure. Kuhn would have the female viewer be "passionate[ly] detached" (Kuhn 1982, 3). Dialectical viewing, the split viewing that the female reader perforce engages in, is another incarnation of Kuhn's passionate detachment. Weaving outside the text confers power, winding back inside grants pleasure.

Looking at the male canon of modern drama brings the feminist critic to a standstill. Many canonized European playwrights from the mid–nineteenth century on have attempted to be socially progressive and have, in one sense or another, worked with the form to produce change in the audience. Going on this traditional journey from Büchner to Orton, or various other versions thereof, by weaving outside and winding inside enables us to produce new readings that chart the genealogy of difference.

Of the many modernist plays that we could study to carve out feminist spaces in the field of drama studies, I chose those that had staked a claim to representing marginality and that have traditionally been taught and studied as extraordinarily innovative and progressive texts. I myself derived pleasure from them for many years because they spoke from a marginal place and in a different voice. They try to "speak the mad" (Derrida 1978, 31–64). I have deliberately refrained from using feminist theatre as a counterpoint. Juxtapositioning two or three feminist texts to the male canon would be to tokenize them and place them within a male framework.

Bringing a feminist perspective to the canon while grappling with the construction of marginality in the text, weaving and winding, involves double vision. "Revisioning" the canon has meant bringing traditional drama criticism, feminist theory, and semiotics together. In doing so, I oscillate between looking at woman's imaging to looking again at her construction in relationship to the representation of the marginal.

Madness, as a rhetorical and dramatic element in the text, does not immediately invite identification. It has the potential to alienate the reader into a posture of observation. The axis of identification between audience and character is broken when the audience acknowledges the character's madness. The text refuses to create "illusionistic" theatre, or theatre where the production would disguise its status as a play. Anti-Aristotelean, modernist plays on madness displace the spectator and place him/her in shifting ideologically contradictory positions. They do not reconfirm the male viewer's image of himself in any simple way, but challenge it in diverse ways. The depiction of the split self in these plays quarrels with universal notions of subjectivity. Neither the male in the play nor the male reader outside can count on a sense of self that is secure or on any authority in the social world. Because these playwrights are not mouthpieces for the dominant ideology and do interrogate the audience, their representation of women might be more dignifying of women than blatantly sexist modes and genres.

Critical studies on madness in modern plays have concentrated on debating whether the mad person is really mad or not, on analyzing the character of the protagonist, and on universalizing the protagonist's situation to include, first, men and women, and second, all humanity—all classes, all people (Hayse 1976, Feder 1980, Rosen 1983, Robbins 1984, Cohn 1991). Whether psychological, structural, mythical, or inter-personal, and however informative and interesting, the scholarship on madness effaces the sexual politics of the plays. The neutral cast attributed to the "breakdown" or psychic collapse of the character universalizes the mad to recuperate differences between the sane and mad. Consequently, the implied reader is seemingly neutral, obviously male, and lies within the Aristotelean trajectory. The most sophisticated of analyses of these plays as metatheatre stumble into traditional male identification patterns.

Winding inside the text, weaving outside it will empower the female reader to produce feminist readings of these texts and thereby make a space for the feminist reader.

Part I

Male Marginality and the Female Body

Chapter 1

Male Subjectivity and the Female Body: Büchner's *Woyzeck*

> In former times one saw Jaels against Siseras, Judiths against Holofemeses, Charlotte Cordays against Marats, now it must be men who employ this mania, it is the women who are in command now. *I, Pierre Rivière* (Foucault 1975, 108)

Georg Büchner's *Woyzeck* (1836–37), first performed in 1913, startled its audience by its formal innovativeness, its interest in the psychology of the victim, and its radical critique of social structures. The play, though written in the middle of the nineteenth century, displays a tantalizing commitment to depart from the closed structure of the traditional drama. Richard Hornby notes that "Büchner may simply have intended to flesh out the scenes later" (Hornby 1984, 46). Where the traditional play is ordered into five discrete units, *Woyzeck* is composed of a series of scenes that are linked together by an associational logic. Indeed, the sequence itself is largely editorial since we do not know what order Büchner intended. The play strives to achieve new effects, which today we would call cinematic montage: it uses images that are clustered or juxtaposed to produce meaning. The fragments that attempt to depict Woyzeck's interiority do not follow a linear sequence of events that leads to an inevitable conclusion. The fragments seem to contest with each other in an attempt to problematize the audience's response. The play certainly challenges the notion of a self-enclosed, autonomous, coherent dramatic world in its rapid shifts from image to image. Hornby comments on the difficulty involved in producing a play with 28 scenes. The text also demands that the director decide whether Woyzeck is mad or not, whether the murderer is motivated internally or externally (Hornby 1984, 49). Hornby himself wanted the play performed as incomplete, as ambiguities to be played through. He also staged several events simultaneously in order to show the complexity of the action. In his production, when the audience first enters, they see soldiers around the building, Woyzeck shaving the captain, Marie telling stories, and the doctor engaged in experiments (Hornby 1984, 53). The performance stressed the fluidity of form.

Erwin Rosenthal (1965, 273–74) states that Büchner rejects the form of the classical theatre and describes Büchner's use of the "open" form:

> Diese Dramenform (geschlossen oder tektonisch) weist Büchner energisch zurück. Ihm scheint die Szenengliederung wichtiger als die Einteilung in Akte (die beim *Woyzeck* nicht einmal besteht); die Ganzheit und Einheit, als Prinzip wenigstens wird zerschlagen; die Sprache ist nicht des "gehobenen Tons," sondern benutzt jedmögliche Nuancen des Alltags, vielfacettierter also und charakeristischer für die einzelnen Personen und Begebenheiten als im "tektonischen Drama."[Büchner rejected the closed or "techtonic" form of drama forcefully. The structure of the scenes seemed more important to him than the division into acts (which does not occur in *Woyzeck* even once); totality and unity, at least as principles, are shattered; the language is not elevated but uses the tints of everyday language whenever possible; consequently it is more multi-dimensional and more characteristic of individual persons and incidents than in the "techtonic" drama.]

The play is characteristically modern in that it captures an individual's subjective impressions in a nonlinear fashion. Büchner's manipulation of point of view in the play, which is composed of fragments, magnifies the play's aura of modernity. Despite the play's overall deconstructive gestures in presenting fragments, the fragments are connected to make an informed comment on the relationship between the mad subject's subjectivity and his need to possess the female body. The depiction of Woyzeck's class ressentiment during the opening sections is not at counterpurposes with his jealousy during the latter half. The fragments' formal disparateness works to highlight Woyzeck's difficulties in reconciling his class consciousness with his class ideology and gender ideology.

The play opens with Woyzeck, the barber, who is minion to his employer, the captain. He is also the object of scientific experimentation for the doctor. Woyzeck tells us that he is devoted to Marie, the woman he lives with. When she is unfaithful to him, he kills her. The play's basic "story" has a historical reference point. Albert Meier, who documents the sources of the play, charts the manner in which Büchner might have experimented with the dramatization of the story of the 41-year-old Johann Christian Woyzeck, who had killed his lover, Johanna Christiane Woost, in Leipzig on June 21 (Meier 1980, 18). When the case came up for trial, the issue of Woyzeck's insanity was raised. Apart from this criminal case, the case of Pierre Rivière of Normandie, who murdered his mother, sister, and brother in 1835, has some bearing on Büchner's theme and technique in *Woyzeck*. Pierre Rivière was apprehended for his crime and wrote his memoirs, in which he explained the circumstances and motivations that drove him to kill his mother, brother, and sister and attempted to justify his actions. Rivière indicated that he had committed the murders in order to regain the power that men of that age had lost to women (Foucault 1975, 108). Büchner does not explicitly attribute the same motive to Woyzeck, but he points in that direction fairly clearly. As Meier states, Büchner does attempt to present things from Woyzeck's point of view. Meier (1980, 20) describes the similarities between Rivière's and Büchner's texts:

> Büchner hat mit seinem *Woyzeck* Ähnliches unternommen: die Entwicklung zu einem Verbrechen von der Situation des Täters aus darzustellen und zu erklären. Die literarische Struktur des *Woyzeck* simuliert die Selbstdarstellung bzw. gibt ihr Surrogat, indem Woyzecks Umwelt vorherrschend im Bezug auf diesen dargestellt wird, so dass das Geschehen im Drama im wesentlichen in der Perspektive Woyzecks erscheint und von seiner Person aus verständlich wird. [Büchner undertook a similar project with his *Woyzeck:* to represent and clarify the development of a situation to the perpetration of a crime from the perspective of the perpetrator. The literary structure of *Woyzeck* simulates this self-representation, or substitutes for it, as the case may be in that Woyzeck's surroundings are primarily presented with respect to the above so that the acts in the play are essentially seen from Woyzeck's perspective and are understood through his character.]

The initial sequences of *Woyzeck* do image a world tinted by the colors with which Woyzeck imbues it, and we understand the world from his subjective version of it. The subjectivity of his vision is, however, validated because it is seen within the framework of a class system that is objectively presented. In revealing the oppressiveness of the class system, Büchner sanctions Woyzeck's reading of it. His "madness" is rendered as his subjectivity: his ability to perceive his position vis-à-vis his class superiors. By the same token, the exposure of the captain's and doctor's manipulations clarifies that Woyzeck's madness is a function of their construction of him as Other. The imaginative hypostatization of Woyzeck as Other allows Büchner to denaturalize the seemingly intrinsic power of the dominant group to name, define, and objectify. We, the audience, are caught within a dialectical movement because we experience Woyzeck's interiority while we also grasp society's appraisal of him. The later sequences focus on Marie's victimization and specifically challenge the female viewer's "understanding" of Woyzeck's plight. Far from hiding from the social by recourse to the psychological as Lukács claimed, Büchner by speaking of gender relations makes explicit connections between the conditions of Woyzeck's class subservience and gender positionality (Lukács 1951, 66–69).

The complex issues that the text evokes through a series of sharp, jagged scenes have led to doubt about the dominant theme of the play. Büchner's interest in depicting the world of Woyzeck through Woyzeck's eyes invites a psychological interpretation. The description of the class system calls for a Marxist interpretation. The fact that Büchner did refer to a contemporary account of a man named Woyzeck who was indicted for the murder of the woman he was living with makes it viable for us to read the play as a Zolaesque account of brutalization and victimization of the lower classes. The choice of a protagonist who resembles an Albee character more closely than he does a Shakespearean hero suggests that *Woyzeck* is characteristic of a new kind of tragedy that highlighted the interest in the commoners. Indeed, the play has been read with emphasis on the economic, the material, the naturalistic, the metaphysical, the social, the psychological and the universal (respectively, Dosenheimer 1949, 66; Lukács 1951, 66–69; Stern 1964, 118, and Schwarz 1978, 104; Hauser 1974, 122; Richards 1977, 189; Otten 1978, 125; Eskelund 1982, 43). Attention has been paid to the sexual leitmotif in the text, both in productions of the play and in the criticism. It has been examined most elaborately by Dunne, who asserts that the play argues in favor of a more "natural" attitude to sexuality (Dunne 1990, 294). Interesting and informative as these readings are, they nevertheless ignore the construction of gendered subjectivity in the text. The Mitbestimmung or concurrence of the critic allows him/her to make the liberal humanist gesture of sympathizing with both oppressor and victim because of an increased understanding of them. While the female spectator is caught in the dialectic produced by the text's structure, the female withholds her sympathy for the male and resists universal understanding.

Büchner attempts to show that Woyzeck was perceived as mad by the doctor. By showing us the doctor's single-minded obsession with proving that Woyzeck is mad, Büchner indicates that Woyzeck's "disturbance" is a response to the pressures the doctor and the captain impose on him. Ironically, Büchner's caricature of the doctor almost persuades us that the doctor is demented. Woyzeck's responses can be understood as a sign of the marginalized Other's class ressentiment. Woyzeck can articulate his anger, but the doctor and the captain, his oppressors, have a stake in silencing him. Both of them are shown as tyrannical and arbitrary in their conduct toward him. Thus, in the opening section, through his portrayal of Woyzeck as victim of the doctor and captain, and by extension, society at large, Büchner persuades us that the play will emerge a radical indictment of society.

By validating Woyzeck's critique and showing the doctor and captain as oppressors, Büchner constructs Woyzeck's subjectivity. Marie's infidelity threatens his notion of manhood which has remained intact even during the challenges issued to his sanity by the captain and doctor. Woyzeck has loved

Marie and has also believed that she was the cardinal certainty in his life. His subjectivity, his authority in the "symbolic" in the realm of language and law controlled by the Name of the Father, is closely tied in to his relationship with Marie (Gallop 1982). As long as she remains faithful to him, his manhood is not called into question. Although Woyzeck's intelligence is mocked, his perceptions are challenged, and his rationality is questioned, his sense of his manhood is not shaken. Hornby believes that "castration fear [is] expressed through Woyzeck's sexual impotence" (Hornby 1984, 48). It is interesting that Hornby asserts Woyzeck's sexual impotence, surely a transference of the character's social inadequacies. Hans Wetzel points out that the third version of the text implies a sexual motive to the murder: "Nicht nur die beiden, in deren Dienst sich Woyzeck aufreibt, richten ihn zugrunde. Weit mehr treibt ihn das sexuelle Verlangen seiner Geliebeten, vor dem er, der Verhetzte und Abgearbeitete, versagt, und ihre Untreue in die Verzweiflung" [Not only these two (doctor and captain) in whose service Woyzeck is worn down destroy him. The sexual demands of his lover drive him to a greater extent; he—the exhausted and overworked—failed and is in despair over her unfaithfulness.] (Wetzel 1992, 242). Büchner implies that Woyzeck's perception of who he is, is inextricably twined with his sense of his manhood. When Marie is unfaithful, he loses possession of the female body which is a precondition of his coherent male subjectivity. All semblance of order in his life is now a question of the past. His sense of subjectivity collapses. The two strands in the play—the social and the psychological—are problematized by the jealousy motif, which highlights the personal but situates it within the public domain. Woyzeck's distress at Marie's infidelity indicates that he shared dominant nineteenth-century beliefs about women and their roles in life. The woman is expected to be faithful to her lover, the father of her child. Her unfaithfulness brands her morally and lays her open to the male's wrath. We are now critical of Woyzeck's politics.

Marie's unconscious assertion of her right over her own body unwittingly places her in a liberatory posture which invites the female spectator to align herself with the woman against the man. It is a marginal spectatorial position which the female spectator cannot accept because of Büchner's portrayal of Marie as the crippled object and victim of class and patristic structures. When Woyzeck murders Marie, the female viewer is momentarily seduced into feeling that society has no choice but to punish Woyzeck in the interest of its own sanity and safety. Thus, we too occupy the position of the Other and question and resist the protagonist's actions. Curiously, the "open-endedness" of the initial scenes is contradicted by the closure at the end. The ordering of scenes seems to indicate that the play will not come to a well-defined closure, but will allow the audience to come to its own conclusion about the meaning of the scenes. At the end, however, there is no way out for either Woyzeck or Marie. Henry Schmidt indicates that "At the end of the play, the situation remains unchanged: Woyzeck's murder and the (assumed) death have no impact beyond the dry fact that two lives are terminated. Woyzeck is rejected even by his own child, and no one within the world of the play either pities or understands, as the remark of the policeman about the 'beautiful murder' indicates" (Schmidt 1970, 52–53). The closure at the conclusion, which reinvokes the opening image, reiterates Woyzeck's contradictory subject position as both oppositional to the hegemonic received class system and bound to dominant ideologies.

Büchner begins with the striking image of bondage. He sets up the authority and morality of the ruling class. The opening scene visually introduces Woyzeck as an underling, as an instrument. The captain lounges in his chair; the servant shaves him. The captain is less a fool than a clever manipulator. He is deliberately presented as a caricature—a caricature that is representative of his class. Henry Schmidt points out that Büchner insists that the caricature is the norm. By implication, the captain is like the rest of the other members of the ruling class (Schmidt 1970, 51). His grotesqueness and his individuality are significant because the former emphasizes his class position and the latter describes the specificity of his relationship with Woyzeck. Woyzeck sees that the captain is symbolic of the upper class, but Woyzeck is at the same time helpless because his knowledge does not allow him to liberate himself from the oppression of the individual. Precisely because of his class position, the captain is a figure of looming terror and at the same time he is ridiculous because he cannot make contact with Woyzeck. Woyzeck's response to the captain controls our perception of him, for the captain is defined solely in terms of his relationship with Woyzeck. Thus, the captain's conversation appears vacant, repetitive, and inane. Schmidt suggests that "Büchner lets the Doctor undermine himself through his speech; the same process unmasks the Captain, the Drum Major, and Andres" (Schmidt 1970, 53).

In contrast to the captain, Woyzeck appears neither empty-headed nor frivolous. While the captain's conversation may initially appear to both Woyzeck and the audience as harmless, if absurd, it soon acquires sinister resonances that the audience catches. The captain emerges a bullying oppressor. His gratuitous and condescending geniality does not mask his determination to possess Woyzeck completely. Woyzeck is aware of some of the nuances of the captain's manipulativeness. Woyzeck's actions after the initial scene, though not directly or sequentially linked, are obliquely linked to the captain's treatment of him. At the outset, the captain is annoyed that Woyzeck plans to leave ten minutes early—ten minutes for which the captain has paid. The annoyance triggers a tirade on the endlessness of time:

> CAPTAIN: Easy, Woyzeck, take it easy. One thing after the other! You're making me dizzy. You'll finish up early and what'll I do with ten minutes on my hands? Use your head, Woyzeck. You've got thirty years to live. Thirty! That's three hundred sixty months. And days! Hours! Minutes! What are you going to do with that horrible stretch of time? Figure it out for yourself, Woyzeck! [*Woyzeck*, 3; all subsequent references to the play are from *Woyzeck*, trans. Theodore Hoffman, in *The Modern Theatre: 5 Plays*, ed. Eric Bentley (Garden City, N.Y.: Doubleday, 1955)].

The menial task the barber performs does not fully indicate the extent of the captain's dominion over him. The barber Woyzeck must not only shave the captain, but reflect the captain's class interests by acting the fool for him. Woyzeck has to respond to the captain's idea of him: Woyzeck is a simpleton who does not even know where the wind sits, who does not know a hawk from a handsaw. The captain is captain of the winds. Woyzeck has to revalidate what the captain says to ensure that he (Woyzeck) is seen as a good person. Woyzeck's acceptance of the captain's taunts confirms the captain's sense of his superiority and reassures him that Woyzeck knows his place. When the captain's gambits fail to elicit the responses he is looking for, he woos Woyzeck to folly:

> CAPTAIN: I think the wind's from the north-south.
> WOYZECK: Yes sir, Captain.
> CAPTAIN: Ha! Ha! Ha! North-south! Ha! Ha! Ha! Are you dumb! Disgustingly dumb! [*Woyzeck*, 4].

Stroked into this outstanding proof of his own cleverness, which lies primarily in using his power to force Woyzeck into agreeing with a stupid proposition, the captain rewards Woyzeck: "You are a good man" (*Woyzeck*, 4). Woyzeck is obedient, he panders to the captain, he is good. Woyzeck produces a version of himself that the captain will reward. As it were, he reflects a constructed image, one that the captain has constructed. This image serves to arouse Woyzeck's class consciousness and highlight his class dependency. He is never addressed, even though he is present. He is spoken of, never spoken to.

The captain attempts to control Woyzeck by imposing the religious ethic of the ruling class on him. The religious dogma serves to blur Woyzeck's class difference. The captain's remonstrances are intended to make Woyzeck see himself as a sinner, to terrify him into unquestioning obedience. Unable to deal with Woyzeck's rebuttals, the captain can only conclude that he thinks too much ("But you think too much," *Woyzeck*, 5). Woyzeck, deeply disturbed by the captain's strictures, is bewildered by a feeling of guilt that cannot be attributed to pathological aberration. He responds the way he has been programmed to. It is not coincidental that he feels the place, the field he visits after his stint with the captain, is "cursed" and that some supernatural force will unleash its fury on him. Be it freemasonry or fire, it will get him and make him pay for his "sins."

The earth below his feet moves; in the hollow under it are the freemasons. The freemasons can be read as projections of his fear of retribution for nameless sins. Büchner uses images from biblical texts to delineate Woyzeck's spiritual state. The apocalyptic imagery conspires to give us the impression that the vengeance of a relentless God is at hand:

> WOYZECK: Andres, look how bright it is. It's all shiny over the city. There's a fire running around the sky, and a sound coming down like trumpets. It's closing in on us!—Come on. Don't look back! [*Woyzeck*, 6].

We are to understand that the destructive power of religion—the system of rewards and punishments that the captain has so recently referred to—provokes Woyzeck's response. Woyzeck does not manufacture the religious myth; he succumbs to its terrible power. Weighted down by traditional beliefs, an unnamable fear corners him into a position where he can no longer question authority but merely make obeisance to it. Andres, too, falls victim to the "mystery"; he is afraid. To Woyzeck, the fear is unnameable:

> WOYZECK: Marie, it happened again. Plenty. Doesn't the good book say, "And behold, there was a smoke coming up from the land like the smoke of an oven? ... It followed me all the way into town. Something we can't understand, that drives you out of your senses. What's going to happen? [*Woyzeck*, 7].

To us, Woyzeck's reaction is a symptom of his fear of authority—the authority of those who "know," the authority of tradition. His class ressentiment stands in contradiction to his internalized image of nothingness—a reflection of the captain's judgment. Woyzeck fears that he will be punished for his views on morality, ideas that the captain deems immoral.

Büchner shows us that Woyzeck's state of mind, his madness, is constructed by people around him. With a few rapid strokes, through the use of a language that is abrupt and jumpy, Büchner portrays this phenomenon. Woyzeck's entirely reasonable invocation of the Lord in the appropriate context is deemed irregular and incoherent by the captain:

> CAPTAIN: You have no morals. Morals! That's what a man's got who behaves morally! Understand? It's a good word. You went and got yourself a child without the blessing of the Church, as our right reverend chaplain put it. "Without the blessing of the Church." Now I didn't invent the phrase.

> WOYZECK: Captain, the Good Lord's not going to be hard on the little worm, just because no one said Amen before they made him. The Lord said, "Suffer little children to come unto me."
>
> CAPTAIN: What did you say? What kind of crazy answer is that? It's got me all confused, and by "it" I mean "you"! See? [*Woyzeck*, 4].

Woyzeck's comment on his child's status and the Lord's response to it are conventionally acceptable, but the captain imposes his version on Woyzeck. He marginalizes Woyzeck and puts him out of the frame of mainstream society: the church or God rejects Woyzeck's offspring because he is conceived outside wedlock. Ironically, the captain projects his own nervousness on the menial, as though the menial were spinning around with no center/axis. The captain says: "Easy, Woyzeck, take it easy. One thing after the other! You're making me dizzy" (*Woyzeck*, 3).

At a subterranean level, the language already accuses Woyzeck of having no balance, of making the captain dizzy because Woyzeck is too much in motion himself and cannot stabilize himself. Similarly, the captain muses, "You always look so moody" (*Woyzeck*, 3). Thus, when the captain comments: "Yes, I felt it before. It's really whizzing around," his comment could be connected both to the weather which they are ostensibly discussing or the effect Woyzeck has on him (*Woyzeck*, 3). Marie serves to isolate and accentuate Woyzeck's anxiety and fear, albeit unwittingly. She says he looks disturbed and ghostly, or even possessed (*Woyzeck*, 7). She echoes the captain's dismay with Woyzeck's contemplativeness: "He'll crack up with those ideas of his" (*Woyzeck*, 8). Like the captain, Marie attributes her unease to Woyzeck's stance and his feelings. She speaks to her little son: "Why so quiet, little fellow? Are you scared? It's getting so dark it's like going blind. Only that street light shining in. It gives me the creeps" (*Woyzeck*, 8). Almost without being aware of it, she names the malady, but in universal terms: "Good God, if fools make sense, then we're all fools. What a crazy world!" (*Woyzeck*, 8). She does not call Woyzeck mad, but makes the suggestion at the universal level. Having established that Woyzeck is a victim of traditional notions of morality and sanity, that he is constructed as insane, and that he is not disturbed, Büchner now artistically indicates that he will become a victim of society's notions of sexuality.

The action of the play moves to Marie. She is singing to the beat of pounding drums: "Oh, soldiers are such handsome guys," an invitation to the virile drum major (*Woyzeck*, 6). Influenced by dominant ideas on "maleness," she believes that a male "does," he does not think. Dunne notes that Marie is attracted to the drum major's "essential maleness" (Dunne 1990, 296). Woyzeck thinks too much, while the drum major performs. Implicit comparisons between the two men force us to set them up as contrast points. Because the drum major is coarse and sees only a female body in Marie, the female spectator is forced into a paradoxical, conservative, and momentary alignment with Woyzeck. The drum major is aggressively "masculine" and objectifies her. He rhapsodizes over her thighs, her hips, her childbearing potential. Of her eyes, he croons: "Like looking into a well, or staring up a chimney. Let's go! After her!" (*Woyzeck*, 9). Both images are redolent of darkness, water and depth. The female is seen as a sexual cavern. Dunne mentions that the well "suggest[s] an underlying image of the vagina." She also notes that "the images of mouth and lips, with their vaginal connotations, are repeatedly associated with Marie" (Dunne 1990, 297). For her part, Marie is attracted by the drum major's social position and his flamboyant masculinity. His earthy, animal sexuality is irresistible when she contrasts him with Woyzeck, who comes to visit her immediately after she exchanges greetings with the drum major. She thinks the drum major is a fine specimen: "A chest like a bull and a beard like a lion. In a class by himself: no woman is prouder than I am" (*Woyzeck*, 14). Ultimately, the drum major is also attractive because he enjoys a higher class position than Woyzeck.

Although Dunne acknowledges the social dimension of Marie's attraction, she emphasizes her sexual drive. If she is correct in her assessment of Marie's "desire," Marie is self-conscious about her "choice." For Dunne, "It is important to establish the positive evaluation of sexuality because it is how Marie is seen by the reader/viewer; whether she is seen as overwhelmed by the power of her libidinous desire or as a callous Jezebel or as a character combining these possibilities" (Dunne 1990, 299). My own sense is that Marie's response to the drum major is significant not only at the level of the plot, but also because it reveals that Marie internalizes societal construction of the female as sexual, and does not express female desire so much as a reified version of it.

Woyzeck's gloomy forebodings differentiate him radically from the drum major, for the latter literally burgeons with brutal vitality. Woyzeck's "What's going to happen?" is grim and unappealing (*Woyzeck*, 7). Marie finds Woyzeck incomprehensible: "He'll crack up with these ideas of his" (*Woyzeck*, 8). The differences that Marie sees between the two men are visually staged by the settings in which she meets them. Darkness and gloom frame her meeting with Woyzeck; light and mirth her encounter with the drum major.

The spookiness and "blindness" she experiences at home with Woyzeck are dramatically contrasted with "the interior of the brightly lit booth" in the fairground with the drum major (*Woyzeck*, 9–10). The drum major commands respect and admiration because he is free of anxiety, is exultant about his masculinity, and can settle any dispute by dint of sheer drunken force. The scene that depicts his only direct encounter with Woyzeck begins with the drum major's declamation: "I'm a real man!" (*Woyzeck*, 24). His position in the army adds to his power. His brief skirmish with Woyzeck inevitably ends with Woyzeck's humiliating defeat. Metaphorically and dramatically, the scene enacts the emasculation of Woyzeck. When Marie is attracted by the flashy drum major, whom Schmidt calls the "decorated phallus," Woyzeck has lost (Schmidt 1970, 54). Not only has she betrayed him sexually, but she has tacitly agreed with society that Woyzeck is less of a man than the drum major.

The barker's eulogy to brute reason embodied by horse/beast (brute reason) celebrates the "natural" at the expense of the "intellectual" (*Woyzeck*, 9–10). In this context, his speech implies that the drum major follows his instinct like a beast while Woyzeck thinks too much. The mindless revelry at the fairgrounds and the carnivalesque riotousness over the "natural" as opposed to the rational emphasize Woyzeck's discomfiture and difference from the mob. Woyzeck cannot enjoy the fair because he begins to philosophize about it. He has social responsibilities that he broods over. Unlike the drum major, Woyzeck is committed to Marie and loves her. He believes that she is the sole purpose of his existence: "I have nothing else in the world" (*Woyzeck*, 16). He ekes out the most painful of all livelihoods to help support her, to be part of a family with her. He earns a little extra money for Marie and the child by allowing the doctor to conduct experiments on him. The doctor puts him on a diet of peas to study the effects it has on the human body. Woyzeck's very body serves the interests of his enemies and oppressors. He does not have the freedom to pee. He is berated soundly when he pleads nature's urges:

> DOCTOR: I saw you, Woyzeck. You were pissing in the street. You were pissing against the wall, like a dog! Three groschen a day and board for that! Woyzeck, that was bad. The world's going bad, very bad.
>
> WOYZECK: But, Doctor, when Nature calls.
>
> DOCTOR: When Nature calls! When Nature calls! Nature! Didn't I prove the *musculus constrictor vesicae* can be controlled by the will? Woyzeck, Man is free! Through Man alone shines the individual's will to freedom! Can't hold his water! [*Woyzeck*, 12].

Woyzeck tells the doctor of the voices that plague him. The doctor, apparently forgetful of his experimentation, decides that Woyzeck has "the most beautiful *aberratio mentalis partialis*, secondary order, nicely developed" (*Woyzeck*, 13). Büchner unambiguously declares that it is the doctor who will send Woyzeck to the madhouse. The doctor, aligned with the other figures of authority, is excited about a revolution in the arena of knowledge that is based on a treatment of Woyzeck as less than human, as beast. Paradoxically, the knowledge the doctor garners is catalogued logically and conventionally; he seeks to understand not Woyzeck but the disease in an abstract sense. The doctor wills that Woyzeck fulfill the experimental conditions that he has already predetermined. Woyzeck's tentative description of nature and the way it controls human beings is dismissed. His dissertation on nature is not a simplistic deterministic view; indeed, one remembers that at the fairground, he insists on deliberate thought. Rather, the doctor seeks to fit Woyzeck's experience into the framework of his scientific analysis and thus appropriates it to suit his rational ends. Büchner indicates that the sane cannot understand the insane; they can merely impose their own forms and shapes on them to suit their own interests.

The doctor is painted in expressionist hues and emerges a macabre figure, a sinister man who machinates in order to enhance his dominion over people through his control over the medical discourses. The scene that dramatizes his examination of Woyzeck presents him as a towering, looming figure who stoops to direct his pawn. Schmidt states that "Woyzeck's fate is all the more tragic and unavoidable precisely because of the *smallness* of this particular adversary, who by chance happens to occupy a higher position in society than Woyzeck" (Schmidt 1970, 50–51). Büchner's savage portrayal of class relations moves the audience from shock to anger. The antisociety theme is firmly established, and Woyzeck has been isolated. As Meier succinctly summarizes the action of the play up to this juncture: "Woyzeck ist nun in seinen drei wichtigsten Sozialbereichen Beruf, Freundschaft und Familie isoliert [Woyzeck is now isolated from the three most important social domains: profession, friendship, and family.]" (Meier 1980, 54).

The dramatist now problematizes the course he has followed and presents Woyzeck as a half-crazed animal incapable of compassion and irrational in his anger. The connection between the social and the personal is mediated through gender. By contrasting Woyzeck favorably with his oppressors, Büchner has implied that Woyzeck's perspective is eminently comprehensible. Büchner has stressed that Woyzeck's wrath and agony have a strictly concrete source—society. That he should want to revenge himself against his oppressors is inevitable and indeed revolutionary. But Woyzeck does not attack his enemies, he attacks their victim—Marie. Marie is society's victim because she is powerless as a lower-class woman. She is compelled to accept society's verdicts because of her limited vision and extreme poverty. She cannot afford the luxury of rebellion; indeed, she is too fettered by the beliefs and thoughts of her society and class to be able to see Woyzeck's point of view. She is also a victim because her death does not ultimately affect that stratum of society that Woyzeck deplores. Society will not agonize over the loss of Marie.

Büchner articulates Woyzeck's conservative gender ideology, which deflects his class ressentiment. While the earlier fragments of the play show us the oppressor and the victim, the latter fragments show us the victim expressing his minimal agency against another victim. What we apparently witness is Woyzeck's struggle against his "bestial nature." Schwarz sees the depiction as an expression of Büchner's "controlled nihilism" (Schwarz 1978, 353). And we see it from outside. We are alienated. Our acknowledgment of Marie's assertion of her autonomy is severely counterbalanced by our knowledge that her choice of the drum major does not insert her as an agent, but keeps her at the level of an object. Hitherto a victim, who was "saner" than his fellow beings, Woyzeck is now transformed into a grotesque creature whose "suffering is animal-like" (Schwarz 1978, 353).

Woyzeck acts with missionary zeal to repossess Marie. Ownership of the woman constitutes his gender identity, and his killing of Marie expresses an attempt to recover ownership. The female spectator's withdrawal does not discursively align her with Marie because Marie has even less agency than Woyzeck. The text structurally lends Woyzeck power by allowing him to dominate and annihilate Marie, but she remains the voiceless victim who is terrorized and silenced for her single act of autonomy. Displeasure informs the female spectator's stance. The scenes that lead to the murder move at a rapid pace and lend the audience distance from Woyzeck so that the audience now moves from sympathy to distaste. Ultimately, the audience does not rest completely in either posture. We reaffirm our sanity in terms of opposition toward the Other, the insane, but, male readers understand Woyzeck, who, in the first instance, has been constructed as insane, while the female viewer refuses such "understanding." We move from Woyzeck, who has to tolerate the captain's taunts, to Marie. Marie is haunted by a sense of shame and sin. She attempts to pray. She blames herself for an immorality that is socially prescribed.

Woyzeck feels himself enclosed and breaks out of the psychic closure and his impotence: "I've got to get out" (*Woyzeck*, 18). Büchner's portrayal of Woyzeck credits him with some marginal power in his madness. He gains power, but the power is at the cost of Marie and lasts only an instant. Moreover, his brief escape does not obliterate his pain. Thus, while he succeeds in expressing his anger, he stays impotent at the social and psychic levels. His inability to strike back against his real oppressors highlights his helplessness. His anger against society is displaced by his bitter revulsion against Marie.

At yet another level, the text now suggests that Marie is ultimately responsible for Woyzeck's disintegration. His fury is kindled by a despairing jealousy. Büchner implies that Woyzeck's encounter with the drum major makes him decide to kill Marie, for Büchner follows up the scene of Woyzeck's defeat with the fragment at the Jew's, where Woyzeck buys a knife. The "inevitability" of the movement of the play after his purchase subverts the movement its opening sequences initiate. The opening sequences image a hero whose hostility is directed against the oppressor, the latter scenes a madman who seeks to avenge himself on a victim. The brutal murder of Marie forces the audience to reread the initial scenes, which now seem to foreshadow Woyzeck's madness—site-traversing class ressentiment and male subjectivity.

Marie is shocked when Woyzeck comes to take her away. The grandmother's story, replete with pathos, has just come to an end. Woyzeck's comments are threatening:

> WOYZECK: Do you know how long it's been, Marie?
> MARIE: Two years, Pentecost.
> WOYZECK: Do you know how long it will last? [Woyzeck, 29].

The murder dramatizes the climactic point of Woyzeck's frenzy:

> WOYZECK: Take that, and that! Why can't you die? There! Ha! She's still twitching. Still can't? Still twitching? (Stabs again). How are you dead? Dead! Dead! (He drops the knife and runs away) [*Woyzeck,* 29].

Presented on stage as a sexual act, an act that overpowers the woman, the murder serves to distance us from the conflict between Woyzeck and his oppressors. Dunne is unequivocal about the sexual quality of the violence and, following Larsen, reads the knife as a phallus substitute used to signify "phallic revenge on female sexuality that has castrated the owner (by preferring another lover)" (Dunne 1990, 304). Woyzeck's actions after the murder are also devised to make us watch him, to observe this phenomenon who kills and then literally dances. The audience is distanced from the protagonist because of the cruelty and brutality of his act.

Büchner is now concerned with Woyzeck's "problem," which he presents as rooted in both the psychic and the social context. The social criticism is compounded by the depiction of Woyzeck's disintegration, for Büchner shows us the effect of societal and sexual relations on the psyche. That Büchner intended the play to inspire social change is borne out by the insistent, anguished dramatization of Woyzeck's exploitation and by the successive versions of the manuscript which increasingly expand and fill in the social dimension (Krause 1969). The language of loss attributed to Woyzeck is influenced by Othello's accents:

> WOYZECK: A sin, so big, and so wide. It should stink, until the angels are smoked out of heaven. You have a red mouth, Marie. No blisters on it? Marie, you're as beautiful as sin—but can mortal sin be so beautiful? [*Woyzeck*, 17].

Woyzeck expresses anguish by seeing signs of it outside him—in the landscape. He discusses Marie's infidelity, however, in precise moral terms which are not expressive of the bewilderment he expresses earlier. Perhaps the social framework in which he operates places him in the "right" as male and Marie in the "wrong" as unfaithful female. Dunne makes the crucial point that "Woyzeck's right to dispose of Marie has been prepared in the text by a number of images." She refers to society's view of the woman as property and the theme of the hunt in *Jäger aus der Pfalz* (Dunne 1990, 304). Büchner suggests that the female, though a victim herself, is perceived by Woyzeck as the bringer of madness because of his extreme jealousy. And it is her enjoyment of her own body that drives the man mad. That the text invests Woyzeck with power at Marie's expense without making it possible for us to see her as a viable subject indicates that Büchner validates received mythologies on femininity even while allowing the female spectator an oppositional entrance into the text. Textually, the construction of the marginal Woyzeck's subjectivity defines Marie as object and thus wins the mad subject his speech at the price of the female's silence within a framework that suggests that ownership of the female is the precondition of male subjectivity.

Chapter 2

The Name of the Father— The Body of the Mother: Strindberg's *The Father*

August Strindberg's influence upon twentieth-century dramatists and his exploration of the human psyche mark him as modern. His plays' concern with the interiority of the subject and his canvasses of the mind reveal his kinship with Büchner. Aside from a generalized inclination to distance themselves from the predominantly realist European theatre of that period, both playwrights worked with "intimate" material in experimental rather than mimetic modes. Strindberg's *The Father* (1887), although ostensibly a high realist text, plays with realist conventions. The play has several intertextual connections with Büchner's *Woyzeck*.

Both plays are framed by a discussion between the sexes that seeks to articulate the meaning of maleness or femaleness, what a man must be, what a female may be. While they approach the dramatization of sexual politics very differently, their focus on jealousy and male ownership of the female body forges the beginning of an influential historical lineage that has left its imprint on the twentieth-century male canon.

Strindberg's strongly articulated opinions and his life experiences have had a strange palimpsestic effect on his work. It is as though his work were shackled by his opinions and framed by the scenarios of his life. The dramatist's several marriages and his famed misogyny have hampered students from examining the pattern his text delineates. Over the last twenty-five years, much of his later work has been recuperated from the traditional speculations on the uniqueness of his personality and the intensity of his perceptions and reconsidered. The earlier work has not been reassessed, however.

The Father revolves around issues of paternity. When the protagonist is torn with doubts about his daughter's paternity, his sanity is questioned and he is straitjacketed. The play has been variously seen as "grandiose naturalism"

(Madsen 1962, 48), as a naturalistic battle for survival (Williams 1966, 9), as a powerful rendition of a transhistorical battle of the sexes (Paulson 1968, 448), and as a reflection of Strindberg's paranoid fear of a matriarchy on the ascendant, a response to his traumatic experiences with his first wife, Siri von Essen (Paulson 1968, 437–49). Strindberg is unfavorably contrasted with Ibsen and emerges in these critical writings as a relentless spokesman for patriarchy's modes and mores. One would assume that *The Father* was an anachronistic play, the sour burnt offering of a rabid misogynist.

Kela Kvam views the play very differently, however, and sees it as "an attempt to inquire into the problems of the male and his relationship to his sexual role" (Kvam 1983, 112). Robert Brustein points out that the play was a response to Ibsen's *A Doll's House*. He contrasts the two plays: "One might say that both plays attack conventional sexual attitudes, Ibsen dramatizing the woman's revolt against the tyrannizing male, and Strindberg the male's revolt against the tyrannical woman" (Brustein 1964, 105). He considers the possibility that the play may not be one-sided: "The two faces that Laura shows the Captain lead him to act with alternating tenderness and hostility towards her, an ambivalence reflected in the mood of the play where the energy of battle is occasionally broken by nostalgic interludes," but he concludes that the play is in fact "slanderous, prejudiced, one-sided" (Brustein 1964, 108 and 112).

Indeed, *The Father* has had impressive detractors, Peter Szondi and Eric Bentley among them. Szondi suggests that the play attempts to blend the naturalistic style with the subjective and consequently does not succeed in achieving the effects of either style (Szondi 1963, 41). Bentley says that he is tired of Strindberg's earlier work, that the early plays are excessively and single-mindedly "well-made," that they are not "seriously dramatic enough, not seriously human enough" (Bentley 1971, 99). Walter Johnson considers the play straightforward: a woman drives a man mad by casting doubts on his daughter's paternity (Johnson 1976, 142). I suggest that *The Father*, far from being solely the relatively simple enactment of a naturalistic dilemma or the reactionary outpouring of a male gored by his wife, is a complex play which is radical in its conclusion and its perception of the conflict between its main characters. The contradictions the play articulates make it an exemplary site to study the intersections between sexuality and insanity.

Büchner's *Woyzeck* locates madness in the space between the social and psychological. The play traces the construction of the mad subject as Other and also sketches out the impact of the social construction on the subject's perception of his own gendered identity. Strindberg's *The Father* shows us how the social saturates the psyche of the individual and similarly places madness in the perilous site between the exterior and the interior. The protagonist of

The Father, although "driven mad," experiences the confrontation with Laura and his family in terms of his sense of subjectivity and authority, which he derives from his tenuous position as both husband and father. While *Woyzeck* only partly claims that the woman's sexual freedom or autonomy over her body and self drove the man to madness, *The Father* unequivocally declares that Laura's very claims to autonomy, whether proven or not, edge the man to madness.

Strindberg suggests that the female's autonomy causes the male's madness, for the male is unable to accept the fact that he has no control over the female's body or the female's psyche. I contend that the structure of Strindberg's text validates the female's position, for Laura emerges free and powerful. The text shows that Adolf, the captain and Laura's husband, is constructed as the Other by the characters in the play; it also constructs Laura in like manner, for she is viewed as the Other by the captain, whose perspective we see. Strindberg stages a double drama and articulates a double discourse: one that asserts and another that questions and undermines what is asserted. Never one without the other. And in this dialectical movement, the moment he celebrates is the woman's freedom, the moment he mourns is the man's acceptance of failure. Strindberg shows the viewer that the subject is produced in history and in the family. We know how and why the captain and Laura are who they are and why they act the way they do. And they are not presented as unchanging, stable entities. The heterogeneity of discourses that inform the play makes it a powerful analysis of the conflicts that feminism provokes.

Büchner's *Woyzeck* is an example of a text with a radical program which is not realized; the opposite is true of *The Father*. I would argue that *The Father* emerges as a radical text on two counts: it is formally innovative, and it stages a dialogue between feminism and patriarchy that is not collapsed into a univocal conclusion. Kvam points out that Strindberg's era experienced a shift in attitude toward male and female roles because of the women's liberation movement. According to her: "The role of the male does not appear in the play to be biologically determined, but rather a historic anachronism, a myth defiantly maintained" (Kvam 1983, 125). I would add that biological difference is insignificant in this play because Strindberg locates sexual difference in an institutional context and views the relationship between men and women as one mediated by hierarchical social structures and by male anxiety about paternity rather than biological differences. His emphasis is on gender as constructed rather than given.

The long history of the production of *The Father* has perhaps contributed to the impression that the play is one-sided in its presentation of the conflict between its protagonists. Only occasionally well acted, most productions of the play have tended to emphasize Laura's malevolence. The captain has been cast in the role of tragic hero. Kvam indicates that Strindberg intended the captain and his costume/uniform to signify a masculinity that Strindberg describes by saying "To me particularly here, he represents a masculinity which they have tried to denigrate, steal from us and transfer to the third sex!" (Kvam 1983, 122). The actors who played the role raved and ranted in an absurdly melodramatic fashion, though Strindberg suggested that the captain be played in a subdued key (Paulson 1968, 437–39).

So slanted an interpretation of the text, which celebrates the father as tragic hero, has effectively contributed to the universal image of Strindberg as a misogynist par excellence, a view which in turn has discouraged students from reevaluating the play. The play circumvents the tragic by its conclusion, which envisions the woman Laura as free and powerful, the father as weak and spent. The father's tragedy is to some extent Laura's victory. The father does not come to an understanding of his flaws. *The Father* explores the connections between sexuality and insanity. At the level of the plot, *The Father* appears to follow a bold and simple line of dramatic action (Madsen 1962, 66). The motivation of the action is not, however, located around a single, stable nucleus. Strindberg manipulates the point of view from which the action is staged so that the lines of certitude vanish, perspectives shift, and doubt is thrown on the narratives the protagonists tell. This is not the same as saying that one is never quite certain why Iago plots against Othello but rather to say that the play is directed and enacted by the main characters, Laura and Adolf. On this stage, uncertainty becomes a key principle in the dramatic text. One is never quite certain which course of action the dramatist approves of. The credibility of both Laura's and Adolf's narratives is questioned, which makes it problematic for the audience to determine where their sympathies should lie. The effect of the play approximates the metatheatrical technique of Pirandello, but in a less self-conscious way, so that the plurality is further enriched by the semblance of an impersonal or omniscient dramatist at work. And Strindberg does not resolve the ambiguities he draws out; rather, he invites the audience to pay attention to the fact that the players on stage are their own directors. While Laura and Adolf enact and react to self-staged dramas, the dramatist plays the part of the deus ex machina who terminates the production but does not resolve the problem.

The Father strikes the chord of uncertainty in its opening scene. The pastor, presumably staunch in his beliefs by virtue of his profession, veers toward doubt rapidly. From the position of the judge, he slides into the position of the doubter. The pastor is initially reluctant to get involved in the sordid proceedings of attempting to arbitrate on a ticklish matter: the paternity of the maid Emma's child. Regarding Nöjd, he asks, "how much impression ... God's word is likely to make on a trooper" (*The Father*, 9. All subsequent references to the play are from *The Father,* in *Six Plays of Strindberg,* trans. Elizabeth Sprigge [Garden City, N.Y.: Doubleday, 1955].). Paradoxically, the trooper's word makes a powerful impression on both the pastor and the captain. Nöjd's response to the captain's query suddenly questions the absolute certainties on which the captain insists on basing his life, for it has never occurred to the captain that the male cannot be certain of paternity:

> CAPTAIN: Once and for all—are you the child's father or are you not?
> NÖJD: How's one to know? [*The Father,* 10].

Nöjd's refusal to take responsibility for Emma's pregnancy because a man can never be certain of a child's paternity strikes a chord in the captain. The captain is struck by the validity of Nöjd's argument, but he is also disturbed about its implications. The captain, who had taken the cudgels up in Emma's defense, is now swayed by Nöjd's point of view almost as though he were subconsciously acknowledging the problematic nature of paternity. He had wanted to know why Nöjd had not been hauled over the coals, but he reverses his judgment completely. The pastor's "sympathetic" attitude provokes a similar response from him (*The Father,* 11). The captain blames Emma: "Maybe the boy is responsible—that's what you can't know. But one thing you can know—if anybody's guilty, the girl is" (*The Father,* 11). In one delightfully brief comic episode, Strindberg has shown us the attitudes of three men who briefly agree that sexuality is women's business. In an equally important way, the episode ironically frames the father's anguish at the very uncertainty that Nöjd is happy about. The conversation between the captain and his brother-in-law apparently shifts to everyday talk about the captain's family, but in reality stays on the same register: the problems that women create. At this point, the captain starts to stage his play. The controversy in the family concerns the upbringing of his daughter Bertha. The women in the house question his exclusive authority over his daughter:

> CAPTAIN: The house is full of women, all trying to mould this child of mine. My mother-in-law wants to turn her into a spiritualist; Laura wants her to be an artist; the governess would have her a Methodist, old Margaret a Baptist, and the servant girls a Salvation Army lass. Meanwhile I ... I, who have more right than all the rest to guide her, am opposed at every turn. So I must send her away [*The Father,* 12].

The space in the house is overrun by women, and each woman has her wishes for Bertha. The captain's rights over Bertha are challenged, so he wants to move her away from the influence of these women. The house is a "lunatic asylum" because the women have too much power and will not heed the captain (*The Father,* 13). The pastor concurs with this notion: "You should keep your womenfolk in order, Adolf. You give them too much rope" (*The Father*, 12). The smooth ordering of the family which depends on strict hierarchization is threatened. Instability and disorder are on the threshold because the women "talk about men being made to see that women can do this and that" (*The Father*, 14). The women's challenge, particularly Laura's, which casts doubt on Bertha's paternity, threatens Adolf's authority and confidence, which depend on his hierarchical position as male and head of the family, biological father of his daughter, symbolic Father of the other women.

Before Bertha's paternity is questioned, the situation appears different. Adolf implies, for instance, that the confusion over Bertha's future is a result of Laura's illness. Laura's temperament is ultimately the cause of the problem: "She was brought up with romantic ideas and has always found it a little difficult to come to terms with life" (*The Father*, 12). Her anxieties are similarly glossed over: "As a matter of fact, she does sometimes get so overwrought I'm frightened for her and think she must be ill" (*The Father*, 13). The captain constructs Laura as the Other: the weak, overwrought female. He is, as it were, elaborating on essentialist notions of gender. In telling his own story, the captain has contradicted himself, which implicitly questions his claims to "reasonableness." Earlier, the discussion on Nöjd's behavior with Emma had already confused him. Now, he contends, for instance, that the women only want Bertha to be married. He has donned the garb of a victim, while he prepares to make a strong effort to wrest all the power that has seeped back into the women's quarters. He makes no mention of parley with his wife over their daughter's future, which he envisions in a characteristically traditional fashion. It is significant that he dismisses suggestions that Bertha may have artistic talent. Of course, the young man who had thought she had talent was in love with Bertha and hence hopelessly subjective. Inevitably, the captain goes on pure surmise; he has no proof:

> PASTOR: Was he in love with Bertha?
> CAPTAIN: I take that for granted [*The Father*, 14].

The captain wants her to become a teacher—an authority figure—and hence have a traditional education and also further transfer those values she has learned to her students. Paradoxically, such an education would lend her a certain independence from "female" roles. The professions the women in the house favor are grouped around the humanities. Laura has hopes that Bertha will pursue an artistic career; the mother-in-law/stepmother wants her to study the occult, and the servants want her to help humanity in the name of Christ. Thus, even before Laura is on stage, the house appears to be polarized. The feminine is the lunatic, the artistic, the psychic. The masculine is the rational, the ordered, the stable. But Strindberg calls into question what he has established. He suggests that Laura's association of the artistic with the feminine might be simplistic.

The action of the play challenges the concept of the old stable order that expresses itself in rigidly hierarchized structures and in the notion of the stability of the human identity. The human character is no longer composed of an integral core that determines and defines identity. The stable ego is dissolved. Strindberg delineates the phenomenon in a few simple strokes. Almost before the pastor leaves, the audience begins to question the captain's hard core of rational argumentation. The pastor is concerned about the captain's condition. Why is he anxious about the well-being of Adolf when he has been in perfect harmony with Adolf's ideas throughout the evening and has even provoked some of Adolf's more bitter outbursts? The pastor assumes that the captain is unduly disturbed: "You aren't very well, are you?" (*The Father*, 14). The dramatist has subtly undermined the captain's position, for it is not an enemy who questions him, but a sympathetic friend and ally. The female spectator cannot but be alienated by the construction of the captain's subjectivity. Male critical readings of the play implicitly sympathize with the captain at this juncture because anxiety over paternity is subtly depicted as a universal (male) concern. When Laura first makes her entrance, the captain acts on his resolve to take a firm stand from the start. He is the master, and Laura must submit accounts of the household expenditure. Kvam also records the captain's assertiveness and reads it as a desire to "maintain patriarchal dominance" (Kvam 1983, 122). She compares Laura to a slave and defends her because she has no other choice: "Yet what can Laura do otherwise than use the somewhat ignoble strategy of the slave?" (Kvam 1983, 123). No option that leads a slave out of chains can be "ignoble," however. Laura's structural position in the text, moreover, is not that of a slave. The captain is not called upon to account for *his* expenditure, because the social norm that invests him with his sense of self confers this right on him. He is quite the feudal chief demanding that his vassal-housekeeper-wife abide by the law.

The scene, performed today, would invite the audience's sympathy for Laura. The little tableau vivant is complete in all its particulars, right down to Laura's "ironic bob" à la housemaid (*The Father*, 16). The relationship between economic power and familial authority is emphasized. The captain draws from this power as he tries to intimidate Laura. Laura is sensitive to the insidious link between the economics and politics of the family. She recognizes that her daughter's life has been "settled" as a matter of trade would be at a business conference. In the person of the captain resides the sole authority of the house. And he is supported by the law—norms forged outside the house—norms that adjudicate business affairs. The whole episode deserves to be quoted because of the swift way in which these propositions are formulated and the even swifter way that the premises that underlie them are unearthed:

> LAURA: By the way, do you keep accounts yourself—of what you spend outside the household?
>
> CAPTAIN: That's none of your business.
>
> LAURA: True. As little my business as the future of my own child. Did you gentlemen come to any decision at this evening's conference?
>
> CAPTAIN: *I* had already made my decision, so I merely had to communicate it to the only friend I have in the family. Bertha is going to live in town. She will leave in a fortnight's time [*The Father*, 16].

In the discussion that follows, the captain invokes the law to support his decision (*The Father*, 16). He also rejects Laura's attempt to effect a compromise. Laura has no choice but to challenge him because she is faced with the prospect of losing her daughter. The alternative would be to succumb to a domestic tyrant's yoke. And she challenges him by affirming her sexuality. In a hierarchical society, when a woman exults in her sexuality, the man's honor, his position, and his authority over the family are seriously jeopardized. Laura asserts her autonomy over her body and implies that she has been untrustworthy by insinuating that Bertha may not be the captain's child. Lacanian thought on the question clarifies and theorizes the trajectory Strindberg dramatizes:

> The Name-of-the Father is the Law. The legal assignation of a Father's name to a child is meant to call a halt to uncertainty about the identity of the father. If the mother's femininity (both her sexuality and her untrustworthiness) were affirmed, the Name-of-the-Father would always be in doubt, always be subject to question of the mother's morality. Thus the Name-of-the-Father must be arbitrarily and absolutely imposed, thereby instituting the reign of patriarchal law [Gallop 1982, 39].

Laura challenges the reign of patriarchal law in her house by the simple question: "But supposing the wife has been unfaithful?" (*The Father*, 17). The conflict between Laura and the captain is outlined in terms of a debate between an abstract law that does not recognize the truth of a situation and a humane law. The abstract law serves to secure pleasure and privilege for the male. The woman is excluded from the enjoyment of pleasure because Laura's role comes to an end after the act of reproduction. The captain expresses the law in unambiguous terms:

> CAPTAIN: According to the law as it now stands, children are brought up in their father's faith.
>
> LAURA: And the mother has no say in the matter?
>
> CAPTAIN: None at all. When you have sold something, you don't get it back and keep the money too [*The Father*, 16].

Marriage protects the captain from the danger of Laura's unhampered sexuality: "But of course in marriage there is no doubt about paternity" (*The Father*, 17). The institution of marriage, ratified by law, secures the captain's position and consolidates his privileges. Laura's fidelity is the fountainhead of the captain's power that ensures his personal feeling of security as a sexual being. When Laura flaunts her sexuality, she explodes the whole system:

> LAURA: Supposing I am telling you the truth now when I say: Bertha is my child but not yours. Supposing...
> CAPTAIN: Stop it!
> LAURA: Just supposing ... then your power would be over [*The Father*, 28].

The rest of the play traces the loss of the captain's power and the resulting insanity. Strindberg assumes that a stable, hierarchized society is the precondition for the ordered working of the family and the "sanity" of its head. He shows us that this stability is fragile, for when women assert their rights over their own bodies, a revolution is in the offing: the old relationships between male and female, father and daughter, master and servant collapse. While the play foregrounds the destabilization of the relationship between man and woman, it also displays the connection between the social system and the collapse. Laura manipulates the captain on the basis of his law, within his framework, because he will not listen to new voices, new sensibilities:

> CAPTAIN: Are you joking? [about Bertha's paternity].
> LAURA: No, I'm simply applying your own theory. How do you know I haven't been unfaithful to you? [*The Father*, 27].

The perspective of the play changes as Laura now initiates the action, enacts her own play. The metatheatrical venture gives the female viewer an entrance into the text through Laura. Her first question articulates the contradictions of the system the captain accepts:

> LAURA: Can't one tell who a child's father is?
> CAPTAIN: Apparently not.
> LAURA: How perfectly extraordinary [*The Father*, 17].

She merely follows the captain's reasoning through to its logical extreme at a later stage but uses it to suit her own purposes. If the law cannot tell if the trooper is responsible for Emma's child, how can it guarantee the captain the privileges of fatherhood? Strindberg implies that the very institution of the law was established because of male fear of women. Thus he reverses the conventional notion of the female as weak.

A quick shift introduces a different register by which Laura will be perceived. Paradoxically, the drama that Laura stages forces the audience to view the captain with sympathy, as the captain's drama has invited sympathy for

Laura. Strindberg dramatizes the oppressive assumptions of Laura's position and forces us to view the matter from Adolf's perspective and vice versa. Access to the captain's subjectivity does not necessarily ratify the framework within which he operates. He earns our sympathy because he is constructed as Other, not because of his actions. In contrast, Laura does not invite the female spectator's sympathy, but the spectator aligns herself with Laura because of her subversive feminist politics. Laura tells the doctor that the captain's mind is affected. The captain is constructed as the Other who is mad. Laura appears manipulative and overarchingly domineering. She has interfered with the captain's scholarly activities, opened his mail. The impression one has of her manipulativeness is reinforced by the difference in Laura's and the captain's roles. The captain fast loses mastery over himself. The dramatist achieves these perspectives by emphasizing the differences in tone, register, and rhythm between Laura and the captain so that the director of the play, Laura, is highlighted. From the mode of dramatization, the audience unearths the biases of the "director." Laura's biases are highlighted during her scenario: her scorn for the scientific and her incredible commitment to autonomy over her self and power in the family. The biases of the captain emerge quickly, linked as they are to the mores of patriarchal society: insistence on rationality and commitment to a hierarchically organized society and family. The play contrasts the scientific ways of knowledge and the intuitive ways of perception. All hellfire is let loose when Laura tries to persuade the doctor that the captain is on the verge of insanity, which the captain himself had already hinted at. The family is on the brink of chaos.

Bentley objects to Strindberg's representation of anarchy. He argues that there is something "wrong which cannot be put right, as some have tried to put it right, by accepting Strindberg's disorder as that of his age. The artist's task is not to portray vagueness vaguely, disorder disorderly. On the contrary! He cannot show chaos to others, if he himself is lost in it" (Bentley 1971, 98). Strindberg's modernity, however, lies in the effort he makes not to collapse disorder into order. That is, he can dramatize insanity from the site of insanity and expose Laura's contradictions from her position and the captain's from his. While Strindberg does not resolve the problems the text poses, he does draw out some pattern in the disorder he dramatizes.

The pattern the first half of the play sets up is inverted in the second half to display the phenomenology of the changes the family undergoes. At the outset, the captain is in possession of women, power, and reason; he ends up dispossessed of women, power, and reason. He has no control over those he used to command. Bertha, Laura, and even the faithful nurse reject the captain. He is isolated as the Other and finally straitjacketed by the women. The changes are occasioned by female bonding. The bonds forged between the women through the action of the play change the quality of the relations between men and women.

Carlson, who analyzes the play within the framework of the myths that Strindberg uses, discerns an interesting pattern in the seeming vagueness of the relationships. According to him, the Omphale-Hercules myth is the key to the text. Carlson's insight into the role of the mother-in-law/stepmother is invaluable. He suggests that she is the "secret heart of the play, hidden and mysterious" (Carlson 1982, 51). More than other women in the text she embodies the irrational forces. She never appears on stage. She seems to symbolize an aspect of Laura's divided psyche: she is the woman who mocks the rationality of the captain and who punishes him for his blithe disregard of the "dark world of unconscious impulses" and his disdain for the psychic, occult dimension of life by rendering him subject to the forces he has scorned (Carlson 1982, 52). At the level of myth, such a pattern can be discerned. One can also perceive, however, that the relationship between the two women forges a solidarity that threatens the captain's position. Further, the idea that the father is crushed by powerful irrational forces dramatizes the father's perception of his situation (Carlson 1982, 52). *The Bacchae* dramatizes a similar ritual. Dionysos avenges himself terribly on the all-too-rational son for ignoring the Dionysiac rituals. The captain pays for his valorization of the rational at the expense of the irrational. In a very important sense, the fight over Bertha's education is between the old woman and the captain. She it is who initiates Bertha into the mysteries of spiritualism from her sequestered quarters. We do not know where she lives but guess that she is separated from the main living quarters. The only space she is associated with is the attic, a place of enclosure and secrecy, setting for a mysterious happening.

Bertha, panic-stricken, tries to resist the influence of the old woman. Her fear is highlighted by her dramatic entrance. She rushes to her father, screaming, "Father, Father! Help me! Save me" (*The Father*, 24). On the one hand, she seeks her father's help in averting the wrath of her grandmother; on the other she seeks to clarify and understand what her grandmother tells her. An insidious question is posed—who is more powerful, more correct, grandmother or father? It is presented artlessly: "Grandmother says there are things she can see and you can't" (*The Father*, 25). The captain cannot effectively prove his greater power of vision over the natural world but can offer an acceptable alternative that will rescue Bertha. In other words, he asserts his greater control over the social world. He can simply send her away so that she is no longer exposed to her grandmother's experiments with the spirits. Later, the sound of music emanating from the attic convinces Bertha that the old lady was correct: "I'm sure there are ghosts" (*The Father*, 33). The nurse, Margaret, unhesitatingly believes Bertha and thinks that it is an omen that bodes no good. If Bertha learns to trust the old woman, she learns to distrust and fear her father. Ironically, it is because he has broken the social contract, the compact between father, mother, and child. She disowns him in a scene edged with irony. Although she does not know that her parents are debating her paternity, the captain's violence and indifference provoke her into rejecting him. It would appear that the social bond is indeed more important than the biological one:

> BERTHA: (going to him) Are you ill, father?
> CAPTAIN: (looking stupidly at the word "Father.") Me?
> BERTHA: Do you know what you did? You threw a lamp at mother.
> CAPTAIN: Did I?
> BERTHA: Yes. Supposing she'd been hurt!
> CAPTAIN: Would that have mattered?
> BERTHA: You're not my father, if you talk like that.
> CAPTAIN: What d'you say? Not your father? How d'you know? Who told you? Who is your father, then? Who?
> BERTHA: Not you, anyway [*The Father*, 51].

The captain has lost his daughter because he has imprisoned himself in his ego and cared little about her sensibilities. When he throws the lamp, he throws his light, Bertha, away. She has been the terrain of his struggle with Laura and has merely been the instrument of his will. He has not considered her an individual. Bertha's allegiance is with Laura. The captain's isolation now merely remains to be accentuated by his incarceration. He is the Other, whose perceptions will no longer be validated by society. Paradoxically, he has come to occupy this position because he sees the world scientifically and society uncritically. Laura, who perceives the world intuitively and who commands knowledge through the realm of art, is sane. Thus the father does not emerge a renegade but a reactionary. The old woman "sees"; he does not. Strindberg, however, questions both positions.

The captain's earlier attempt to regain his place in the family comes to nought. Act II, which follows the process by which he becomes insane, makes it clear that he loses his sanity because he cannot regain his position. The captain's insanity is intimately bound to his wife's sexuality and fidelity and his failure to maintain proprietorship over it. He bargains with her to regain control:

> My judgment is fogged and my mind is beginning to stray. This means that the insanity you have been waiting for is now on its way and may come any moment. The question you now have to decide is whether it is more to your advantage for me to be well or ill.... Free me from doubt and I will give up the fight [*The Father*, 38].

The captain wants her to cede her power in her "own interests." He surrenders himself to despair when she refuses to grant him ownership (*The Father*, 40). He vents his fury on her when he finally acknowledges his own helplessness. His sense of self, his ego, has dissolved, and doubt has corroded his assurance. Act II ends with the captain throwing the lamp at a triumphant Laura. The binary oppositions between rationality and irrationality, subject and object are now reversed. Adolf would have Laura declare that she has been virtuous, that his life has been meaningful, that his honor is intact. He throws away his reason. His irate gesture against Laura appears both peevish and puerile. Bertha's reaction to the episode conclusively influences our response. Roles appear to be inverted; the father is childish, the child is mature.

The captain sees his dilemma in universal terms and tries to communicate his sharp perceptions to the pastor and the doctor. His gibes at them—that they too have been cuckolded—fall on deaf ears. They complacently assume their wives' fidelity and are not aware of its cardinal importance to the smooth ordering of their lives. Had they the knowledge Adolf has, they too would go mad. The captain's knowledge, of course, within the framework of the play is partial, confined as it is by the parameters of rationality:

> PASTOR: I suppose you know, brother-in-law, that you're not in your right mind?
>
> CAPTAIN: Yes, I do know. But if I had the handling of your decorated heads, I should soon have you shut up too. I am mad. But how did I become mad? Doesn't that interest you? No, it doesn't interest anyone [*The Father*, 50].

The captain's knowledge does not help him transcend his situation because he cannot see the problems in terms of his need for authority and control, his conventional deportment as patriarch, his rational, scientific grasp of human affairs. Unlike the Shakespearean hero, the captain cannot overcome his distress and accept the kind of responsibility for his anguish that Lear was capable of. The doctor and the pastor, oblivious to the implications the captain's plight has for them, enter into a conspiracy to stow him away. Ironically, both characters typify the same kind of authority the captain has characterized. The doctor commands a rational discourse similar to the scientific knowledge the captain has mastered. And this very quality prevents him from realizing the source of the captain's anxiety. The doctor, who has the legal power to confine the captain, is himself cloistered by his knowledge. Although he is not diabolic, his treatment of the affair serves to marginalize the captain. Perhaps the pastor and the doctor ignore the captain because he has come too close to the truth for comfort. Thus, they move away from the captain. Conversely, the women come together.

The captain's second important dialogue with his daughter shows him that she is now completely at one with her mother. He insists that Bertha must follow only his will (*The Father*, 52). A terrifying scene witnesses his desire to "devour" her. He will cannibalize her, ingest her, if she will not acknowledge her fleshly bondage to him. Significantly, he is pacified by the nurse, who renders him as weak as a newborn infant. The nurse, hitherto loyal, straitjackets the captain. Yet another stable relationship has been undermined. The captain seems to succumb to some age-old, preadult rites. He is not afraid of the nurse's sexuality and hence trusts her. He is duped into underestimating her ties with Laura.

The horrible spectacle of the straitjacketed lunatic is contrasted to the image of amity between mother and daughter. In yet another inversion, the captain does not save Bertha from the irrational; Laura saves her from the captain's irrational rage. Laura is free of the captain. Carlson points out that "in her role as wife, Laura is often interpreted as the epitome of feminine treachery" (Carlson 1982, 56). This interpretation ignores the captain's rigid adherence to norms hostile to Laura's free spirit. *The Father* concludes with a double image—a superimposed image—the father in a straitjacket, fettered by his fears, and the mother and daughter, freed from the patriarch, exulting in their togetherness. The play ends on a note of freedom and enclosure: freedom for the woman, confinement for the man.

Bentley finds that the conclusion of the text is not organic to it, that it "does not quite grow out of the human resources of the story" (Bentley 1971, 99). Indeed, the conclusion of the play stems from the intersections between the social and the psychic that the play explores. Laura wants authority over her daughter at one level and at another, authority over her body. The two blend. Faced with obduracy, she sets out to win her freedom, buries the woman who wails, and takes on the guise of her other self, the old woman. At the level of the plot, the woman is the harbinger of madness. She is motivated, however, by the need to rebel against a patriarch who disdains the artistic associated with the feminine. Her success and her freedom lie in her sanity.

It is a function of the complexity of the play that the conclusion mourns for the father while celebrating the mother's freedom. A certain inevitability marks Laura's actions, an inevitability determined by the social and psychic conflicts set up between a spirited woman and an authoritative man against the backdrop of enormous social upheaval and change. The play dramatizes a radical insight into the nature of sanity—a society that reinforces a man's ideology is the precondition of his fragile sanity. The dramatist reinforces the insight in the manner in which he deploys a variety of perspectives that capture both the failure of the man who realizes that the center is hollow and the problematic nature of the victory of the woman who discovers autonomy and a new freedom in the breach at the center but only at the expense of having played up to stereotypical convictions on the connections between the feminine and the intuitive. Laura has vanquished the father, but her victory is qualified for us by the knowledge that she succumbs to the patriarchal structure that represses her when she takes on the role of the father in her relationship with Bertha. Ironically, in refusing the possibilities that the patriarchal education would offer Bertha, she both liberates and confines her, for Bertha is now literally tied in to the preoccupations of her mother and the muttering old lady in the attic. Laura too seems partially confined by an essentialist notion of femininity. Although Strindberg has located the struggle for power in the social space, in the last instance, his dichotomization of the spheres according to the essentialist categories which structure the play and which are reaffirmed at the end of the play renders his celebration of the female suspect and restricts the female viewer's pleasure because Laura replays an authority position that mimes patristic ideologies. Thus, the text powerfully dramatizes the complicated, almost tragic, price a woman pays when she wins a battle in a patriarchal society.

We need a new production of *The Father*, one that will blazon the exergue in all its daring.

Part II

Male Fantasy and the Female Spectacle

Chapter 3

The Female Pantomime: Pirandello's *Henry IV*

With claims to a precocious postmodernity and an unrivaled reputation for practicing metatheatre, Luigi Pirandello would at first appear to have little in common with either Strindberg or Büchner. Indeed, one could insist that Pirandello's plays signaled a departure from nineteenth-century theatre, even theatre that was antirealistic. Pirandello's drama evinces a concern with developing an antiillusionistic theatre that resembles both Büchner's and Strindberg's approaches. Nevertheless, the mode in which Pirandello tackles the problem is substantially different from that used by either of these dramatists because Pirandello hails the spectator.

Formally, Pirandello's commitment to a theatrical dialogue with his audience separates him from both Büchner and Strindberg. However, his emphasis on the subjective world of his characters, his deep interest in staging the Weltbild of the male marginal, and his intuitive placement of women in the middle of this problematic serve to link him with the other two playwrights. That the connection is stronger than the mere deployment of the theme is made patent by the focus on the antiillusionism. More concretely, the accent on the male's sexual stress in the constitution of his subjectivity, placed within a modernist frame, brings Pirandello's work close to Büchner's and Strindberg's.

Pirandello's *Henry IV* decisively includes the spectator in its theatrical world. The spectator is spoken to, addressed directly, and, most importantly, shown how the theatrical world is assembled, put together. The world on the stage is assembled under our very noses, so to speak. We are not observers of a world that is independent of us, nor do we identify with the protagonist of a world that purports to be imitative of ours. We are duped, deluded, and left hanging in midair. We are asked to produce the meaning of the play.

The play *Henry IV* (1922) is about madness as a constructed reality. Pirandello's concern with dramatizing the ways in which reality is not a natural given, but a socially constructed phenomenon, is revealed in *Six Characters in Search of an Author*. The oppositions between madness and sanity that *Henry IV* plays with are similar to the oppositions between face and mask that are delineated in *Six Characters in Search of an Author*. Whereas Pirandello blurred the lines of demarcation between illusion and reality in *Six Characters in Search of an Author*, he blurs the lines between madness and sanity in *Henry IV*. Whether the protagonist of *Henry IV* has constructed himself as mad in the most theatrical gesture possible, or whether the characters in the play have perceived him as mad because of his "insane masquerade," madness is viewed as a construction rather than an intrinsic quality. Because Pirandello does not authorize the unnamed's narrative, we cannot with absolute assurance decide that he has indeed been "sane." (Since the protagonist's name is never mentioned, I will refer to him as the unnamed.) After all, the unnamed's "sanity," reconstructed by him as it were, could be another shade of the delirium of madness. Further, since *Henry IV* is a play about plays, the "madness" is clearly also to be seen as a theme that the playwright has played with in order to evoke not only the different ways in which madness is constructed but also the different ways in which madness is manifested. The confusion that ensues as a result of a rather ironic and problematic distinction between "real" and "pretended" madness destabilizes the notion of the stable ego and leaves us in a Pirandellian universe where "real" madness is not completely real, for the unnamed has been "playing" a role with remarkable consistency for 12 years. At the same time, "pretended" madness is not exclusively a matter of pretense, for the protagonist wounds Belcredi when he is presumably "sane." Even if the protagonist's act is viewed as characteristic of Pirandellian characters in that they desire to remain within the realm of the fixed, the static, the world of theatre, the choice itself can be considered to display a passion or an obsession that is tinged with the hue of Otherness as "madness." Thus, in this play which unleashes the element of madness onto the dramatic stage, the sanity of the protagonist, the counselors who help him, and the troupe that comes to cure him are questioned.

Pirandello also operates with the idea of gender as culturally constructed, rather than biologically given. Unfortunately, the unnamed clings to a private conception of femininity which does not speak to the reality of the women in the play. His vision of women congeals them, so that they resemble the frozen portraits he gazes at. The portraits of the unnamed and Donna Matilda in costume in their youth furnish an example of this construction of both the subject and the woman. In these formal elements, the play links women with madness but woman remains unnamed as madness. The mise-en-scène which focuses on mirrored images of women and the unnamed plays with the trope of woman as madness.

Identity, for the chief character, is contingent on reflection. Judith Butler, using Lacan, declares that "ontological characterization presupposes that the appearance or effect of being is always produced through the structures of signification" (Butler 1990, 44). Pirandello elaborates on the trope of reflection in a number of ways. The portrait of Henry IV that dominates the mise-en-scène functions as the Lacanian mirror image, giving the unnamed a sense of power and coherence that he does not have. It reconfirms an image of the self that is reassuring. Following Butler's notions on reciprocity between male and female, one notices that the portrait of Donna Matilda hints at a reciprocity whereby the male is dependent on the image of the woman to remain secure in his identity. The thematic of reciprocity with the female is later enriched by the fact that the daughter who looks like the mother's image functions as woman, not the mother herself (Butler 1990). Women then are interchangeable because from a male reference point, their significance lies in their "image," their value, not in their ontology. The reconfirmation of male identity through the female image is, however, marked by loss rather than plenitude because of the fantastic nature of the self-construction. The unnamed's presentation as mad illustrates the fabrication of masculinity in general. The unnamed's madness then alerts us to the construction of gendered subjectivity by estranging us.

The play opens with a portrayal of three young men dressed as German knights of the twelfth century. They are waiting for the appearance of a person called Henry IV. The noblemen identify him as Henry of Germany, as opposed to Henry of France. The master of the house, di Nolli, accompanied by his fiancée, Frida, her mother, Donna Matilda, and Matilda's lover, Belcredi, comes to the castle. The troupe is headed by Genoni, a doctor. They have come "to shock" the unnamed back into sanity. They believe that he is mad and that in his madness, he has clung to the persona of Henry IV, a role he once played in his youth. According to Donna Matilda, the unnamed's friend, he had a bad fall and never recovered from it. By reenacting the masquerade they all engaged in twelve years ago, members of the troupe hope to bring the unnamed back to the realm of sanity. Pirandello, however, views neither the unnamed nor madness in the light they do. Indeed, the play problematizes the very notion of madness.

As Pirandello is different formally from Büchner and Strindberg in that he is metacritical, i.e., stages a theatre on theatre, so is he also radically different in the structural function he assigns madness in *Henry IV*. Where both Büchner and Strindberg dramatized madness as a signified, as an entity that had a specific meaning and invoked a specific response and formed part of the whole of the dramatic text, Pirandello makes it impossible to talk with any degree of validity about the signifier and signified of madness. The material vehicle is the signifier. The mental concept is the signified (Elam 1980, 6). We neither know what acts betoken madness, nor what words can be broken down to spell madness, nor what madness means. Pirandello does not use it as a structural device to resolve the exigencies of the plot, nor does he diagnose madness. He problematizes the notion of the signification of madness and pushes the dramatic situation to an extreme position in an attempt to allow madness to speak itself. The authorial voice or the directorial voice is mediated to such an extent that the very identity of the protagonist remains unspoken, unnamed. With that gesture, Pirandello indicates that he will not objectify, "name," and describe the reality of the mad. While the characters refer to madness and the doctor rationalizes it, the dramatist does not commit himself to a single definition. Rather, he will play "masquerade," neither to mask nor to unmask but to revel in the masquerade itself, to show that the unnamed's "act" is neither "real" nor an "act." A phenomenology of both the theatre and madness, *Henry IV* is an unusual effort in the history of both theatre and fiction to articulate the difficulties about both thinking of madness and dramatizing it without objectifying it.

The themes of the criticism on the play—the focus on identity, the speculation on madness, and the metaphor of the theatre—are significant to an understanding of the play (Oliver 1979, Matthaei 1973, Paolucci 1974, Patterson 1984, Ragusa 1980, Levenson 1981, Proser 1981). My purpose in this chapter is to explore the connections between the three discourses. I assume that the significance of the play lies in the context of the enunciation, i.e., the midspace between the play and its spectators (Elam 1980, 6–20). The spectator produces the text in interpreting it; thus the boundaries that separate performers from the spectators are obliterated. Pirandello's phenomenological study of madness links the theme to the themes of identity and the theatre. In the light of the shifting identities of the women, the projection would seem to be on woman rather than specific individual women. In Pirandello's system, the spectator's presence is invoked and considered by the self-conscious construction of mise-en-scène which invites us to watch/write the play. By addressing all three issues, I will suggest that Pirandello's play concerns itself less with the identity or fate of the individual than with the status of the discourses of madness, sanity, and gender and its connections to the constitution of subjectivity and the status of the theatre. My purpose is to evoke the spaces madness etches and explore its connections to the structure of the play as a whole. In particular, I will address the critical notion that *Henry IV* ends on a note of enclosure with the unnamed "cabined, cribbed, confined" as a Beckett character up to the waist in earth or up to the neck in a jar" (Bentley 1972, 44). While this is true in terms of the fact that the unnamed is entrapped, perhaps in the role, certainly in the castle, madness nevertheless protects him from the tentacles of the Genoni troupe. The tentacles metaphorically represent the tyranny of meaning itself, for when the unnamed's behavior can no longer be explained and packaged into meaning, it can no longer be objectified. In other words, personal experience remains unquantifiable and undiagnosable, albeit in a solipsistic fashion. It is a tragedy that this small freedom has to be won at such a terrible cost. Thus Pirandello neither celebrates the madness, nor the murder. Since the unnamed's act can be seen as either mad or sane and both mad and sane, Pirandello does not say that madness has no meaning, he merely says that its language is not univocal and that it cannot be defined or understood in any single mode.

Act I of *Henry IV* starts out on an uncertain note. The mise-en-scène deliberately deludes the spectator. The furnishings of the room are arranged to reproduce a setting from the twelfth century, though the actors smoke cigarettes, which indicates that the play is set in the modern period. Deception follows deception, for the actors on stage are also dressed like knights from the twelfth century. The very first lines confuse the audience because Landolph, Harold, and Ordulph have not decided what particular milieu the furnishings are supposed to represent. It could be the throne room at Goslar, at the castle in the Hartz, at Wurms, in Saxony, Lombardy, or on the Rhine. The knights decide what the setting will be and hence permit the dramatist to let us know that this is not a self-contained mimetic representation, this is not a self-enclosed world:

> (When the curtain goes up, the two valets jump down.)
> LANDOLPH (to Berthold as if explaining): And this is the throne room.
> HAROLD: At Goslar.
> ORDULPH: Or at the castle in the Hartz, if you prefer.
> HAROLD: Or at Wurms.
> LANDOLPH: According as to what's doing, it jumps about with us, now here, now there.
> ORDULPH: In Saxony.
> HAROLD: In Lombardy.
> LANDOLPH: On the Rhine [*Henry IV*, 140. All subsequent references to the play are from *Henry IV*, trans. Edward Storer in *Naked Masks*, ed. Eric Bentley (New York: Dutton, 1952)].

At this point, the audience is free to outline the space the stage is intended to represent. It is not fixed to one particular local habitat. As the valet lights up a cigarette, the time frame is dislocated. Surely this cannot be the twelfth century. It seems clear, then, that these are actors who are acting out a play who invite you to understand that the action on stage is composed of illusions woven together. Indeed, the point is emphasized by the fact that the opening scene covers Berthold's entrance into the ranks of the actors.

Berthold comments on the disjointedness of the mise-en-scène. Referring to the modern paintings of Donna Matilda and Henry IV, he says: "Well, the thing seems to me somewhat out of place, anyway: two modern paintings in the midst of all this respectable antiquity!" (*Henry IV*, 145). Further, the three pseudo-counselors dictate the part Berthold will play but will not give him the prompt-book. They tantalizingly throw lines at him that he may be able to use. Strangely, Berthold has studied the "wrong part" and has come prepared to play the part of retainer to Henry IV of France. Berthold's comic mistake underlines the fact that the actors are putting the play together right now. Harold emphasizes the problem when he tells Berthold: "But the trouble is that not even we know who you are" (*Henry IV*, 142). The audience finds it difficult to follow the orientation of action; so far the dramatist does not appear to have made up his mind on the central locus of the action of the play. Berthold's plea might as well be the plea of the audience: "Well, for Heaven's sake, help me a bit! Give me the main lines, anyway" (*Henry IV*, 146). The other three counselors, we are told, are merely period names. We do not know if Landolph's gripe is about not knowing who he is in relation to the unnamed, about not having a large part to play, or about not knowing who he is outside of the frame of the court of Henry IV:

> Cheer up, my dear fellow! We don't any of us know who we are really. He's Harold; he's Ordulph; I'm Landolph! That's the way he calls us. We've got used to it. But who are we? Names of the period! Yours, too, is a name of the period: Berthold! Only one of us, poor Tito, had got a really decent part, as you can read in history: that of the Bishop of Bremen. He was just like a real Bishop. Tito did it awfully well, poor chap! [*Henry IV*, 143].

Their identities/roles are compromised firstly by their awareness that they do not know if the parts they play are roles made to measure, roles that are defined, and by their awareness that these amorphous roles may or may not be their identities. There are cues, however, stage-managed by a figure who set the wheels in motion but is not there to direct the show: "Ah no, old sport, not quite that! We've got to give the proper answer, you know. There's trouble if he asks you something and you don't chip in with the cue" (*Henry IV*, 144). The invisible stage-manager, the unnamed, has no coherent, stable identity but a shifting image of himself which the prompters flesh out. Acting and identity intersect here, except that the unnamed never plays a role in a finished production. He defines the overture and lets the text write itself. The members of the cast, however, believe that the text writes itself according to prearranged signals. Thus, at the conclusion they find out that they have been acting in an unwritten text that does not get written. In one sense, Pirandello's schema for the play strives to create the effect of being a mime of the unnamed's play.

Pirandello implies that identities are constituted arbitrarily. Identity defined by Aristotelean or existential terms is invalidated by his disdain of the notion of the individual who expresses his character by his actions. Indeed, Pirandello suggests that identity is a construction that has little validity, and if it does have any validity at all, it is in the space midway between the individual and his/her observers. Where the characters of the Renaissance stage celebrate the world as a stage, Pirandello's characters are poised between believing that they possess identities and believing that they are constructed by other entities. Madness intertwines with the theme of identity. The four counselors are also in doubt as to whether the world they live in is mad. When Berthold expresses the fear that he may go mad, Harold responds wryly and trenchantly: "Go mad, be hanged! You'll have a fine time!" (*Henry IV*, 145). Harold connects madness here with acting and the pleasure the self takes in both madness and acting: the pleasure of evading the self and the pleasure of discovering the self. One acts in an unscripted text, one assumes the identity of an unfinished, unformed, unstable "persona."

The audience knows that the young men play charades, but the rest is left to speculation. The arrival of Donna Matilda with her party is the first verbal indication that people believe the unnamed is crazy. The whole situation then becomes crazy fantastic. The fictitious site of the play itself is the site of craziness, but it is not necessarily embodied by the personage of the unnamed. First, the troupe that comes in is clearly a troupe of actors. Their purpose in coming to the castle is to play out a charade that will shock the unnamed into the present. Matilda is cast in the role of the emperor's mother; Doctor Dionysius Genoni will play the part of Hugh of Cluny. The only difference between this troupe and the Harold, Landolph, Ordulph, Berthold troupe lies in the Genoni troupe's conviction that their script has been written out. The play they will perform has been predetermined by the Freudian psychoanalyst, Dr. Genoni. I call him the Freudian psychoanalyst because he uses popularized versions of Freudian psychoanalysis in an attempt to cure the unnamed. Ironically, his first name, Dionysius, invokes the Greek god Dionysos, who incarnates the principle of madness. Dr. Genoni systematically concentrates on delving into the unnamed's past and psyche. He makes an attempt to understand why the unnamed has gone crazy. Instead of Freud's "talking cure," Dr. Genoni substitutes his "acting cure." Like Freud, Dr. Genoni theorizes, based on what he knows of the unnamed's case history.

Donna Matilda, the doctor, and Belcredi have to make their entrances into an unscripted play and divert the course of that production. Pirandello thus invites the audience to be aware of the spectacle that is being assembled for them as much as for the unnamed. The responses of Genoni's troupe are an objective correlative of the reading that the audience might have produced of the opening scenes. They express the audience's reading. Neither the Genoni troupe nor the audience has yet seen the unnamed. Based on the performance of the counselors, the audience locates itself within the troupe's reading. Both the counselors and the audience imply that the unnamed lives in a fixed, unchanging point in time and has to be jolted out of it. Submitting to the expertise of the psychoanalyst, the troupe surrenders to a Freudian reading of the unnamed's situation. The audience is guided by the Genoni troupe's reading and, perhaps, half expects the performance to be executed as the Genoni troupe planned. Neither the audience nor the Genoni troupe is allowed to stick to the authoritative reading of the unperformed play. It is unperformed because the chief character is mentioned but has not appeared on stage. Berthold, the reader/spectator turned actor, repudiates the claim that the unnamed is crazy and confuses the audience further by questioning the sanity of the three counselors:

> BERTHOLD: Yes, sir, but I can't stand it any longer, and I ask you to let me go away this very minute.
>
> DI NOLLI: Oh, you're the new valet, are you? You were supposed to begin this morning, weren't you?
>
> BERTHOLD: Yes, sir, and I can't stand it, I can't bear it.
>
> DONNA MATILDA (to Di Nolli excitedly): What? Then he's not so calm as you said?
>
> BERTHOLD (quickly): —No, no, my lady, it isn't he; it's my companions. You say "help him out with his madness," Marquis; but they don't do anything of the kind. They're the real madmen [*Henry IV*, 160].

Landolph problematizes the situation even further by accusing Berthold of making Henry mad. Is the mysterious man mad or not? Will the real madman stand up? Di Nolli's mother, at whose behest the Genoni troupe is here, seems to have believed that the unnamed was on the verge of a cure. The unnamed—who for the audience has been an absent signified—has not appeared and has not been named.

The members of the Genoni troupe are unshaken by the inconsistencies of the tales they hear. They persist in their belief that the unnamed, always a brilliant actor, was shocked into an attachment to his role and can be just as easily jolted out of it. Pirandello shows us how casually their interpretation of the unnamed's actions is put together. Much of the history of the unnamed's madness is recounted either by Donna Matilda or Belcredi. Belcredi in particular appears to know the unnamed's character and believes that the role of Henry IV suited the unnamed's temperament and brought him in touch with himself. Pirandello subverts Belcredi's testimony from the start, however. We are aware that Belcredi is implicated in the whole imbroglio and cannot really be a reliable raconteur. Further, Belcredi's version conflicts with

Donna Matilda's version. Donna Matilda, portrayed as a woman hungering after her youth, would twist any story to cast herself as the chief actress. Indeed, she tries to play a dual role—her role as the mother of her daughter and her daughter's role. The squabble Belcredi and Matilda have about the portrait illustrates her desire for a role that she can play directly opposite the chief actor. Indeed, they are actors hustling for the limelight. Belcredi too attempts to highlight his own importance in the play they all staged twelve years ago. His aspirations are grander, for he claims that he was the director of the whole theatrical effort. The disagreement between Belcredi and Matilda serves to cast doubt on a vital portion of the unnamed's biography. Several different versions of the play, staged twelve years ago, contest each other. Underlying the narrative is the implicit assumption that the unnamed's identity is being constituted by these actors, who have a memory of the role he played but can no longer be certain what role he will play. It is as though the unnamed has decided to stage his performance on a site to which they have no access. Paradoxically, the Genoni troupe superimposes a biography on a nameless character and then constructs his present identity.

Through much of the play, the unnamed seems to be the one who has power to signify. He produces meaning through acting, gesture, and assumption of identity. Much of his power relies on the women, however, even though they may not be aware of it. Judith Butler succinctly talks about the male need for female reflection at a theoretical level:

> But that process of meaning constitution requires that women reflect that masculine power and everywhere reassure that power of the reality of its illusory autonomy. This task is confounded, to say the least, when the demand that women reflect the autonomous power of masculine subject/signifier becomes essential to the construction of that autonomy, thus, becomes the basis of a radical dependency that effectively undercuts the function it serves [Butler 1990, 45].

Butler's observations also provide us with a different key to the motivation of the murder. When the members of the Genoni troupe threaten to smash the reflection and show the unnamed Matilda instead of Frida, they challenge the unnamed's sense of sanity and security. Quite as much as Büchner's Woyzeck and Strindberg's captain depended on the female's sexual fidelity, the unnamed depends on the reflection to see himself as sane and powerful.

Clearly, no one in the text can understand the different registers that the unnamed uses. Pirandello's critique of Dr. Genoni could be read as a spoof of Freud and the attempt by psychoanalysts to structure and pattern their patients' lives according to their presuppositions. As of yet, however, the members of the Genoni troupe believe that the unnamed will come out of the role of Henry and reassume his earlier role as a young nobleman (who has by now turned old). No kernel of certitude lends the spectator a touchstone by which to understand the plays that are being enacted. Even as Belcredi's, Donna Matilda's, and Dr. Genoni's readings of the unnamed's character could be projections of their own personae, so could our reading of the events on stage. Pirandello implies that our efforts to give the events on stage a coherence and framework are as skewed as theirs. The contradictions, however, make us cautious. Pirandello invites the reader to interpret, takes the interpretation into consideration, and casts doubt on it. Significantly, he implies that we insist on accepting as coherent what presents itself as process, unfinished and tentative. Like the Genoni troupe, we read and interpret and act to construct realities that are seemingly logical but are actually only readings.

Since Genoni's reading is tentative, we are tempted to identify with a different axis of action—the action around the unnamed. Pirandello implies that even if we sympathize with the unnamed, we see the play through the eyes of the Genoni troupe. We can actually identify with the unnamed with any seriousness only if we completely believe his version of his history. This would be to lend credibility to a narrative that Pirandello quite clearly presents as a theatre—a theatre of improvisation, a narrative framed by fantasy and acting. The unnamed's story is after all the story of his acting. If the unnamed's version is colored, so is the Genoni troupe's. We know fully well that Dr. Genoni has constructed a pathological case study based on Freudian theory. Since Pirandello insists that neither version has the status of truth, an interpretation of the unnamed's state of mind is open to speculation. We are certain only of two things throughout the play: that the unnamed did have a fall and that he does attack Belcredi. Belcredi and Donna Matilda do agree that he was intense and that he had a penchant for Matilda, but they interpret both themes differently. The rest of the disquisition merely reflects our several readings of event and character.

Even before the unnamed enters the stage, Pirandello delicately implies that the members of the Genoni troupe are not as secure in their scientific discourse as they seem to be. Donna Matilda is visibly shaken when she sees her portrait: "But I would never have believed it! (Shaking as if with a chill.) What a strange feeling it gives one!" (*Henry IV*, 150). The doctor himself is "frightened at the disturbance" he has caused (*Henry IV*, 152). When Belcredi and Donna Matilda disagree about when they first knew that the unnamed was frozen in the role of Henry IV, Donna Matilda insists that they did not immediately realize it because Belcredi and the others had been "like mad folk" (*Henry IV*, 158). Berthold's excited entrance in the middle of this recapitulation gives rise to an alarm that both reveals and conceals the emotional unease of the troupe. Frida confesses that she is "frightened" and attempts to run away. Landolph accuses Berthold of having made the protagonist "quite mad" (*Henry IV*, 161). Interestingly, the doctor hesitates when he is asked to go in to see the unnamed on his own: "What do you mean? ... I? Alone?" (*Henry IV*, 162). When the unnamed enters the stage, he overturns their expectations. His demeanor and dialogue lead the actors of the Genoni troupe to believe that he is wise to their masquerade. The unnamed is certainly in command of the situation and monopolizes the conversation. The speeches that Pirandello attributes to him function as double entendres. They are edged with an ambiguity that makes it hard for us to discern if the unnamed is indeed aware of the charade the Genoni actors play or if he merely plays the part of Henry IV to perfection. He says, for instance, "Nothing satisfies them! I was a little boy, Monsignor.... One passes the time, playing even, when, without knowing it, one is a king—I was six years old..." (*Henry IV*, 168). The context suggests that he is speaking of Henry's childhood; but the ellipses contradict this perception and imply that he may be talking about the present where "he plays the king" or that he played the king even as a child. Some sections of his speech hint at a remembrance of the past, when he knew Donna Matilda:

> HENRY IV (looking at them): Ah yes! And I can postpone my grief to another time. (Shows the MARCHIONESS almost with coquetry the tint he has given to his hair.) Look! I am still fair.... (Then slowly as if in confidence.) For you ... there's no need! But little exterior details do help! A matter of time, Monsignor, do you understand me? (Turns to the MARCHIONESS and notices her hair.) Ah, but I see that you too, Duchess ... Italian, eh? [*Henry IV*, 168].

The unnamed does not persist in this vein, however. He does not renew his acquaintanceship but goes on to talk about the power that limits the will. Further, he even seems to offer a rationale for his "imposture" or "masquerade":

> HENRY IV: It's like this: When we are not resigned, out come our desires. A woman wants to be a man ... an old man wants to be young again. Desire, ridiculous fixed ideas of course—But reflect! Monsignor, those other desires are not less ridiculous: I mean those desires where the will is kept within the limits of the possible. Not one of us can lie or pretend. We're all fixed in good faith in a certain concept of ourselves. However, Monsignor, while you keep yourself in order, holding on with both your hands to your holy habit, there slips down from your sleeves, there peels off from you like ... like a serpent ... something you don't notice: life, Monsignor! (Turns to the MARCHIONESS.) Has it never happened to you, my Lady, to find a different self in yourself? Have you always been the same? My God! One day ... how was it, how was it you were able to commit this or that action? (Fixes her so intently in the eyes as almost to make her blanch.) Yes, that particular

> action, that very one: we understand each other! But don't be afraid: I shall reveal it to none [*Henry IV*, 169].

The text conflates the marchioness with madness. The unnamed accuses the marchioness of committing a secret, unmentionable act. It is plausible that he blames her for her instrumentality in the fall or for scheming to unsettle him, then and now. We are struck by his steady emphasis on concealment of the dreadful secret. Since the fall temporally marks the beginning of his madness, we read madness as the unmentionable signifier: what cannot be named. Because he speaks to the marchioness and attaches culpability to her, albeit obliquely, we forge an association between the horror of madness and the horror of femininity, which Lacan has characterized as lack (Gallop 1982). The dramatist does not develop this theme as a singular strand. Nevertheless, the link established between femininity and madness in the male imaginary is foregrounded by the formal technique of the plot's enunciative strategies, which revolve around the images of women either as masquerades or portraits.

The unnamed's role as penitent also informs the speech. The members of the Genoni troupe are flabbergasted by the dual edges of his speech and wonder what the exact state of his mind is (*Henry IV*, 173–75). Donna Matilda is convinced that he has recognized her. Belcredi disdains her perception, but simultaneously insinuates that the unnamed has recognized him (*Henry IV*, 175–76). The doctor has his own interpretation of the unnamed's behavior. The doctor insists on fitting the unnamed's actions into a framework in which he feels comfortable. Genoni's explanation is theoretical and ingenious:

> DOCTOR: (with a smile of pity of the competent person towards those who do not understand) We must take into account the peculiar psychology of madmen; which, you must know, enables us to be certain that they observe things and can, for instance, easily detect people who are disguised; can in fact recognize the disguise and yet believe in it; just as children do, for whom disguise is both play and reality. That is why I used the word childish. But the thing is extremely complicated, inasmuch as he must be perfectly aware of being an image to himself and for himself—that image there, in fact! (Alluding to the portrait in the throne room, and pointing to the left.)
>
> BELCREDI: That's what he said!
>
> DOCTOR: Very well then—An image before which other images, ours, have appeared: understand? Now, he, in his acute and perfectly lucid delirium, was able to detect at once a difference between his image and ours: that is, he saw that ours were make-believes. So he suspected us; because all madmen are armed with a special diffidence. But that's all there is to it! Our make-believe, built up all around his, did not seem pitiful to him. While his seemed all the more tragic to us, in that he, as if in defiance—understand?—and induced by his suspicion, wanted to show us up merely as a

> joke. That was also partly the case with him, in coming before us with painted cheeks and hair, and saying he had done it on purpose for a jest [*Henry IV*, 174].

The unnamed leaves them quarreling among themselves. Each of them is certain that he or she has understood the unnamed; yet, each of them offers a different interpretation. Donna Matilda thinks that the unnamed's remarks were addressed to her; Belcredi believes the same. The doctor is convinced that the unnamed has manifested signs of "lucid" dementia. All three of them, however, agree that the unnamed has surprised them and made them feel uncomfortable. The fact that the three do not have a uniform interpretation of the unnamed's state of mind makes it all the more difficult for the audience to situate itself in the action of the play. The actors in the Genoni troupe are neither callous nor cruel; they are merely very unreflective about scrutinizing their interpretations of the two plays: the pageant twelve years ago and the play that has been on stage since then.

The narrative of the pageant is blurred and confused because of the speed with which the whole affair took place and partly because Belcredi and Matilda shroud some fragment vital to the coherence of the narrative. We know that is the case because their personal biases make it impossible for them to see the unnamed except in connection to themselves. And we are never told what these fragments are. Rather than acknowledge that, we are tempted to superimpose a coherent framework on the sketchy outlines that the members of the Genoni troupe give us. The ambiguity is enriched by the audience's awareness that the episode is very important to both Belcredi and Matilda. Mundane possibilities mingle with the existential in the audience's attempt to unravel the skeins of this story of many seams. Did Matilda and Belcredi consolidate their relationship after the unnamed's accident? Is either of them hiding a secret vital to the plot of the narrative? Who is Frida's father? Did Belcredi actually engineer the accident, as the unnamed would have us believe? Did Matilda stay with Belcredi to acknowledge her complicity? Are their biographies bound up to the unnamed's in some horrible, nameless way? Have they vested their lives to defend their versions of the episode? Is it a part of the past in which they have invested a glamour and romance that they will not demystify?

Despite these murky, uneasy uncertainties, the audience finds its entrance through the actors of the Genoni troupe because it cannot get into the skin of the unnamed's radically different consciousness. Further, the audience chooses to ignore the unrepresentable incongruities and gaps in the narrative because it feels more secure when it fabricates a coherent narrative outline—frame, point of view, motive, character, resolution.

Pirandello subverts the tightness of the narrative and imbues it with the colors of delirium, for after the unnamed presents himself as the central intelligence of the narrative, he acts in a manner contradictory to his claim to rationality when he lunges on Frida. The unnamed is in command of the situation when the members of the Genoni troupe, disguised, come to parley with him for the second time. He dismisses both the doctor and Donna Matilda summarily. Once they have left, he tells his three counselors:

> Oh, look at this imbecile watching me with his mouth wide open! (Shakes him.) Don't you understand? Don't you see, idiot, how I treat them, how I play the fool with them, make them appear before me just as I wish? Miserable, frightened clowns that they are! And you (Addressing the VALETS) are amazed that I tear off their ridiculous masks now, just as if it wasn't I who had made them mask themselves to satisfy this taste of mine for playing the madman! ... And it's a bad look out for a man who finds himself labelled one day with one of these words which everyone repeats; for example "madman," or "imbecile." Don't you think it is rather hard for a man to keep quiet, when he knows that there is a fellow going about trying to persuade everybody that he is as he sees him, trying to fix him in other people's opinion as a "madman"—according to him? Now I am talking seriously! Before I hurt my head, falling from my horse... (Stops suddenly, noticing the dismay of the four young men.) What's the matter with you? (Imitates their amazed looks.) What? Am I, or am I not, mad? Oh, yes! I'm mad all right! (He becomes terrible.) Well, then, by God, down on your knees, down on your knees! (Makes them go down on their knees one by one.) I order you to go down on your knees before me! And touch the ground three times with your foreheads! Down, down! That's the way you've got to be before madmen! [*Henry IV*, 189–90].

Again, the unnamed casts doubt on his own narrative. He says he is not mad: he says he is mad. He also points out that madness is constructed. Is he testing his "secret counselors"? Does he want to find out if they have played their roles in the spirit of a trivial and practical joke or have played them out in the spirit of a dream from which they do not want to wake? The counselors believe that his sanity has been unimpaired all those years. At this point, the audience is perplexed, even though the counselors are convinced that the unnamed is sane. The audience could have been persuaded that he was sane, if he had not suddenly asked his counselors to go down on their knees. Whether he is feigning madness or is truly mad, he remains inaccessible to us because he does not remain in either position long enough for us to be persuaded conclusively of either. His shifting positions make it difficult for us to resolve the problem. When John comes in at the end of the act, he says that John has come in to "play the monk" (*Henry IV*, 196). Nevertheless, he greets John after the manner of Henry IV. The act ends with his dictating the document of his trials as Henry IV to his "faithful monk" (*Henry IV* 196).

Act III opens with the "acting cure." The sound of Frida's voice emanating from the frame of Donna Matilda's portrait stuns the unnamed. When Frida stretches her hand out, he lets his lamp fall and tries to run away. Attention is diverted from him, as the others rush to comfort a terrified Frida. Despite the fact that the unnamed has said nothing, Donna Matilda and Belcredi are sure of his newly found sanity:

> DONNA MATILDA: He is cured, Frida. Look! He is cured! Don't you see?
> DI NOLLI (astonished): Cured?
> BELCREDI: It was only for fun! Be calm!
> FRIDA: No! I am afraid! I am afraid!
> DONNA MATILDA: Afraid of what? Look at him! He was never mad at all!...
> DI NOLLI: That isn't true! What are you saying? Cured?
> DOCTOR: It appears so. I should say so...
> BELCREDI: Yes, yes! They have told us so.
> (Pointing to the four young men.)
> DONNA MATILDA: Yes, for a long time! He has confided in them, told them the truth!
> DI NOLLI: (now more indignant than astonished) But what does it mean? If, up to a short time ago...?
> BELCREDI: Hum! He was acting, to take you in and also us, who in good faith... [*Henry IV*, 198–99].

They believe in this newly found sanity despite the fact that at the end of the unnamed's "revelation" of his sanity, he continues to play the role of Henry when John comes in to act the monk. In the final scenes, Pirandello shows us that the unnamed's state of mind can only remain hidden from us. During the initial part of the encounter, the unnamed says: "Cured, yes! I am cured!" (*Henry IV*, 200). As the conversation proceeds, however, the situation becomes less stable and more fragile. The unnamed abruptly points to Belcredi and says, "He believes that I have been carrying on a jest" (*Henry IV*, 201). The unnamed takes them through a whole story whereby he seems to explain the reasons for enacting a "fantasy." The whole narrative, which claims that he sought refuge in madness and further that he is sane because of "conscious madness" persuades the others of his rationality to the extent that Belcredi insists that he, Belcredi, is mad (*Henry IV*, 204–6). Towards the end of the speech, the unnamed says to the doctor: "But I am not a madman according to your way of thinking" (*Henry IV*, 207). But finally, he draws close to Frida, claims her for himself, and orders the valets to hold the others. We are as shocked as the members of the troupe are. Belcredi lunges forward, yelling that the unnamed is no madman. The unnamed immediately responds in a manner that contradicts Belcredi's assessment:

> HENRY IV: (in a flash draws the sword from the side of LANDOLPH, who is close to him) I'm not mad, eh! Take that, you!... (Drives sword into him. A cry of horror goes up. All rush over to assist BELCREDI, crying out together)
> DI NOLLI: Has he wounded you?
> BERTHOLD: Yes, yes, seriously!
> DOCTOR: I told you so!
> FRIDA: Oh God, oh God!
> DI NOLLI: He's mad, mad!
> DI NOLLI: Hold him!
> BELCREDI: (while THEY take him away by the left exit, HE protests as he is borne out) No, no, you're not mad! You're not mad. He's not mad! [*Henry IV*, 207–8].

The conclusion is characteristically ambiguous about the unnamed's (in)sanity.

The unnamed wounds and kills Belcredi when he (Belcredi) attempts to keep the unnamed from reaching out to Frida, whom the unnamed sees as the young Matilda. The Genoni troupe's plot revolves around the role women are said to have played in the unnamed's life. Significantly, Donna Matilda implies that she played a crucial role in the happenings that led to the accident that presumably caused the unnamed's madness. In recounting her story to the doctor, she says that she was the object of "a pair of eyes glaring [at her] with a contained intense promise of devotion" (*Henry IV*, 156). She senses that his fervor may have been excessive:

> When I laughed at him then, it was partly out of fear. One might have believed a promise from those eyes of his. But it would have been very dangerous [*Henry IV*, 156].

Soon afterwards, she describes his madness in the same register. His madness "burned and blazed there in the terrible obsession which lit his face" (*Henry IV*, 159). Yet Pirandello makes no explicit connection between the unnamed's madness and his relationship with Matilda because he later casts doubt on Matilda's narrative. Thus, although Pirandello does not with any certainty suggest that the male/female relationships in the text breed madness in the male, he introduces the motif in an oblique way. The figures of the women act as crucial motivating devices. Belcredi's taunts about the marchioness and the unnamed, as also his attempt to keep Frida back, spur the unnamed to action.

The motif is brought into play at the opening of Act II when Donna Matilda emphasizes her physical resemblance to Frida. When Matilda sees the portrait, she recognizes that the portrait represents Frida as well as herself. Matilda debates the point heatedly with Belcredi and concludes to the doctor that "she cannot recognise herself in me as I was at her age; while I, there, can very well recognise myself in her as she is now!" (*Henry IV*, 152). Frida is not only an extension of Matilda, she is Matilda for the unnamed quite simply because he has never seen the aged Matilda but has lived with the portrait of the young Matilda for a few years and the memory of the young Matilda for even longer. The notion is dramatically strengthened when Frida first appears in the marchioness of Tuscany's costume. Donna Matilda exclaims: "One would say it were I! Look!—Why, Frida, look! She's exactly my portrait, alive!" (*Henry IV*, 179). The unnamed sees Frida in a similar light. When he talks about the insolence of the Genoni troupe, he points out that Donna Matilda can no longer be either Matilda or the marchioness of Tuscany, for she has lived all these years and is a ravaged version of the image he had of her:

> (Indicates the MARCHIONESS) She has enjoyed them [these years] and has become—look at her!—a woman I can no longer recognise. It is so that I knew her! (Points to Frida and draws near her) This is the Marchioness I know, always this one [*Henry IV*, 207].

It is crucial to emphasize that he claims madness at the same time that he claims Frida. When he leaps at Frida, he repeats that she was his. He regards her as an image that belongs to him; she is his possession. He considers that he is reclaiming what had been snatched away from him. As he claims Frida, so does he claim madness. While the members of the Genoni troupe do not reckon with the unnamed's perspective on Matilda and Frida, they do play with his secret affection for the marchioness in his role as Henry I and his affection for Matilda to draw him out of his "madness." Thus, the women are the linchpins around which the "acting cure" is built. Ultimately, the unnamed's passion for Frida as Donna Matilda causes him to kill Belcredi and thus draw the mime to a close.

In conclusion, even before the unnamed acts "irrationally," the audience has been able to observe and sympathize, mediated by the rational intelligences of the Genoni troupe. That is the point of view accessible to the audience. Identification with the unnamed is impossible because we can understand, as the Genoni troupe does, the unnamed only in terms of a rationality secure in itself. If we were to assume the subject position of the unnamed, we would be mimicking a deliberate exit from a recognizable world to an unrecognizable, unimaginable world. Pirandello does not presume to suggest that the unnamed chose to express his angst by sliding into solipsism and exile. He does not maintain that the motive or impulse to madness is definable nor that madness is a charted course with a plotted destination.

Pirandello does not try to "rationalize" madness by attempting to lend it logical motivations. Rather, he acknowledges that madness is unrepresentable and presents *Henry IV* as a production that draws out the thematics of a signifier whose referent cannot be located but can only be mediated through a system of signifieds that cannot even identify the signifiers of the radically Other system. Belcredi and the unnamed operate in different systems. This is not to suggest that the play is exclusively about the construction of private languages that isolate and incarcerate individuals who have mislaid the primary signifiers of the other system. The unnamed does have a grip on the Genoni troupe's endeavor: their signifiers are consistent with their signifieds and are part of a well-established system. They have an authoritative frame of reference—their referent is clearly Freud. This consistency of language clearly emphasizes the Genoni troupe's rationality. Their venture may be foolish and unsophisticated but within their own system they have scientific authority to reinforce their positions. The space of madness is one they can neither envision nor enact. Thus their play collapses, while the unnamed's is a runaway hit, complete with a horrendous climax.

Pirandello evokes the spaces of freedom that madness/the unrepresentable create by linking madness to the theatre and the question of identity. By showing us that we can visualize madness only from a point of grievous certainty, from a core of rational certitude, he confesses that even to dramatize it would be to objectify it. The topos of rationality intervenes in our perceptions of madness. Since to talk about madness would be to objectify it, he attempts to dramatize it from the site itself. But this is possible only through theatre, through mime. Hence, the play opens in Goslar/Wurms, etc., without giving the audience the mooring either of sanity or insanity. It presents itself as a play that contains within itself the same pressures of possibility that sites of madness can offer. It signifies the possibility of difference. Even as Pirandello initially presents the scene without identifying it as either mad or sane, present or past, he has to submit to defining it in terms of opposition to the world of rational certainty. Simultaneously he problematizes that world so that we are aware of its uncertainties, but the very uncertainties go unnoticed because of the semblance of certainties. We may know that the Genoni troupe's version is compromised but its members do not. Even as they act, they are aware that they act and believe that they can find themselves when the show is over. The unnamed, on the other hand, seems to move through the worlds, seems to act several roles without troubling to identify them. Mime, because of its uncertain status, could represent madness. The female pantomime—the female as male reflection—concretely signifies male madness. Pirandello surveys the possibility that madness and acting are indivisible and that they hold and harbor a multitudinous imagining, a possibility to live without fixed meanings. It is a radically different consciousness that is unconcerned with the desire to unravel meaning. Pirandello presents the unnamed as a persona gliding in a world that is seemingly stable but inherently incoherent. Even if one accepts the various reports of the unnamed's shift to a different space, one is conscious that the so-called stability of a fixed point in time and space is absent. The unnamed's world is perilous because it depends on the interaction of the counselors, who sometimes play their parts beautifully and are word perfect and at other times slip up, and then it is all a Pirandellian version of "let's improvise tonight." Further, we cannot fix meanings onto signs because as one of the counselors says, they have very little information and are in constant doubts about the plot that they are a part of. The unnamed, for instance, addresses his counselors on his perfect understanding of the twentieth century and then moves back to being Henry IV. The unnamed for Pirandello has no signifier attached because he/we cannot name madness. We cannot lend it the contours of clarity because in so doing we rationalize it. At the same time, Pirandello is aware that even for us to perceive madness, we need to be on the side of the line that guarantees rationality. Inevitably, then, the theories on madness that Freud strung out are false for the dramatist because they emerge from a rational perspective.

Pirandello discredits theory on madness and attempts to speak it, profoundly aware that the only speech he can make on it is about its unrepresentability. It is its very lack of connection with the referent that lends madness a "freedom": a freedom from being impaled by meaning. This freedom is marginal, however, and won at the cost of the female. The female viewer then is doubly distanced and cannot support the universalist stance that locates the tragedy in the life sentence the unnamed serves in a theatre where he has little choice but to replay the same script. For the female viewer, the tragedy lies in the relentless female pantomime of the male imaginary.

Chapter 4

The Erotic Female Body: Weiss's *Marat/Sade*

Peter Weiss's *Marat/Sade* was a theatrical coup when it was first staged in 1964 at Berlin's Schiller Theatre. Its metatheatrical apparatus, while inviting comparison with Pirandello's innovations, has a political dimension that acknowledges Weiss's debt to Brecht. Antirealist from the overture that lists the dramatis personae, the play is akin to Pirandello's *Henry IV* in its framing of the spectacle. The physicality and the significance of movement in Weiss's theatre cannot be underestimated. Weiss had worked with the filmic medium before he came to the theatre. His sensitivity to film is discerned in his approach to theatre, where he is scrupulously precise not just about the verbal vehicle but also about the visual impact. Weiss does not produce Brechtian alienation theatre, although he uses many of its stock elements, including song, interruptions, and the all-important epigraphic summary of action before each scene. Weiss's technique in M*arat/Sade* is very specific to a filmmaking strategy originally borrowed from Brechtian praxis. Jean-Marie Straub and Danielle Huillet, Jean-Luc Godard, and Peter Weiss himself had experimented with avante-garde forms of filmmaking that challenged conventional narrative schemes. Whether it actually uses a film technique exclusively or not, the play *Marat/Sade* works with spectacle in a manner that is reminiscent of classical film, but uses a spoken text that clashes with the visual to alienate the audience. The audience is invited to gaze and is rejected at the same time. The deliberate enticement of the audience is effected by the movement or by the physicality prescribed in the stage directions, while the withdrawal is enjoined by the dissonance between visual spectacle and verbal context. Because of the foregrounding of the performative dimensions embedded in the text, interpretation of movement can alter the construction of meaning profoundly. This is of course true of the performance of most or all theatrical texts, but here I emphasize the shift in actual physical movement as marking a tremendous change, as opposed to, say, variations on interpretations of character or changes in the mise-en-scène or music. The importance of movement and the emphasis on physicality are so central in this play because it seemingly sensationalizes madness, which is signified by the gestures and movement of the actors. Their physical deportment becomes a crucial part of the production of meaning of the text.

The text has been a play in process in that the dramatist himself wrote six different conclusions to it at various times in order to clarify its political significance and even to make authorial position unambiguous.

Darko Suvin, in studying the production history of the play, compares three different versions and finds that each has its own ideological accent. He establishes the limits of the text, that is, interpretive parameters that foreclose the possibility of infinite readings because of cultural and social constraints. Suvin implies that the Verfremdung of the text is an invariant because of the relationship between the illusionistic and parabolic, or the overlapping inner and outer circles of the play. The first performance earned the approval of Peter Weiss, who, along with director Swinarski and Gunilla Palmstierna-Weiss, worked on the set. It highlighted the debate between Marat and Sade in a playful way but resulted in a "liberalism that cannot really imagine a political alternative to the madhouse status quo" (Suvin 1988, 411). The second production, probably the most well known, was directed by Peter Brook and made Marat a character in a Sade play on revolution and copulation. If there are both Artaudian and Brechtian elements in the text, Brook emphasized the Artaudian to approximate the effect of cruelty. The third production, in Rostock in the G.D.R., showed Marat as precursor to Marx. Suvin considers Swinarski's version to be a limit case, the other two versions to be adaptations.

When he produced the play in Santiago, Chile, William Oliver broke with theatrical conventions by having the mad inmates attack not only the audience in the play, but also the paying public. Oliver also tried to use the inmates to add thematic significance to the production while retaining the spectacular effect. Simonne Evrard, for instance, ran screaming down into the audience (Oliver 1967, 486–501). This production clearly tried to keep the audience in a state of unease.

At the Marat/Sade forum held at St. Mark's Playhouse, director Brook, critics, actors, and theatre professionals discussed the effect of the play on them. One group argued that it was a great play because it made the viewer want to start the revolution. Leslie Fiedler confessed to being moved by the play because it was "congruous to a world in which [he was] particularly uncomfortable." Interestingly, he wondered if he were masochistic (Schechner 1966, 218). Fiedler's point is that the play pulled him out of a notion of the Left as comfortable and cozy and forced him to identify with the real rejects of society. He hated Marat's politics and also the "chic—the anti-humanism of the play" (Schechner 1966, 220). According to him, the audience is cast as Coulmier's liberal crew. Podhoretz considered the play to be a comment about Communist self-cleansing. Discussants debated the relationship between sanity and madness (Schechner 1966, 214–37).

Critical and production histories of the play focus on the ideological conflict between Marat and Sade. Critics have also been sensitive to the trope of madness and sexuality in the text, both foregrounded by the Peter Brook production. In her review of the Brook production in New York in 1965, Susan Sontag stressed that "insanity proves the most authoritative and sensuous kind of theatricality" (Sontag 1966, 164). Sontag's point about the theatricality and insanity being at the center of the intellectual debate between Marat and Sade is well taken, especially her reminder that *Marat/Sade* is not "simply theatre of the senses" (Sontag 1966, 167–68). One would only add that this debate is also formulated by the body and its performance. Given the crucial significance of body as signifier of madness, sexuality, and power in the text, Weiss's sexual politics are also written on the body, specifically the female body.

Among modern playwrights to use the trope of madness, Weiss makes a spectacle of the body in a manner that would seem to invite objectification of the mad. Sensationalizing the mad by having them perform on stage as mad and as specific characters would appear to demand the voyeurism that was historically the case with Sade's productions in Charenton. Foucault too notes that audiences came to see the mad perform their madness, so to speak. He comments that under the Empire the specularization of madness reached a pitch unknown in the history of exhibiting madness. Paradoxically, the mad were visually displayed but otherwise confined to asylums. Speaking specifically of Coulmier's productions, Foucault says: "Madness became pure spectacle, in a world over which Sade extended his sovereignty and which was offered as a diversion to the good conscience of reason sure of itself" (Foucault 1973, 69–70).

Yet the very notion of *performing madness* argues against ideas of essential madness and credits the marginal with some power over self-presentation and the constitution of identity. Weiss's play asks that the inmate play out the madness of his/her performance and also the madness of the character. Both are on stage and neither is more real than the other. Judith Butler theorizes the relationship between performance and identity:

> Acts, gestures, and desire produce the effect of an internal core or substance, but produce this *on the surface* of the body, through the play of signifying absences, that suggest, but never reveal, the organizing principle of identity. Such acts, gestures, enactments, generally construed are *performative* in the sense that the essence or identity that they otherwise purport to express are

> *fabrications* manufactured and sustained through corporeal signs and other discursive means [Butler 1990, 136].

Reading the bodily movement of the performers then questions notions of their essential madness. Their movements themselves present their madness, so that it is not as though paranoid male inmate plays paranoid Marat, but that the corporeal gestures of the mad invest Marat with an identity whose essence is also questioned. The movements represent both the actor/inmate and Marat. In other words, all characterizations remain provisional at the level of essence or permanence. Performance constitutes the identity of character/inmate or inmate/character.

The emphasis on the body in the text, as constitutive of identity of both character and inmate, resurrects the question of whether the pleasures of the text are voyeuristic, especially in the light of the performances of the two women, "Simonne Evrard" and "Charlotte Corday." (I put the names in quotation marks once to show my hesitation about which role each woman "plays" but follow the convenience of convention by using these names through the rest of the discussion.) Oliver, for instance, discovered that some versions of the play completely revealed Corday's breasts, though doing so is unnecessary for the development of her role. The presentation of Corday's killing of Marat, Corday's lashing of Sade, and Evrard's tending of Marat could reconfirm the classic male gaze in its objectification of the female. The relay of looks in the diegesis solidifies this gaze. The bourgeois audience on stage and the male director on stage, Sade, observe the action. Because the audience in the play surveys, we too scrutinize. However, the passive pleasures of voyeurism as described by Mulvey are withheld by the level of unpredictability of the performance of the mad and the extent to which their actions are curtailed by their surveyors (Mulvey 1975, 6–18). Foucault's observation of the inscription of law on the body, desire on the body, and the law of desire on the body screens the mad/female from the sane/male gaze of both audiences (Foucault 1980, 186).

At the level of the action of the play, Weiss again withholds voyeuristic pleasure by his presentation of the murder of Marat. He underscores the aspect of performance by having Corday come to Marat's door three times before she kills him. He denies the viewer the traditional pleasure of narrative fulfillment. Critics have registered the Brechtian stamp of some of these caesuras in the action (Cohn 1967, 478–86). The most intrusive of these, which draw us into the drama of the performance and thereby produce an illusion rather than counteract one, are those that pull Corday out of her role. The first time, Sade tells her that it is not yet time, forestalling the satisfaction of narrative completion, but bringing us to the problem of performance, whether Corday will be able to play the role or whether she will muff it. Sade reminds her: "Not yet Corday/You have to come to his door three times" [Corday stops short, hides the dagger, and withdraws to her bench. The sisters and Duperret follow her as she leaves.] [*Marat/Sade,* 17. All subsequent references to the English translation are from *The Persecution and Assassination of Jean-Paul Marat as Performed by the Inmates of the Asylum of Charenton under the Direction of the Marquis de Sade,* translated by Geoffrey Skelton, verse adaptation by Adrian Mitchell (New York: Atheneum, 1965).].

History, of course, tells us that Corday did kill Marat, but Weiss gets us involved in how Corday's performance will go over or whether there will be some horrible, violent slipup. The second time Corday goes to Marat's, she sinks into herself. The third time, she does succeed, as we had been told she would. The heuristics of performance, meaning as derived from the body's significance in culture and theatre at this moment as opposed to the historical setting of Sade's play or the time Sade's play was produced, could actually counter the Brechtian interruptions. The interruptions are to have the effect ostensibly of engaging us in the debate between Marat and Sade.

The arbitrary dichotomization of the play into action (the move to kill Marat) and philosophy (the debate between Marat and Sade) can be criticized because both take place in the theatre of the body. Marat is after all in his bath through the action and is driven by his body.

The description of Marat's skin as spraying poison from his body is historically accurate as far as Marat's skin disease goes. In placing Marat in the bath, Weiss immobilizes him, which is perhaps a comment on the sequestration of the inmates. Historically, Marat's freedom was curbed, and his skin itched because he had to hide in cellars. Marat lacked "freedom" of mobility, just as much as the insane who were in the asylums. Weiss returned to this thematic with *Trotsky in Exile* (1970). Foucault notes that the isolation of the mad was a crucial indication of the power that the sane exercised over them in the Napoleonic age: "Power over madness was in its most important manifestation at least, exercised in the form of exclusion; thus one sees madness caught up in a great moment of rejection" (Foucault 1980, 184).

The emphasis on the skin disease viscerally accentuates Marat's exclusion: he cannot be touched, like the lepers of a bygone era. Thus Marat has to be washed continuously and keeps Evrard chained to him as he is to the body. Sade's eloquent intellectual defense of the body entering the pore of every intellectual debate, while rejected by Marat, nevertheless shows them to be more alike than dissimilar. Sade, after all, either directs the passages that Coulmier as Napoleonic spokesman deplores, or Sade sits back and enjoys the pandemonium that he has caused. His role in the interruptions further serves to mark his difference from Coulmier, his similarity to Marat.

As Otto Best shrewdly observes, Marat and Sade engage in a friendly battle; the real battle is with the Coulmiers (Best 1971, 79). Oliver perceived the importance of the bourgeoisie. In his production, he actually increased the number of bourgeois couples to register their presence (Oliver 1967, 498). Taking the spotlight away from the debate between Marat and Sade also allows us to concentrate on the contemporary intervention of the text.

These interjections work at two difficult levels: they show Sade as a critic of the establishment quite as much as the populist Marat is, and they refer to political issues of the day of performance.

Sade's staging of the play in and of itself with Marat as a protagonist could be irksome to the Napoleonic powers. In addition, the play gibes at Napoleonic imperial ambitions in a Brechtian mode and comments on Euro-American late twentieth-century economic imperialism. Coulmier interrupts the action of the play five times and each time it is to survey, contain, and censor liberty, to uphold the Napoleonic coup. The pattern of interruption speaks against demands for economic liberty on the part of the people, physical liberty on the part of the inmates.

When the people demand a real resolution, access to the means and modes of production, the patients demand their freedom. Coulmier purports to "represent" the voice of reason, "die Stimme der Vernunft" (*Marat/Sade*, 22. All subsequent references to the German text are from 1964 edition edited by Günther Busch [Frankfurt am Main:Suhrkamp Verlag, 1964]).

The second interruption is because Sade has not honored some previous cuts in the text that adopted an antireligious stance. Comically, the herald comes out and pacifies Coulmier with a sophistry about

> Things which happened long ago
> Remember things were very different then
> of course today we're all God-fearing men [*Marat/Sade*, 30].

The pious thought is followed by a patient/clergyman's prayer to the devil and comically capped by a set apology:

> Please understand this man was once the very
> well-thought-of abbot of a monastery
> It should remind us all that as they say
> God moves like man in a mysterious way [*Marat/Sade*, 31].

Coulmier steps out of the "reasonable" role and shouts, mimicking the mad, when Roux makes his populist plea. Roux's speech is very directly antiwar and obviously refers to the Vietnam debacle but also to the Napoleonic wars. In an address resembling Mother Courage's canny view on war, Roux debunks war mythology:

Once and for all
the idea of glorious victories
won by the glorious army
must be wiped out
Neither side is glorious
On either side they're just frightened men
messing their pants
and they all want the same thing
Not to lie under the earth
but to walk upon it
without crutches [*Marat/Sade*, 45].

Coulmier's panic about Napoleonic discipline permitting such utterances that were anti–Napoleonic is seen in his shrill response:

COULMIER: [shouting over him]
This is outright defeatism
At this very moment our soldiers are laying
down their lives
for the freedom of the world and for our
freedom
[turning violently to Sade]
This scene was cut [*Marat/Sade*, 45].

His state of high anxiety is discerned in his next interruption where he "jumps up to protest" (*Marat/Sade*, 75), actually to protect the traitors of the revolution who have now been reinstated by the emperor. A reference to Talleyrand drives Coulmier to the brink, and he threatens to shut the production down if they use passages that were previously deleted by "mutual consent." The sequence of interruptions culminates in Coulmier's "incit[ing] the nurses to extreme violence" while the patients move in ecstasy (*Marat/Sade*, 102).

The pattern of Coulmier's interruptions forestalls the pleasures of narrative fulfillment, that is, the progression to Marat's murder and paradoxically also spectacular fulfillment in watching the mad, except at the end, when the mad dance. Otherwise, whenever it looks as though we will get hypnotized by the sheer show of madness, Coulmier steps in. Coulmier's interjections then bring us to the performance of the mad and with it to knowledge of their status as the dispossessed, and hence to contemporary issues, whether Napoleonic or from the actual date of production.

The movement of the body on stage fixes the moment of performance as the most relevant: the thematic of the mad, their identities, and their freedom. While spectacular fulfillment may be foreclosed, the interruptions nevertheless draw visual attention to the spectacle, specifically bodily movement. Madness remains foregrounded through its inflection on the body.

Charlotte Corday suffers from Schlafsucht: her role is supposed to be played lethargically, somnolently. We are told that she suffers from depression. The imprint of madness on the female body raises the question of whether, despite the narrative and spectacular interventions, the play remains caught in that cultural convention whereby women's bodies are displayed for visual pleasure.

Corday's gestures are not outward; in general, they are inward. Her body itself is used as a signifier. We infer from Weiss's instructions that she is not in complete control of her body and that she is "attended throughout by two sisters, who support her, comb her hair and arrange her clothes. She moves like a somnambulist" (*Marat/Sade*, ix). Such an unawareness of the body is dangerous, to say the least, especially considering the emphasis on her exposed breasts, covered by a "flimsy white cloth" (*Marat/Sade*, viii). Oliver's reading of Corday's body would imply that Weiss used it to signal the inadequacy of her desire to kill Marat. Oliver's interpretation is unambiguous when he describes the girl who plays Charlotte Corday in Sade's play:

> A ripe young girl traumatised into a catatonic state by some sexual experience. Her naive idealism and intense morality are opposed to the sexual demands of her body. Her body is not to be recognised! Sade casts this pathetic creature as Corday knowing that the role will betray the child's psychotic repression [Oliver 1967, 495].

Corday's revolutionary role is seen completely as a sexual one here. Copulation takes over the revolution and the killing of Marat is seen as a sexual act transferred to violence. Bersani has studied such a transposition in male sexuality, rather than female sexuality (Bersani 1976, 13). If Oliver is correct in his estimation of the essentially sexual nature of Corday's act, Weiss constructs a version of female sexuality as dangerously violent because of the female's lack of awareness and control over sexual desire. Perhaps it is in this sense of lack of awareness that Oliver says Corday and Marat are "bodiless persons" (Oliver 1967, 495).

Textually, the repetition of Corday's sinking into herself and the nurses' forcible movement of her away from Marat's door supports the notion of an uncontrolled body. In terms of the action of the mad, Corday's "unreliability," her initial readiness to plunge the dagger into Marat, emphasizes her uncoordinated eagerness. We are also told that she seems to be standing and sleeping ("im Stehen zu Schlafen" [*Marat/Sade,* 34], that she is "led forward" [*Marat/Sade*, 36], speaks with her eyes closed [*Marat/Sade*, 37], thinks of Duperret's sexual advances as a test because she desires to succumb, but twists herself away from him [*Marat/Sade*, 38]. She is dragged behind by the sisters after she whips Sade and is led away again by the sisters after her second conversation with Duperret. At the end of Act I, she is sleeping.

The significance of Corday's body is overinvested by Sade's casting of her, by her madness, and by the audience's perspective of what we *see*. Her body removes itself from the diegesis and produces its own meanings within the space of theatre/culture. Foucault's observations on the connections between sexuality and madness are complex and suggest that Corday's body is a site of conflicts that cannot be explained by the idea that sexuality overcame the body and resulted in violence. He critiques the approach to the psyche which insists on reducing madness and rendering it intelligible by viewing sexuality as the meaning of madness (Foucault 1980, 185). His own project allows us to consider the grafting of sexuality and madness as indices of the impact of sequestration or imprisonment of the mad and hence allows us to see the political significance of Corday's body, Corday as the inmate/actor, and the body's imprisonment in contemporary society. Foucault maintains:

> Power relations can materially penetrate the body in depth, without depending even on the mediations of the subject's own representations. If power takes hold on the body, this isn't through its having first to be interiorised in people's consciousness. There is a network or circuit of bio-power, or somato-power, which acts as the formative matrix of sexuality itself as the historical and cultural phenomenon within which we seem at once to recognize and lose ourselves [Foucault 1980, 186].

Foucault's notion of the impress of power on the body allows us to retrieve Corday's body from signifying sexual repression. Rather, her body marks the imprint of repressive powers, here the asylum directors and in the Napoleonic era the antipopulists. For Weiss, within the theatre of the mad, Corday's body defines the struggle against the oppressor.

Within Sade's theatre, the historic Corday is under siege and is severely criticized for assassinating Marat in a somnambulistic fantasy. Sade himself does not resist Corday, Weiss does. Further, within Sade's play, Corday's discourse is rejected. The first time she attempts to kill Marat, she seems to visualize herself as a revolutionary and berates Marat for having failed the public. Within the Napoleonic frame, she is a hero for having killed Marat and paving the way for that "authentic" populist hero, Napoleon. In other words, Coulmier approves of the play because of its seemingly anti–Marat core. Freedom is invoked in this first attempt:

> And I go
> to murder you Marat and free all mankind [*Marat/Sade*, 15].

She is led away by the sisters with her head bowed (*Marat/Sade*, 15), and later the discourse of freedom is undercut by the "Liebeserklärung" (*Marat/Sade*, 28), the love explanation expressed in explicit phallic imagery of the dagger piercing Marat's flesh (*Marat/Sade*, 17). In the second attempt, Corday is inert and indeed stillness marks her performance here. She has been statically arranged in a pose, much like a picture or a statue. She responds to the herald's cue but is very hesitant about making her demand to enter Marat's bath. She sinks into herself and is quickly drawn away. This sequence visually displays the woman as a portrait, picture, or statuette. Complete absence of the will is played out by the body.

The third time Corday appears to have more energy because she pushes Duperret aside, but this time she seems to be in a trance, possessed.

The distinction between Sade's theatre and Weiss's is after all a sophistic one. It is a purely heuristic device which enables one to see Sade as director/actor rather than as the historical Sade vs. the historical Marat. We see Corday in Sade's/Weiss's theatre so that as inmate she can be seen to perform her oppression and as character she can be seen to be dangerously empty. These two elements characterize the contradictory quality of the female body on stage.

Many of the images that transcend the diegesis—the space of Weiss's and Sade's stories—are "pathological" versions of the culturally sexualized female body. Cixous and Clément point out that the hysterical woman is surrounded by a voyeuristic audience of men "ready to satisfy [their] fantastic desire" (Cixous and Clément 1986, 10). Corday is circled by Sade, the director, who within the diegesis has fantasies about her, and by Coulmier, the doctor/director, and the gaping Parisian audience. The spectacle of Corday's lashing Sade, with her braids in one production, with thongs in another, is definitely played on the stage of male desire. The enactment of Marat's death as a sexual act also seems to mimic a Sadean fantasy fulfillment, again male.

An important sense in which the very body of the woman is appropriated for male consumption is highlighted by Corday's performance. In talking about women who are possessed, Cixous and Clément argue: "The female body served only as intermediary, prop, passage. Passage accomplished, that which is no longer woman but beast, devil, *symptom* is set free [my emphasis]. The girls are not released, the demons are: the girls are *bound"* (Cixous and Clément 1986, 11). Certainly, Corday acts possessed in her vacancy and total obliviousness to her body. Because of the highly restricted nature of her movements, which are variations on her confinement by the nuns and the asylum's "panoptic" gaze, her body kills Marat (Foucault 1979, 195–231). She herself does not kill him. Of course, Weiss's politics, which were left of center, ultimately brought him close to Marat. Consequently, the portrayal of the historic Corday as regressing is to be viewed as an expression of the socialist playwright's solidarity with Marat, but one that is exaggerated by the dramatization of Corday's body. The historical Corday's assassination of Marat is contaminated by the inmate's symptom: Schlafsucht. It transforms a potentially revolutionary murder, not into a conservative right wing coup as Coulmier et al. may have hoped, but into the sexual surplus of the female unable to contain it.

In another crucial sense, Corday's body belongs to the people. Her initial arrival in Paris, her perception of her mission, her rejection of Duperret points to a notion of her will being subservient to the people; her body becomes theirs. After all, it is in their name that she kills:

> I name you names
> Marat
> the names of those
> who have gathered at Caen
> [falling into a sing-song]
> I name Barbaroux
> and Buzot
> and Pétion
> and Louvet
> [as she speaks the names her face is distorted
> increasingly by an expression of hate and lust]
> and Brissot
> and Vergniaud
> and Guadet
> and Gensonné [*Marat /Sade*, 94].

Weiss's *Marat/Sade* uses the trope of the body of the mad in general, and the female body specifically, to critique the imprisonment of the mad, the sequestration of the marginal. The spectacle the performance creates is not contained by the play, so that the move to withhold visual fulfillment is counterbalanced by the accretion of visual pleasure. Because the body of "Corday," the woman who plays the role of inmate and the historical Corday, is marked by contradictions, visual pleasure overlaps voyeuristic pleasure. Corday's absence from her body becomes the condition of her oppression. Corday's rebellion against the normative is counterbalanced by her lack of mobility. As Cixous and Clément say about women in general, "she has not been able to live in her 'own' house, her very body" (Cixous and Clément 1986, 68).

Part III

Political Interventions and Female Subjectivity

Chapter 5

Female Sexuality and Subjectivity: Brecht's *The Good Person of Szechwan*

Bertolt Brecht's theory of "alienation" theatre marks a departure from the practice of Pirandello, Strindberg, and Büchner. His choice of a female protagonist in *The Good Person of Szechwan* (1939–41) might seem to separate his text from theirs, but the problematics of spectatorial positioning, the use of madness as an entrance to the text, and the theoretical, self-conscious distance from Aristotelean theatre are comparable. However, his approach to the psychological through the material does separate him from the other three dramatists. Where Strindberg blended the psychological and social and Pirandello took the high road of the unconscious, Brecht, the Marxist dramatist, grounds his work in the material.

Iris Smith asserts that feminist critics are attracted to Brecht's work because of "the redefinition of spectatorial pleasure" implied by his approach to the construction of the self and his dialogue with viewers (Smith 1991, 491). Brecht's *The Good Person of Szechwan* explores the inherent possibilities of alienating the audience which the sane/mad/observer trajectory offers. The female viewer, enraged by the shameless exploitation of Shen Teh, seeks both to define and to solve the problems that Shen Teh faces. In dramatizing the life of a prostitute who metamorphoses into a male, Brecht does no less than to historicize madness: he gives it a name, a profession, and a gender. In showing the constitution of the female subject as mad, Brecht assumes that subjectivity and agency for the female subject in a patriarchal, capitalist society is fraught with peril that threatens her subject position.

In Brecht's play the gods come down to the earth to find a good person. Brecht equates the gods' notion of obedience with servitude to the status quo. If the gods find people who live by their laws, their norms will not be repudiated and their power will not be endangered. The third god explains what is at stake for them in this allegorically transparent caricature of the ruling class: "The resolution says: the world can go on as it is if we find enough good people who succeed in living a life worthy of a human being." (*Good Person*, 5. All subsequent references to the English translation of the play are from *The Good Person of Szechwan* in *Bertolt Brecht: Collected Plays,* translated by Ralph Manheim, edited by Ralph Manheim and John Willett [New York: Random House, 1976].)

Wang, the water seller, takes the gods to Shen Teh, a prostitute who is considered "good." The gods give her money with which she buys a tobacco store, but she finds that she cannot cope with the problems she encounters. Brecht shows us that she adopts a male persona, the persona of a fictitious cousin. He records her "splitting," which becomes the focal point of the play.

The transformation that Shen Teh undergoes has been approached from the ethical, psychological, and material perspectives. Gender is not foregrounded in these analyses. The critical universalization of Shen Teh's dilemma is symptomatic of modernist humanist critiques which subsume gender under the rubric of a universality which ultimately remains androcentric. Elizabeth Wright approaches the play as an example of Brecht's dialectical practice and takes a material stand on the splitting: "Brecht is able to show the real split of the bourgeois individual into private moral self and public business self. The split person as an embodiment of capitalism has nothing to do with any notions of schizophrenia: s/he is the visible image of the objective contradictions of man/woman in the bourgeois capitalist world, an image of an alienated condition" (Wright 1989, 41). John Fuegi, who privileges gender in his analysis, accounts for the splitting of Shen Teh/Shui Ta in economic terms. He argues that the "double exploitation" of women (because of class and gender position) and the "relations between men and women" in Szechwan can be "unmasked" only by the "masking" of Shen Teh (Fuegi 1974, 191 and 194). In conclusion, he stresses that the two personae merge into a neutral category—that of "mensch." Thus, he too finally concurs with the general hypothesis that the text is about man, not women.

The three major strands of criticism of *The Good Person of Szechwan* that have accounted for the splitting of Shen Teh have revolved around the notions that goodness is impossible in an evil world, that tragedy ensues from the fierce circumstances that enwheel Shen Teh, and that women bear a double yoke under capitalism (respectively, Bentley 1981, Ewen 1969, Swaffar 1979; Gray 1976, Knopf 1982; Sokel 1962). More generally, in considering Brecht's status as a Marxist playwright and his representation of women, Lennox argues that Brecht's women figures are "double edged" and that they "demonstrate both his blindness to women themselves and to a whole range of issues which women have taken to represent, but simultaneously they call forth a potentially utopian dimension which might be elaborated in contemporary reutilisations of his works" (Lennox 1978, 84). Shen Teh of *The Good Person* is not exclusively a classical female stereotype at all. Indeed, some aspects of the stereotype are held up for scrutiny. I argue that the play explores the psyche of the speaking subject as female and mad, that the world of the play is significant in the historical traces it leaves on the woman's formation, and that Brecht scrutinizes male perceptions of women and women's desires. Further, the play is not a self-contained, unified whole whose every part can be tied to the center, but a fabular, fantastic, almost allegorical rendition of women's desire.

Brecht portrays Shen Teh's desire for the power and credibility of the phallus. This is why the play is not about the neutered "mensch" but the female who craves entrance into the symbolic—the realm of law, economics, language that the male sex has appropriated. It is in her desire for the phallic signifier that Brecht locates the madness of the text. Shen Teh may not want to be a man, but Brecht portrays her as a woman who wants to enjoy the effects of masculinity. This portrayal is consonant with the Freudian thesis that the girl child, when she first recognizes sexual difference, desires either to be a male or have a male child (Irigaray 1985, 55–81). Yet, the desire lends Shen Teh an escape into potency and power. That it is only through madness that the female can insert her subjectivity is troubling to the female viewer, who nevertheless sees the splitting as indicative of the extremity and the specificity of the female's material and psychic condition in patriarchy (Cixous and Clément 1986).

Smith is more unequivocal about her reservations regarding the later plays. She notes that the feminist spectator's pleasure is prevented by essentialist dichotomizations that the mode of presentation ignores (Smith 1991, 495). Nevertheless, she too is convinced that in both *Mother Courage* and *The Good Person*, Brecht does in fact work with a main female character's "struggle to avoid victimization" (Smith 1991, 492).

The prologue of the play delights in a parable on the gods' search for goodness, a goodness they must unearth if the world is to continue as it always has been. Wang brings the gods to Shen Teh in his role of public spokesman. His opinion of Shen Teh does little to filter our perception because Wang merely isolates an abstract trait, goodness, and credits Shen Teh with its possession. Unlike Wang, the gods do not have a consistent point of view. They oscillate. The text shows the "goodness" motif to be a decoy since it invalidates the notion of "goodness" on the very same terms that it sets "goodness" up (Swaffar 1979, 65–69). Its viability as a criterion is disproved. The gods value "morality" but accept Shen Teh's sale of her body; the gods value honesty but accept Wang's false bottomed carrier; the gods value hospitality but pay Shen Teh for the price of a night's rest. The goodness motif, though a decoy, acts as a plot device to bring the play to the Shen Teh/Shui Ta transformation. Nominally, Shen Teh/Shui Ta undergoes her metamorphosis to uphold her vestigial "goodness" but the play becomes increasingly concerned with the process of recording her divided consciousness, while the "goodness" motif gets submerged and eventually completely canceled out by the gods' shamefaced encouragement of Shen Teh's persona. Passivity is the cardinal condition of goodness as it reveals itself in the opening scenes when the first god speaks: "We must find one. For two thousand years we have been hearing the same complaint, that the world can't go on as it is, that no one can live in it and remain good. It's high time we discovered someone who manages to keep our commandments" (*Good Person*, 6). She who survives the monstrosities of two thousand years without losing faith in the belief that passivity is its own reward is truly good. The exchange between Wang and the gentleman who spurns the gods is important:

> THE GENTLEMAN (laughing): I can imagine the kind of scoundrels you're trying to palm off on me. (Goes out.)
> WANG (grumbling after him): You swivel-eyed skinflint! Have you no piety?—Pause. There's no one left but Shen Teh the prostitute. She can never say no [*Good Person*, 7].

Goodness is a passive "feminized" commodity; it lies in being the good woman of Szechwan and having the protection of a male. And it lies in negations—in not exploiting men, in not coveting others' goods. Matthews has shown that goodness in a patriarchal society is very much a function of abiding by male edicts. When a woman breaks these rules, she is both bad/mad (Matthews 1984). According to this reading, Shen Teh assumes badness/madness when she becomes Shui Ta, who evades the norm altogether. Goodness is either a question of controlling one's desires or obeying one's hierarchical superiors—fathers, protectors. The man who is a guest in her shop on its opening makes the connection between (feminine) weakness and goodness or benevolence explicit. Shen Teh has just given the unemployed man a cigarette:

> THE WIFE: Was that wise, my dear?
> MRS. SHIN: If you start off like that, you won't keep your shop for three days.
> THE HUSBAND: I bet he had money in his pocket.
> SHEN TEH: But he said he had nothing.
> THE NEPHEW: How do you know he wasn't lying?
> SHEN TEH (angrily): How do I know he *was* lying?
> THE WIFE (shaking her head): She can't say no. You're too good, Shen Teh. If you want to hold on to your shop, you'll have to turn people down now and then.

> THE HUSBAND: Say it doesn't belong to you. Say it belongs to a relative who demands a strict accounting. Can't you do that?
>
> MRS. SHIN: She could do that if she didn't always want to play Lady Bountiful.
>
> SHEN TEH (laughing): Grumble away. I'll change my mind about the room and take back the rice [*Good Person*, 13–14].

Inevitably, the relative assumes the guise of the authoritative male cousin who would presumably be able to keep Shen Teh's goodness or weakness at bay. Shen Teh's response is instructive. She laughingly tells them not to complain, for she could just as well refuse them their living quarters and their rice. When the carpenter, a little later, demands that Shen Teh pay her debt, the man whispers the word "cousin" to her. The wife implies that Shen Teh is not right and therefore is wrong (war das richtig) because she cannot reject people's pleas. She is too good and must learn to be strong if the economic enterprise is not to suffer. The male guest agrees with the wife and thinks that Shen Teh is not able to (kann nicht) refuse and should invoke the authority of a magical figure (ultimately Vetter [cousin]) to help her be stern and unyielding. Shen Teh, however, can refuse people, as she shows by her immediate reminder to them their words could ricochet back to injure them. Shen Teh can but does not wish it (kann aber will nicht).

Shen Teh desires to insert her subjectivity, but the historical construction of her as a weak/good woman does not allow her to wield the power that she has. Later, she finds that people like her cannot exert their wills, not because of their inherent powerlessness, but because of the cultural strictures that enjoin the landlady to demand an exorbitant deposit from her. A female prostitute must by some exigency uncover a male protector to justify her existence. The landlady hikes the price because Shen Teh is a prostitute. Since Shen Teh's goodness lies in her acquiescence born of helplessness, when she does remain firm as Shui Ta, she will be perceived as bad and ruthless. The issues that the text curves towards are female weakness/male strength. "Goodness" itself is sidestepped because the gods give her money with which Shen Teh buys power. This power is for Shen Teh a means by which to transform the lives of people around her:

> Yesterday I moved in here, and I hope I shall now be able to do a great deal of good. There's Mrs. Shin, for instance, the former owner of the shop. Yesterday she came and asked me for rice for her children. And there she is again, crossing the square with her bowl [*Good Person*, 11].

She sees her situation as infinitely more powerful and positive now, but the others do not perceive her differently. Brecht insinuates that her project is hopeless; first, because benevolence is not revolutionary, and second, because as a woman she cannot discipline them into a different mode. It is against this background that Brecht accounts for Shen Teh's mad game with maleness.

Brecht's vocabulary in the play locates madness as the primary signifier which highlights the displacement of Shen Teh/Shui Ta without confining the pattern to a simplistic dialectic of the self and the Other. Both reside in Shen Teh/Shui Ta. Plural voices mark the signification of madness. Initially, the carpenter makes a telling contrast between goodness and madness which equates goodness with passivity and madness with assertiveness. When Shui Ta is firm about offering the carpenter one-fifth of what he wants for the wooden shelves in the tobacconist's, the carpenter, enraged, calls him "crazy" (*Good Person*, 23). Ironically, the carpenter contrasts him to her good cousin Shen Teh "who seems a better sort" (*Good Person*, 23). Shui Ta retorts that Shen Teh is ruined, which of course refers to Shen Teh's financial situation, but also indicates her psychic stress in a pointed way (*Good Person*, 23). The carpenter, frustrated at Shui Ta's obduracy over the price of the shelves, finally turns abusive and calls him an "idiot." Mrs. Shin, Shen Teh's confidante and dependent, also views Shui Ta in like manner. She refers to him as "rabiate," or maniacal. (*Der gute Mensch*, 56. All subsequent references to the German text are from *Der gute Mensch von Sezuan* [Berlin: Suhrkamp Verlag, 1964].) The referents carry different resonances when Shen Teh is named mad. Shen Teh calls herself "frivolous" when she tries on a shawl that she can ill afford because she is beside herself with joy at the prospect of marrying Sun, the flyer (*Good Person*, 41). The mention of money makes her realize that the rent had "clean gone out of [my] mind." Shen Teh asks the old lady: "Would you really lend money to anyone so scatterbrained?" (*Good Person*, 41). At this juncture, the old lady replies that she would prefer to lend the money to Shen Teh rather than Shui Ta, "who is anything but scatterbrained" (*Good Person*, 42). Shen Teh is Shui Ta, so the question of "Widerspruch" or contradiction is rendered complex by the fact that those who exploit Shen Teh call Shui Ta "mad" in the pejorative sense, while the old lady who is genuinely humane accepts Shen Teh's perception of herself as "scatterbrained" in the most positive sense of the word. Shen Teh might be scatterbrained, but she will not scheme to do the old lady out of her money. Her scatterbrainedness is linked not only to her goodness, but also to her "weakness," which formulates her "madness." Shui Ta, on the other hand, is said to have more "sense" and "wisdom" (*Good Person*, 63). The original German text uses the word "vernünftig," which also connotes reasonableness (*Der gute Mensch*, 85). Conversely, Sun tells his mother that while he has a tacit understanding with Shui Ta, who has a "head on his shoulders," he finds Shen Teh too "stubborn" (*Good Person*, 60). He tells his mother that she is "too pigheaded" (*Good Person*, 58).

Without being aware of it, Sun contrasts the two personae explicitly and suggests to Shen Teh that her cousin has "more sense" than she does (*Good Person*, 63). Sun also calls Shen Teh a "little fool" who cannot count as he waits for the sensible cousin to bring him the money (*Good Person*, 64). The original German uses the word "Närrin," which is associated both with the noun *Narrheit* and the adjective *närrisch* (*Der gute Mensch*, 89). Cassell's German dictionary lists foolishness, folly, madness, and craziness for *Narrheit* and eccentric, peculiar, and strange for *närrisch*. Like Yang Sun, Mrs. Shin upbraids Shen Teh for her honesty when Shen Teh hesitates about accepting the barber's blank cheque:

> MRS. SHIN: What? You're not going to take the cheque? That's a crime! Is it only because you feel you would have to marry him? That would be plain madness [*Good Person*, 69].

Shen Teh, however, does not pay attention to Mrs. Shin's scolding and bursts into a song about her love for Yang. Mrs. Shin is emphatic about her disapproval: "I've never seen anything so idiotic" (*Good Person*, 70). Brecht emphasizes the perception of Mrs. Shin, who along with Wang is among Shen Teh's closest acquaintances. She asks Shen Teh if she is "crazy" because Shen Teh has just given Wang the cart to make enough money to go to the doctor. Shen Teh is making amends for having "failed" Wang earlier (*Good Person*, 72). The German words *verrückt* and *Wahnsinn* are woven into the text so that they jar the reader into an awareness of Shen Teh's disjuncture from a coherent, self-contained subject position. The owner of the house shares Mrs. Shin's impressions on Shen Teh, although her judgment is based on different criteria. She comments harshly on Shen Teh's abrupt decision to accept the barber's money. She declares herself "astounded" that young girls should be so "frivolous" (*Good Person*, 76). Shen Teh herself is self-reflexive about her subject position. She claims to the jury of the gods:

> Yes, it is I.
> Shui Ta and Shen Teh, I am both of them.
> Your order long ago
> To be good and yet to live
> Tore me like lightning into two halves [*Good Person*, 100].

The first god validates Sun's, Mrs. Shin's, and the landlady's beliefs that Shen Teh is "mad." He opines that Shen Teh is "muddled, completely muddled" (*Good Person*, 101). The original German makes the point with precision and clarity: "Verwirrtes, sehr Verwirrtes!" (*Der gute Mensch*, 140). *Verwirrtes*, according to Cassell's dictionary, means confused, perplexed, bewildered. Shui Ta also describes Shen Teh's feverish restlessness. When Shui Ta is in conference with Shu Fu and virtually promises Shen Teh to Shu Fu, he says that

Shen Teh is "dreadfully upset" (*Good Person*, 54). Further, Shui Ta promises that Shen Teh *will* be "reasonable," as though to say that she has been senseless up to this juncture (*Good Person*, 54). Whether as Shen Teh or Shui Ta, the lead character is considered less or more than ideally rational.

The Shui Ta posture seemingly liberates Shen Teh from the weight of an age-old burden—male expectation of women. The people of Szechwan expect her to be "good," the policeman expects her to come under male protection, Yang expects her to accede to his wishes. Freed from the constraints of the essentialist conflation of femininity and weakness, Shen Teh is now less soft and pliable and more powerful and assertive in her Shui Ta persona. Indeed, Shui Ta is not a monster; he is merely an efficient manager who enjoys the unexpected privilege of being free to execute his own decisions. For instance, Shui Ta runs the shop the way he wishes. Brecht suggests that the female body confines itself because as a male Shen Teh is able to articulate her desire, which is to control her life and to enjoy an independent existence. Shui Ta has the power of words, as is evident in the scene when he shows up at the tobacconist's:

> SHUI TA: My cousin regrets of course that she is unable to observe the laws of hospitality forever. Unfortunately there are too many of you. This is a tobacco shop and it's Miss Shen Teh's livelihood.
>
> THE MAN: Our Shen Teh could never bring herself to say such things [*Good Person*, 23].

Shui Ta's language is direct, aggressive, and confrontational. It is not conciliatory. Brecht's stark characterization of the female as weak and the male as strong is problematized by the fact that the female becomes the male who is strong, who fights to survive. The historical conditioning of gender roles is completely disclosed by Shen Teh/Shui Ta's quiet eviction of her bothersome unwanted guests: "You're thieves and parasites. If you go quickly and waste no time in arguing, nothing will happen to you" (*Good Person*, 24). Shen Teh is not unable to say these fighting words. Why is it Shui Ta's prerogative to say them? Does language itself assume a more directive force when uttered by a male? Brecht's perception would seem to be that Shen Teh is imprisoned by her body, not her body qua body, but by the prison house of male expectation that will not demur if men speak these words, but will clamor if women speak them.

Brecht's insidious suggestion that helplessness invests Shen Teh with the mad necessity of maleness also implies that the world is not ready for women who seek to control their lives and environment. He drives the point home by portraying Shen Teh not only as a woman whose body renders her a prisoner to male desire and desire for males, but as a woman who in male garb can and will assert herself forcefully. The two pictures are seemingly contradictory because Brecht lends her ascendancy and power even in her male madness, but when she acknowledges what Brecht regards as the essential "feminine"—her pregnancy—she is completely subservient to men. It is a contradiction he does not resolve and hence the ambiguity as to whether the dichotomy male/female is to be viewed strictly as received perceptions that Shen Teh plays out or anatomical constrictions that overcome her. Since Brecht does resort to a closed ending, one where he shows the female form burdened by itself, unable to acknowledge its own growing motherhood, and with no possibility of an extinction of the necessity to be male, the latter seems more likely.

The trajectory of the female who does have the potential to overcome her body but succumbs to it is exposed in the encounters of Shen Teh/Shui Ta with Yang Sun. As Shui Ta, Shen Teh controls Sun, but as Shen Teh, she is subject to him. Brecht explores the limits of the female body and, in direct contrast to Strindberg, suggests that it has no freedom. Strindberg's characterization of women, albeit misogynistic, lent them power and credibility. Brecht initially shows a Shen Teh who has to have recourse to a male protector in more than one way. Although Shui Ta does lend her the aura of male power, he cannot guarantee that the situation can be endlessly perpetuated because Shen Teh will have to give up all claims to her gender. She will not be able to express her desire for men. Besides, Shen Teh cannot be ritually murdered because Shui Ta is Shen Teh and the female will have to emerge if she is not to be consigned to male bachelorhood. Shen Teh/Shui Ta confirms that Shen Teh will have to manage as a female but hopes that as a female she will exert the same authority that Shui Ta is capable of exercising. After the fracas with the carpenter, in which Shen Teh is taken seriously because of her Shui Ta persona, she tells the policeman:

> SHUI TA: But how is someone like Shen Teh to get credit?
> THE POLICEMAN: Then, you're not staying here then?
> SHUI TA: No. And I won't be coming back. I was only able to give her a hand on my way through. I was only able to prevent the worst. Soon she'll be left to her own resources. I can't help wondering what'll happen then [*Good Person*, 29].

The policeman makes the conventional suggestion that Shen Teh be married off to an eligible suitor who will take care of her interests and by implication ensure that she gets the respect she does as Shui Ta. The rich barber, Shu Fu, who is very much taken up with the "angel of the slums," comes forward to cloak her in wealth and respectability. On her way to settling the marriage, Shen Teh runs into a flyer who is on the verge of committing suicide. Yang

Sun's story makes a powerful impact on her. It gives her a glimpse of sky gods winging their way through life. Her imagination is stirred by the passion that Yang Sun shows for flying. Metaphorically, flight expresses her desire. Yang Sun as an individual is less important than what he represents. He is a romantic figure, definitely, in contrast to the widower with three children, and he is capable of such extreme intensity that in her glowing imagination he symbolizes an Icarus ready to immolate himself for his splendid desire. Brecht shows that desire will always wreak havoc in the most well planned of economic enterprises. Shen Teh abandons Shu Fu and decides to marry Yang Sun. Shen Teh strains herself to share in Yang Sun's passion to realize a dream: "One man at least will rise above all this misery; one man at least will rise above us all!" (*Good Person*, 45). Unfortunately, she does not have the power to realize these dreams as a woman:

> SHEN TEH: But we still need 300 silver dollars to get him the job. We must put our heads together, Mrs. Yang. (Slowly) I know someone who might help me. Someone who has already given me good advice before. I didn't want to call him back because he is such a hard, crafty man. This must really be the last time. But obviously a flyer must fly. That is obvious [*Good Person*, 44].

A keen knowledge of her powerlessness as Shen Teh and her efficacy as Shui Ta also prompt her to tell Yang Sun about her "cousin":

> SUN: Have you got a friend?
> SHEN TEH (hesitantly): A cousin.
> SUN: Don't trust him around the corner.
> SHEN TEH: He's only been here once. Now he has gone away and he'll never come back again [*Good Person*, 34].

When Sun comes to the tobacconist's, Shen Teh meets him as Shui Ta, despite her promise to herself not to succumb to the magic of being male. Self-assurance and the ability to protect himself characterize Shui Ta. From this point on the resemblances between Shen Teh and Shui Ta vanish. Brecht's initial portrayal of Shen Teh/Shui Ta had pointed out some classic gender stereotypes such as Shen Teh's sensibility and Shui Ta's sense. Shui Ta had not been radically, irrevocably different from Shen Teh, but merely firmer about clinging to his/her livelihood. The split between Shen Teh and Shui Ta has developed to a pitch where the two are impossible to reconcile in one persona. Brecht has skillfully dramatized the change as though to suggest that the periods of Shui Ta have contaminated Shen Teh and the periods of Shen Teh have stupefied Shui Ta. The two now are distinct personalities; Shen Teh has become schizophrenic. Brecht attributes the classic binary oppositions between male and female to Shui Ta and Shen Teh:

Shui Ta (Male)	*Shen Teh (Female)*
Logical	Irrational
Practical	Passionate
Strong	Weak
Proud	Servile
Cruel	Compassionate
Selfish	Giving
Intellectual	Sensuous

The oppositions unfurl themselves in the encounters between Shen Teh/Shui Ta and Yang Sun over the marriage and also in Shen Teh/Shui Ta's response to the injustice done to Wang. Shen Teh had earlier already made up her mind that Sun must fly. As Shui Ta, she questions Sun closely on both his professional and romantic intentions. Thorough and meticulous as a lawyer, Shui Ta grills Sun on when he plans to sell the shop, how he plans to get the job, and what guarantees he has that he will be able to keep it. Acting the responsible protector, Shui Ta suggests that the sale of the tobacconist's shop might be a tempestuous act. He sensibly urges Sun to consider working there. When Sun leaps up to accept Mrs. Mi Tzu's offer, Shui Ta questions him on the price of the tickets that will take Shen Teh with him to Pekin. Yang Sun reveals his true colors in a scene exquisite in its irony. Yang Sun does not realize to whom he is speaking when he tells Shen Teh/Shui Ta:

> SUN: Don't go into a tizzy old boy. I'll get to Pekin all right.
> SHUI TA: But it must be expensive for two.
> SUN: Two? I am leaving the girl here. In the beginning she'd only get in the way.
> SHUI TA: I see.
> SUN: Why do you look at me as if I were a leaky oil can? I'm only trying to make the best of things.
> SHUI TA: What do you expect my cousin to live on?
> SUN: Can't you do something for her? [*Good Person*, 50].

Despite the shock s/he has received, Shui Ta insists that Yang Sun hand the money back till he can show him the two tickets. Yang Sun is undisturbed about this admonition because he is convinced that Shen Teh is the proverbial putty in his hands. Brecht is ruthless in his portrayal of the way men talk about women when they are not there:

> SHUI TA: You seem to forget that she is human and has a certain amount of sense.
> SUN (amused): It always hands me a laugh the way some people think they can make the females in their family listen to sensible arguments. Haven't

you ever heard of the power of love or the itching of the flesh? You're going to appeal to her reason? She hasn't got any reason! On the other hand, she's been stepped on all her life, the poor little thing. If I put my hand on her shoulder and say: "Come with me," she'll hear bells, she won't know her own mother any more.

SHUI TA (with difficulty): Mr. Yang Sun!

SUN: Mr. ... whatever your name is!

SHUI TA: My cousin is attached to you because...

SUN: Let's say because I've got my hand on her bosom. Put that in your pipe and smoke it [*Good Person*, 51].

Yang Sun's language reveals all too clearly the notes of derision and contempt with which men refer to women. Since a female relative is a woman, not much can be expected of her. Further, her condition as female renders her pliable to emotionalism, which leaves her with no grip over her reason, which in turn lends her only the intelligence and rationality of an animal that can be controlled and enchanted by caresses. For Sun, woman's sensuousness expresses her animality.

The revelation "unmans" Shui Ta, who is now suspended between the two personae. Brecht exhibits considerable skill in this scene in which he shows the binary oppositions breaking down to exhibit Shui Ta/Shen Teh's bewilderment: "The business has gone! He's not in love. This means ruin. I am lost" (*Good Person*, 54). The cry registers both personae in sequence. Shui Ta cries out against economic ruin, Shen Teh cries out against betrayal; Shui Ta reverts to the pressing economic exigency, Shen Teh realizes that she is abandoned. Shui Ta's confusion about the weaknesses that despoil one's livelihood culminates in Shen Teh's bitter knowledge of a girl's fate:

SHUI TA: Caresses turn to strangling.
A sigh of love becomes a cry of terror.
Why are those vultures circling?
A girl is going to a rendezvous [*Good Person*, 52].

Shen Teh comes back to her male self and negotiates as Shui Ta with Shu Fu. Brecht underlines the fact that men alone have the power and ability to sell women. When women sell themselves they find themselves in the plight in which Shen Teh finds herself. The bargain between Shui Ta and Shu Fu over Shen Teh's marriage is struck when Shui Ta unctuously assures the barber of Shen Teh's timely recognition of her folly in having fallen in love with Yang. When Yang Sun returns, the situation is totally reversed because Shen Teh meets him as her female self. She completely collapses and succumbs to Yang Sun's seeming concern for her. Brecht schematically stresses the difference between the genders in this painful episode in which Shen Teh is seduced by Yang Sun's words and charm:

SUN: I want you to come away with me.
SHEN TEH: Mr. Shu Fu, forgive me, I want to go away with Sun.
SUN: We love each other, you see. (He leads her to the door.) Where have you got the key of the shop? (He takes it out of her pocket and gives it to Mrs. Shin.)
SHEN TEH: Please don't call my cousin, Mr. Shu Fu. He doesn't see eye to eye with me, I know that. [We are not of one mind (Willet and Manheim, 1962, 59).] But he's not right, I can feel it [*Good Person*, 59].

It seems appalling that Shen Teh should go off with Yang Sun when she knows what he has said of her. It is doubly ironic that she justifies her move by speaking of feelings which Sun has spoken of as characteristically feminine. Brecht splits the "male mind" from the female body with a vengeance. Shen Teh is portrayed as a woman completely immersed in a destructive love that knows no logic, no pride. Shen Teh acknowledges on her wedding day that she is deeply divided; her need for power seems to have been overridden by her need for love: "The bad things he [Yang Sun] had said to Shui Ta were no lesson to Shen Teh" (*Good Person*, 61). Indeed, she repudiates the sterner counsel of Shui Ta, and although conscious of her contradictions, gives in to the essentialist "feminine" conception. She tells Yang Sun, "If you love me, you can't love him" (*Good Person*, 60).

Feminists have critiqued Brecht's portrayal for its stereotypical representation of the woman as blindly emotional. Sarah Bryant-Bertail has suggested that Brecht's characterization of women falls into four stereotypical categories: prostitute, capitalist entrepreneur, abandoned sex object, and martyr mother (Bryant-Bertail 1983, 40). Shen Teh traverses these roles. A prostitute, she sells her goodness to the gods in return for the money that she accepts from them. An entrepreneur, she borrows money against her capital: her shop and her body. Curiously enough, she cannot raise money as Shui Ta. A sex object, she takes pleasure in pleasing Yang, who abandons her. Shen Teh/Shui Ta finds herself pregnant when the distance between the two personae is the greatest. A mother to be, Brecht portrays her allegorically as the earth that would crack open before she let harm fall upon her creatures:

—Then I
Will fight for my own at least, even if I have to
Turn tiger. Yes, now
That I've seen this, I will break
With them all and never rest
Until I have saved my son, at least my son [*Good Person*, 74].

Lennox's notion that Brecht overcomes objectification of the female by deeroticizing her is relevant in this context. That the divestiture of the sexual renders her powerless becomes in the first instance stereotypical. It is important to note that there is no real discrepancy in both stereotyping the maternal figure and using it as a vehicle for one's ideas, because of the conventional veneration of motherhood (Lennox 1978, 86). While Brecht deconstructs the icon of maternity in *Mother Courage*, he is far less ambivalent in *Good Person*. Pregnancy may fulfill Shen Teh's desire, but it prevents her from accepting Shu Fu's offer of money. Mrs. Shin articulates Shen Teh's dilemma in no uncertain terms: "If only it's not a little stranger! (Laughs.) He certainly fixed you. If that's how it is, you can forget about your big cheque. It wasn't meant for this kind of thing" (*Good Person*, 70).

Shui Ta must intervene to reestablish order in Shen Teh's house because Shen Teh cannot really avail herself of the barber's generosity, which is hollow. The barber had given the retainers the shed because his stock of soap was going rotten there. The unemployed man calls for Shui Ta to save the situation: "She's got to send for her cousin! Tell her, all of you, to send for her cousin! He's the only one who can do anything" (*Good Person*, 75). Shui Ta returns, having buried Shen Teh, and assumes the grotesqueness of a male pregnancy. He restores order instantly but imposes conditions on them. They must work, including the carpenter and the unemployed man. Shui Ta holds out the promise of Shen Teh to the barber and keeps the project flourishing with true entrepreneurial zeal. Shen Teh's existence itself would be problematic because the barber would no longer be generous to the mother of Yang's child. His generosity has already been sorely tried by Shui Ta's expanding projects:

> Mr. Shui Ta, I feel a profound reluctance to discuss your constantly expanding projects. I suggest a little supper with your cousin, you bring up your financial difficulties. I offer your cousin houses for the homeless, you set up a factory in them. I hand her a check, you cash it. Your cousin disappears! You ask for 100,000 silver dollars and tell me my houses aren't big enough. Where is your cousin, sir? [*Good Person*, 90].

Shen Teh had to be murdered, if she was to provide for her child. Brecht dramatizes the metaphorical slaying of Shen Teh ironically because Wang and Sun begin to suspect that she has really been murdered by Shui Ta. The final scenes witness Shui Ta's trial, where he is accused both of symbolic and real murder. The gods are as fatuous about goodness as they were in the opening scenes. When Shui Ta discloses the horrible dilemma he is locked in, the gods say that she lay "hidden" (*Good Person*, 102). *She* stands for both Shen Teh and goodness. Thus, the gods do not accept the contradictions of her situation at all. They cannot give her new life but insist that she accept the burden of being feminine. Of Shen Teh's change, Lennox comments that "spectators are again confirmed in their belief that such stereotypical male and female behavior is natural to the sexes" (Lennox 1974, 92). Smith adds a different dimension to the question when she states that the difficulty with Brecht's portrayal of mothers is his inability to represent their desire (Smith 1991, 496). Shen Teh is in the worst situation she has ever been in. She will have to face the rascal Sun. Shu Fu will withdraw his support if she reveals that Shui Ta is female. Things have come full circle and have merely deteriorated for Shen Teh. The madness of being Shui Ta cannot help her continue indefinitely because of her pregnancy. No future invested with power awaits her as Shen Teh, only imminent disaster.

Registering her disappointment with Brecht's desexualization of Shen Teh and consequent effacement of female desire, Iris Smith makes the suggestion that: "The desire [of the woman] could be foregrounded in the actor's playing of Shen Teh, if she expanded on the feminist possibilities of Brecht's early scenario, in which Shen Teh continues to sell herself when not forced to" (Smith 1991, 502). Although Smith's point regarding the erasure of female sexual desire is well taken, her view on the female body in the text does not consider that Shen Teh makes one of her more powerful symbolic moves as a woman when instead of selling herself, she sells a commodity. This also allows Brecht to emphasize the difficulty of her completely withdrawing her body from the market, as witnessed by her beholdenness to Shu Fu. Further, to suggest that pure sexual pleasure is possible or that it is detachable from its context is disturbing. At least, Brecht does not domesticate Shen Teh by leaving her to Yang Sun's tender mercies, a sign that he sought a less conventional kind of resolution for the text.

The so-called "open" conclusion of the play invites the spectator to resolve the problem in his/her own way. The epilogue asks us to conclude the play. Yet, it is difficult for the female viewer to envision any kind of resolution to the play. Shen Teh's options have been shut off. Trapped by her body, she can no longer claim the male effect that empowers her. One can only suggest that Brecht's depiction of the way society hedges Shen Teh is compromised by the introduction of the biological. Shen Teh herself is left in the dark amd pleads for answers. In restricting madness as a possibility, the text indicates that the powers of the woman in madness betoken a rebellion contained by her body/the body of the text. The stark contrast between the powerlessness of women and the potency of men can be read to mean that history and society conspire to solidify these vicious constructions. Yet, despite the weight of history, the madness that converts Shen Teh to Shui Ta is neither tragic nor universal; it is a political act of protest against the ways people think of women. Brecht demolishes these conceptions by showing a Shui Ta who has none of the so-called essentially feminine qualities. And yet in debarring the pleasure the female viewer takes in the construction of female subjectivity by confining Shen Teh, the text uneasily, if mockingly, echoes Freud's dictum that anatomy is destiny.

Chapter 6

The Female Grotesque: Dürrenmatt's *The Physicists*

Post-Brechtian theater, both in Germany and England, witnessed a variety of different kinds of theatre that were interventionist without adopting the dogma of alienation theatre. Among playwrights of the antirealist tradition, Friedrich Dürrenmatt takes his place as a maestro of the macabre effect and devastating resolution. Dürrenmatt has been compared at one time or the other to Büchner, Pirandello, Strindberg, and Brecht, but his platform is not readily equated with the ideas of any of them. Dürrenmatt's ideas of the theatre are instructive in that they attempt to blend certain premodern notions of structure with postmodern quasi–Ortonesque techniques of enhancing the spectacle.

Dürrenmatt's understanding of the complexity of the modern world and its emphasis on facticity enabled him to ask a number of questions crucial to the development of theatre. Chief among these is whether the theatre is adequate for the representation of the modern world (Innes 1979, 41). Dürrenmatt's thoughts on the "grotesque" as a form most appropriate to the nuclear era place him with those practitioners who avoid realism fervently.

Dürrenmatt defines the grotesque as "a physical expression of paradox" (Innes 1979, 109). The tangibleness or tactility of the grotesque heightens its impact on the viewer. The physical distortion of perspective that Dürrenmatt works with makes for exaggerated theatre that threatens the viewer's everyday response. Innes explains the grotesque as "a way of gaining precision, objectivity and distance, of forcing the audience to take a moral stand while retaining the playful artificiality of a literary game" (Innes 1979, 109).

The grotesque, as an unfamiliar entity, must estrange the viewer or distance him or her. Although Dürrenmatt wants an absorbed audience, he does not necessarily demand one that identifies with the characters. Speaking of *The Physicists* (1962), he said he wanted the audience to resist identifying with the physicists despite the temptation to do so. *The Physicists* has political pretensions, and even if it does not completely break with conventional forms of persuasion, it brings two disparate elements together. On the one hand, the content of the play is overtly political, concerning as it does the future of the world; on the other, the form is classical rather then documentary or experimental. Further, its mode is grotesque.

Indeed, Dürrenmatt believed that the grotesque was appropriate to the post–World War II generation as a technique of intervention. Further, he considered that it was dramatic to pursue an incident or event to its worst end. He put these ingredients together in the recipe for *The Physicists.*

The Physicists invited world attention because of its focus on the ethical dimensions of scientific and technological advancement. Imminently threatened by nuclear annihilation, European capitals were engaged by this play. Set in a sanatorium for the mad, the play works through the relationship between justice, power, and knowledge. The discourse on gender impinges on the three themes and constructs the female as grotesque.

Dürrenmatt combines heterogeneous elements. His expedient of placing three physicists who may or may not be crazy in the sanatorium clearly enabled him to discuss the relationship between knowledge and power. The introduction of the criminal element—the murder of three nurses by three inmates, further allowed him to introduce notions of justice, which in the text are seemingly differentiated from larger humanitarian issues of ethical responsibility. A unified thematic is dispersed in two separate theatres of action. In one, Dürrenmatt tackles the evasion of responsibility by exaggerating the profusion of identities the three inmates sport. In the other, he questions the terms by which ethical responsibility is accepted by considering what the relationship of power is to justice. By concretizing one theatre of action and rendering the other abstract, the dramatist allows us to see connections between the personal life and the public act. In this respect, Dürrenmatt is comparable to both Büchner and Strindberg, who unraveled the psychic underpinnings of the public persona.

Critical attention conferred on the play has tended to concentrate on the global theatre. The play is routinely placed with Brecht's *Galileo* and Kipphardt's *In der Sache J. Robert Oppenheimer.* Viewed as a political intervention, it is judged on how effectively it makes a statement about the nuclear era. Among the most hotly contested points is whether the physicists' resolve not to publish their findings actually changes the course of world destiny or whether their decision does not even stay nuclear advances momentarily.

Linked to political concerns are moral concerns. This perspective has Dürrenmatt as moralist interrogating the virtue of the physicists (Fickert 1972, 50–58). Innes compares Möbius to Icarus; this vein of interpretation follows the model of the portrait of the physicist as arrogant (Innes 1979, 122). Reno takes a different approach by suggesting that Dürrenmatt juxtaposes science and religion, physicist and prophet. Reno concentrates on how both discourses are about the possessors of knowledge. He argues that Dürrenmatt regards Möbius as arrogant but also considers him to be chained by his discoveries because he does not know that he owes them to God (Reno 1985, 70–79).

Another area of interest is the genre of the play. Dürrenmatt himself called it a "satyr play" (Weimar 1966, 446). Weimar finds it a "tragicomedy of the modern paradox, a paradox which insists that something must be done, while at the same time implying that nothing can be done" (Weimar 1966, 442). Beckmann is not convinced that the play has any appeal beyond its time and considers it a farce. He asks, "Sind A*tomstücke* möglich? [Are atom plays possible?]" (Ritter 1991, 163). Whitton considers the play a model of "what could happen if the individual does not make himself aware of the consequences of his actions" (Whitton 1990, 124). Ernst Brüche christens the play a "Weltuntergangsfarce [farce of the demise of the world]" and argues that the playwright sees "das Erschrecken als die einzige heute mögliche Form der Ergriffenheit [terror as the only form of emotion possible today]" (Ritter 1991, 169–70). Suter thinks of it as a "Denkspiel [play of ideas]" (Ritter 1991, 166). Murdoch views the play as a tragedy because of Dürrenmatt's rendition of Möbius's hamartia and hubris (Murdoch 1970, 271). The interest in classification has meant that other equally important areas have been overlooked. Inevitably, the manner in which the political or public is imbricated in issues of gender is not acknowledged, not even tacitly. While the female characters are discussed, their roles are analyzed from a male-centered perspective so that the critics also see them the way the physicists do.

Whether or not critics are sympathetic to the physicists' resolve not to share their knowledge in the interests of humanity, the debate implicitly assumes that the physicists' acts are motivated by altruism, even if it is wrongheaded. Some critics quarrel with Dürrenmatt because of his inadequate characterizations of the physicists, others because they are not drawn in a sufficiently sympathetic way for the audience to appreciate their dilemma. Innes comments pithily that "clockwork has replaced characterization" (Innes 1979, 123). Beckmann wants to know when we will care for the characters Dürrenmatt creates (Ritter 1991, 161). Kaiser too thinks that the play is not convincing (Ritter 1991, 163). Voser admires the play tremendously, especially its inversions. She finds, however, that the murder of Monika is insufficiently motivated (Ritter 1991, 154–56). Nagel is emphatic about finding in the mixture of genres a unique virtue (Ritter 1991, 159):

> Dürrenmatt ist ein Autor des Heterogenen, ein Spielzerbrecher. Er lötet zusammen, was nicht zusammengehört um in der Paradoxie der Form eine Paradoxe des Gehalts sichtbar zu machen. Er will die Rationalitätals Wesen

> des Wahns, den Wahn als Zielpunkt der Rationalität entlarven [Dürrenmatt is an author of the heterogeneous, one who smashes the play. He solders together what does not belong together in order to make visible the paradox of content through the paradox of form. He intends to unmask rationality as the being of madness, madness as the goal of rationality].

The significance of the mixture of the other two genres is minimized.

The Kabinettspiel and the detective narrative are subsumed by the public plot. The two subgenres are significant in that they work with issues of identity and motivation. As a genre, the detective narrative is concerned with psychological motivation. Although in this instance, Detective Voss gratefully accepts the official story on motivation, identity remains crucial to the audience because it reveals motivation. The director has after all opened with the cliché of the detective narrative: a dead body. To spice it up, the mise-en-scène exhibits clear signs of struggle. In the first instance, knowing who these men are will help us solve the mystery of why they killed the women. While Pirandello in *Henry IV* raised issues of identity by leaving Henry IV unnamed, the characters in this play have several identities, and thus identity is rendered problematic.

The physicists sport several identities. One of the three, supposedly Beutler, is also seemingly aware of the projections he casts. "Newton" passes himself off as Newton because he does not want to disturb Ernesti, who is convinced he is Einstein. Newton claims he is the real Einstein, however. We are only half-certain that the men are physicists. The emphasis on the psyche and on identity initiated by the murder of the three women makes it quite clear that this private theatre will also have a say in the future of the world. Motivation after all cannot be neatly separated into public and private spheres.

Dürrenmatt's grotesque framework in *The Physicists* and *The Visit* (*Der Besuch der alten Dame)* enables the audience to locate the humor of the text. Humor gets displaced but does not get quite absurd as in the theatre of Tom Stoppard or Samuel Beckett. Dürrenmatt's absurdities are meaningfully loaded in a painful way. And unlike farce, the dark side of sexuality or the psyche does not really become the occasion for laughter. In *The Physicists,* pain is not dissolved by laughter.

Dürrenmatt chooses to work with a strongly realist stage setting to balance the parodic humor that erupts. The mise-en-scène poses the greatest challenge for the antirealist metteur. Dürrenmatt's stage directions describe a picturelike stillness that would suggest muted normalcy but is overdone, so that its artifice does not allow it to be merely background. It works to parody the concept of quiet rest; it is no sanatorium in quiescent Switzerland, but a madhouse. The sanatorium itself bears not just the imprint of a struggle, but is transformed into an asylum. The period furniture strewn around jars or clashes, perhaps to emphasize the two levels that interlock: sane and insane. The mutedness of the mise-en-scène also contrives to shock the viewer in retrospect because of the general disarray that reigns at the conclusion when the madhouse/sanatorium becomes a prison-house. Despite these contrasting effects and the bright artificial tone, the mise-en-scène remains quasi-realistic, a point of difference from the faintly unbelievable quality and direction of the action of the play.

"An anti-bourgeois satire," the play is antiillusionist with a vengeance (Whitton 1990, 125). The fate of humanity is decided from the most unlikely of locales—an asylum for the mad. Absurdist, on the face of it, but extraordinarily rational in that it puts together a "model." Two men who believe they are Einstein and Newton live with a man who claims to be the legendary King Solomon. When the play opens, the audience does not know if these men are really physicists or men pretending to be not only physicists, but Einstein and Newton. They are grouped together because of the liberal psychotherapy of the owner, Dr. Martha von Zahnd. The spectator's interest in the identities of these men is aroused by the play's sensational thriller opening. It begins with a police inspector investigating the murder of Irene Straub. She was apparently strangled by her charge, Einstein, whose ID proclaims him as Ernesto Ernesti. The criminal's identity becomes important because motive can be secured only through the psychology of the criminal, whose sense of identity is crucial to his/her understanding of the motive. Even at the outset, we know that the act is not random and motiveless because another nurse has been strangled, but not by the same man. Dorothea Moser's murderer was Newton, who also believes that he is really Einstein. His ID proclaims him Beutler.

The physicists' sense of who they are ultimately determines their actions. Yet the play only partly concentrates on eking out the motive for murder. Despite the overture's emphasis on the detective narrative, complete with dead body on the margin of stage and signs of struggle, the action of the play is overinvested by abstract motives that the detective frame cannot accommodate. Classically "unified," the motive ostensibly leads into the thematic of the play: the ethical responsibility of the physicists or their perceptions of their identities. The detective narrative is overtly diverted by the inspector's investigation. Far from being the typical detective in search of knowledge, the inspector is easily fobbed off by the chief nurse. Investigation leads to diagnosis. The detective's lack of interest in ascertaining motive creates mystery but also accentuates the audience's distance from the physicists.

Inspector Voss, the sane police investigator, finds very soon after his entrance into the asylum that his norms do not hold in this space. The seeker of knowledge of the mystery narrative, the detective/hero is blocked at every step. His authority is completely undermined because of the milieu. Nurse Martha Boll is punctilious about the liberal ideologies of psychotherapy and drives the inspector batty by her unreal attitude towards the murder of Nurse Stettler. Voss is not allowed to see the director or the assailant. The director is apparently soothing the murderer by accompanying him in a duet. The murderer's needs are regarded as much more important than either the inspector's duties or the rights of the two dead women. The inspector's theory about the female nurses not being physically strong enough to work with the male patients is also mocked by Nurse Boll, second in command, who informs us that Nurse Moser was a crack wrestler, Nurse Straub expert at judo, and she herself a weight lifter. If the women could not have been overpowered by sheer brute strength, they must have been killed when their guard was down. The dialogue is peppered with corrections of the inspector's nomenclature: the murderer is the patient, the murder is the incident. Voss is told twice that the man who killed Stettler is ill and that he is not the murderer but the "assailant." Voss is also reprimanded for referring to the "murder" and is asked to substitute the term "unfortunate incident." Apparently liberal, the medical establishment nevertheless evades the question of the scientists' responsibility. In itself reasonable, the inspector's acceptance of the evasion is slightly more disturbing, especially in Act II when roles are switched symmetrically. The inspector insists that it is an "incident," the director; a murder.

The grotesque surfaces in both parties' indifference to the fate of the victims in Act I. The mise-en-scène is a visual reminder of the nurse's struggle to live and the body an even starker one of her defeat. Their placement on stage underlines the manner in which the nurse's life is marginalized.

The elements of humor are patent in the inspector's having to wait while the patients' nerves were soothed. The inspector is also not allowed to see the director and not allowed to smoke. He does not have even the modicum of authority. He appears to have lost all judicial power in the space of the asylum. Dürrenmatt suggests that a different law operates in this world, one which the inspector can only view as spectacle and cannot control. Yet these reversals are not absurd in that they are not without meaning. Where Dürrenmatt's comedy differs from the absurd is in the deathly moral significance attached to every macabre twist. The inspector's lack of information and his antigeneric behavior do not draw us into identifying with him. Because the first physicist we see has already killed and is in a sanatorium, we are not immediately urged to identify with the physicists. We are distant spectators who increasingly get persuaded by Möbius because of his rhetorical manipulation. When Möbius convinces the two scientists, he comes close to taking us in. Dürrenmatt works with emotions to examine them.

In order not to divert us from the grotesque, Dürrenmatt also keeps us from identifying with the nurses. We know very little about them and in fact none of them survives the first act. Murder mysteries are often structured around exploring the victim's psyche to enable capture of the murdered. *The Physicists* does not belong to this genre, nor does it fit in with studies in psychopathology like Fritz Lang's *M.*

The detective's lack of knowledge and indeed his submission to the official story are particularly startling in Act II. The detective now corrects the personnel on their vocabulary. He insists that the assailants are patients, the killings are incidents. He claims that it is exhilarating to give justice a holiday. By the end of Act I, the suspense produced by the detective narrative is heightened.

Similarly, the Kabinettspiel also explains the psyche. Möbius is here viewed in the midst of his family. Like Strindberg, with whom Dürrenmatt has been compared, the playwright once again forges connections between the personal and public theatres of action. After the Kabinettspiel of the Rose family's visit to Möbius, Möbius has a long discussion with Nurse Monika Stettler, confesses that he is not mad, and strangles her. The curtain falls.

An exploration of these two genres in the text also accounts for the effort Dürrenmatt took to structure it according to premodernist theatrical law. The play has been much praised for its unimpeachable practice of the classical unities, devices that welded the personal or psychic with the public. Indeed, Dürrenmatt claimed that because the play was set in a sanatorium, it was essential that the unities lend some semblance of order.

The detective narrative provides the basic motivation for the physicists' imprisonment at the end of the play. More importantly, their relationship with the three women undergirds their decision not to publicize their discoveries. The four women in the play, their interaction with the men, and the men's perception of them become completely instrumental to the physicists' choices and the world's future. Dürrenmatt grounds the abstract problematic of the limits of power and knowledge in the politics of sexuality, family, and madness.

Both genres have been most often used in the realistic mode. The murder mystery's digression into the space of the grotesque is achieved through the underscoring of the thematics of madness. The grotesque mode grafted to the detective genre deforms it. In taking the detective genre and deflecting its narrative goal, Dürrenmatt directs our attention to the dividing line that separates the criminal from the heroic, the genius from the demoniacal, and the sane from the insane.

The play does boast many moments when the tables are turned on the inspector and the sane. Newton's discussion with Voss in Act I is exemplary of the space between the two. Like Pirandello's Henry IV, Newton appears in eighteenth-century costume to present a hypnotically convincing image of his madness. The inmate raises rationality and logic to a new peak while the bumbling detective falters through his own cross-examination. Newton frames his own conversation by puncturing the association of madness with disorder. He straightens the mess made by the aftermath of the murder calmly with the explanation:

> NEWTON: I simply can't stand disorder. Really it was love of order that made me become a physicist—(He rights the standard lamp)—to interpret the apparent disorder of Nature in the light of a more sublime order [*The Physicists*, 18; all subsequent references are to the translation by James Kirkup (New York: Grove Press, 1964)].

Ironically, Newton also provides Inspector Voss and the audience with a motive for the murder. He says: "My mission is to devote myself to the problematics of gravitation, not the physical requirements of a woman" (*The Physicists*, 19). We are not given any indication whether Voss believes that this is a rational motive. Newton continues to puzzle Voss by mocking him for accepting that he is Newton. When Voss is sarcastic with him about how old he must be (if he is really Newton), he asks Voss directly: "Are you out of your mind, Inspector, or are you just having me on?" (*The Physicists,* 20). Dürrenmatt does not use elaborate inversions to debate the sanity of either Newton or Voss. Indeed, the theme seems almost peripheral in that he complicates the relationship of the mad with society to such an extent that their status as mad is overdetermined by their roles as scientists, actors, criminals.

The mise-en-scène as an antisocial space that is nevertheless a refuge from the power of the state is a more important element in the play than the status of the inmates as mad. In comparison to Pirandello's *Henry IV*, for instance, *The Physicists* makes no attempt to play with the claims of sanity that the physicists make. At the end we have to take their sanity seriously if the tragic dimension of the apocalypse is to be believed. Of course, we could see them as geniuses beyond the pale, which again does not really separate them from the sane. While Joe Orton claims that everyone is crazy, Friedrich Dürrenmatt makes the opposite assumption.

The antisocial space is amenable to giving everyday reality a holiday and forcing the grotesque to speak its truth. Dürrenmatt brings the discussion to the nature of physics at the climax of the Newton and Voss conversation. He implies that the relationship between the physicist and society is the mystery that has to be unraveled. Newton posits a relationship whereby the physicist is God behind the scheme, society unthinking humanity:

All I do is to elaborate a theory about it on the basis of natural observation. I write down this theory in the mathematical idiom and obtain several formulae. The engineers come along. They treat electricity as a pimp treats a whore. They simply exploit it. They build a machine—and a machine can only be used when it becomes independent of the knowledge that led to its investigation. So any fool can switch on a light or touch off the atomic bomb. (He pats the INSPECTOR'S shoulders.) And that's what you want to arrest me for, Richard. It's not fair.

INSPECTOR: But I don't want to arrest you, Albert.

NEWTON: It's all because you think I'm mad. But, if you don't understand anything about electricity, why don't you refuse to turn on the light? It's you who are the criminal, Richard. But I must put my brandy away; if Sister Boll comes there will be wigs on the green. (Newton hides the bottle of brandy behind the wire guard in front of the fire, but leaves the glass where it is.) Well, goodbye.

INSPECTOR: Goodbye, Albert.

NEWTON: Oh, Richard. You're the one who should be arrested [*The Physicists*, 22–23].

Newton's psychic changes clearly reveal the ego of a man who believes that he has completely uncovered nature's wonders. His self-presentation to Voss, through the guises of madness, suggests that whether he is sane or not, his ego projection is intense. Gravity and relativity: the intellectual property of one man. The arrogance explicit in his telling Voss that he should be arrested is a clue to the distance that separates the two. It also implies that Newton assumes a responsibility for the safety of the world that Voss has abnegated by his lack of knowledge. At the level of the detective narrative, it taunts Voss for not keeping the nurses safe.

When Mathilde von Zahnd makes her entrance, she comes across as being even more self-assured than Newton was. Newton's claims are ultimately not viable because he lacks narrative authority. How seriously are we to take a man who is an inmate in an asylum? Hence Newton's games with the inspector seem irascible but nonthreatening. Indeed, one could admire him for subverting the inspector from a tenuous position. Von Zahnd, on the other hand, is shown to accrue authority to herself by her scientific knowledge and more peculiarly by invoking her ancestors, who visually dominate the mise-en-scène.

Dürrenmatt comes closest to problematizing the distinction between sanity and insanity in the persona of Mathilde von Zahnd, who hovers on both sides. Unlike Newton and the inspector, who briefly seem to switch sides, Mathilde von Zahnd cannot be placed on either. Dürrenmatt allows her to let slip her own psychic condition right at the very beginning. Von Zahnd says that her father despised her. Why honor him by hanging his portrait in the room? Her psychic contradictions are as patent as Newton's. She reveals her power when she claims that her patients adhere to what she wants them to think. The effect on the viewer is unsettling. Her own wry comment on her relative sanity despite her ancient pedigree underscores the instability of the scene: both authority figures have either been confused or have qualified their "normalcy." Our consternation about her sanity is further heightened by our knowledge that her great-aunt and cousin are also inmates of the asylum.

Sister Boll's total avoidance of the murders and her spellbound obsession with the intellectually stimulating dimension of the physicists' condition are of a piece with Mathilde von Zahnd's diagnoses. Sister Boll has a startlingly different, if recognizable, value system. Disconcertingly, its values are not those of the "mad" inmates, but Mathilde von Zahnd's megalomaniacal ideology combined with Boll's notions of the scientific. Von Zahnd's grand illusion of controlling the world is not unveiled till the conclusion. For the moment, she discourses eloquently on her superior, enlightened, and rational treatment of the mad. She succeeds in leading the inspector down the garden path and making him feel totally stupid by presenting her preposterous theory about the murderous effects of radioactive material on the two physicists as perfectly obvious.

The question that provides the transition between the detective frame and the abstract metaphysical theme is posed by Newton in the tone of an enfant terrible: "Is it because I strangled the nurse that you want to arrest me, or because it was I who paved the way for the atomic bomb?" (*The Physicists*, 22). He equates the murder of a woman with a scientific discovery when he asks which is the greater crime. A brilliant device on the part of Dürrenmatt, as one commentator has pointed out, to advance the criminal-physicist thesis (Weimar 1966, 438). Yet, the insignificance of the murder is quite appalling and brings us back to justice and sexual politics.

The playwright is inscrutable about opining on the question. He uses irony to pose the question, a grotesque irony possible only in a sanatorium for the insane. Yet the question is presented as a rational one. Several commentators have had difficulty with Dürrenmatt's "demonization" of the atomic bomb as the single source of humanity's annihilation (Ritter 1991, 168). Many others have accepted the physicists' rationalization as Dürrenmatt's ideology and justified the "femocide" (the killing of women) as absolutely ethical on the grounds that the killings were sacrifices in the interest of humanity. One critic alone has asked why the physicists could not commit suicide if their main interest was to protect humanity from their discoveries (Ritter 1991, 170). The physicists' desire for control and the humiliating lack of control they experience in the end would account for why they do not commit suicide.

They are clearly not modern-day heroes, even if they are takeoffs on the classical model of Oedipus. Dürrenmatt's nonrealistic mode and the exaggerated scale of the question would seem to suggest that the play is a model. His conclusion leaves the physicists in jail and divests them of both power and knowledge. Clearly, the physicists are not his mouthpieces. Nevertheless, consistency of the representation of the murdered women as sacrificial offerings does give the female viewer pause.

Frau Rose is the chief character in the cabinet play which forms the other subgenre of Act I. She comes to bid farewell to her husband, Johann Wilhelm Möbius. Her story of sacrifice for the physicist's advancement is instructive in its complete self-effacement. She has already traveled the route Sister Monika wishes to take. She has nine children in all at the moment and has apparently played the role of mother to Möbius too. She calls him "little" the four times she refers to him and directly addresses him as "little" three times. When she recapitulates the story of their life together, it is less the saga of a couple than a mother who tends her young. Möbius in this portrait emerges tremendously weak and Frau Rose, despite her trials, strong and vigorous. Möbius was not only without family, he met Frau Rose as a fifteen-year-old boy. And later, after Frau Rose had completely educated him, he fell sick and was unable to be a "man" and "provider" to her. Her sketch, while seemingly replete with domestic piety, serves as an indictment of an adolescent who never grew up to assume responsibility. Paradoxically, when she finally abandons Möbius, she seems to have stepped into a similar nurturing role with Herr Rose. Dürrenmatt slyly reveals the financial motive lurking beneath the motherly one. Frau Rose's account is sentimental:

> Fräulein Doktor. Try to understand my position. I am five years older than Johann Wilhelm. I first met him when he was a fifteen-year-old schoolboy, in my father's house, where he had rented an attic room. He was an orphan and wretchedly poor. I helped him through high school and later made it possible for him to read physics at the university. We got married on his twentieth birthday, against my parents' wishes. We worked day and night. He was writing his dissertation and I took a job with a transport company. Four years later we had our eldest boy, Adolf-Friedrich, and then came the two others. Finally there were prospects of his obtaining a professorship; we thought we could begin to relax at last. But then Johann Wilhelm fell ill and his illness swallowed immense sums of money. To provide for my family I went to work in a chocolate factory. Tobler's chocolate factory. (She silently wipes away a tear.) For years I worked my fingers to the bone [*The Physicists*, 35].

Presumably, Frau Rose's sacrifice will inspire her husband to make greater sacrifices for humanity. Ironically, his sacrifice will result in the annihilation of a woman who wants to give herself to him. In the hierarchy of sacrifices and stakes on heroism, women sacrifice for men and children, men sacrifice women for the higher good.

Two of the nurses are completely absent. One of them is present only as a corpse. As Oskar Keller implies, Monika Stettler's death works as a motivating device in the action of the play (Keller 1970, 19). While it may seem that the power to initiate action lends the woman agency, this is not the case with Stettler. Indeed, she is punished for attempting to put an end to Möbius's stasis by bringing him out into the world when she dies by his hand. Keller's observation that the playwright's directions do not refer to Monika is well taken. Dürrenmatt's reticence indicates the invisibility of the woman's role in the production. She is more of a "Funktion" than a character (Keller 1970, 19).

Ironically, Monika Stettler has the largest role. She competes with Frau Rose to play the role of Lotte in Goethe's *Leiden des Werthers*. Woman as sacrificial offering dominates the presentation. In the detective narrative, women are victims. Clearly, the victims had to be female in order for the dramatist and the physicist to imply that the woman's pull to the material compromises the men's ascent to the metaphysical. Dürrenmatt's symmetrical organization of the triple murder, each killing stylistically repeated and with the same motive attributed for it, bears this observation out. Perhaps the repetitive motif is designed in part to maintain unity, but it is also clearly intended to intensify the grotesque effect of three strangulations. The female figure is manipulated to construct the grotesque.

We do see one of the nurses, Monika Stettler. And her portrayal as the woman who wants to consecrate her life for the physicist/hero is distressing in that her repeated urgings to Möbius become a variation of the obnoxious "she asked for it." Like Frau Rose, in that she wants to devote herself to the higher cause of male development, Monika is unlike her in that she expresses sexual desire. She is not voided of sexuality because of motherhood in the way Frau Rose is. For the boy/physicist Möbius, Monika's demands could be quite threatening in that sexuality is not presented as a maternal by-product but as an erotic desire. She wants to be looked at, desired. And she takes the sexual initiative. We are to infer that the other two nurses were similarly aggressive about their physical desires. Monika's awareness of her body and her need that Möbius recognize both body and desire could well be the underlying motive for murder. After all, Möbius became sick when he had to assume adult responsibility. For Möbius, the will to stay adolescent is at least as strong as the will to save the world. Perhaps the latter covers up the former and becomes the justification for the physicist's prolonged life as immature adolescent. Newton has also clearly stated that Dorothea Moser interfered with the advancement of physics. Since Dürrenmatt's structure replicates theme and motive, Dorothea's demands clearly paralleled Monika's, and it is equally certain that Newton was unable or unwilling to meet them. Einstein's story is also identical to Möbius's and Newton's. He tells Monika that Irene had arranged their lives together in exactly the same manner Monika had. Einstein emphasizes the pointlessness of women sacrificing themselves almost as though to disavow responsibility for his own act. Monika is deaf to his warnings, including his injunction to run away. Disturbingly, she too is remarkably without feeling for her fellow nurse Irene and sympathizes with Einstein's trauma. To cap the irony, Monika tells both Möbius and the audience that von Zahnd had proclaimed herself madder than Möbius. Monika's faith in both Möbius and Solomon speaks to a simplicity beyond all proportion or perhaps the rare quality of accepting difference with grace. Apparently Monika does the latter, as does Möbius's former teacher who also is not repelled by Möbius's apprenticeship with Solomon. Monika's belief costs her life. The scene ends with Möbius choking her with the curtains.

Newton and Einstein are implicated in this murder. Einstein fiddles and Newton drinks at the close of the scene. Von Zahnd's manipulation subjugates Monika's intelligence and attributes responsibility to her. It lets Möbius, who discourages Monika from her plan, appear increasingly desperate but also larger than life. Such a framing glorifies Möbius's act by insisting that he perpetrated it against his will.

In its presentation of Frau Rose as the only version of femininity worthy of survival, the Kabinettspiel suggests that the play is about the repression of female desire. Frau Rose's sexuality is further submerged by her second marriage, with its missionary impulse and ethic of nurturance. Perhaps the three other women are punished for transgressing the social boundary that permits the mothering role but debars the sexual.

Möbius, however, while rejecting Monika's love, cannot tell her the truth. He goes along with her plans and even tells her that his life has been more supportable because of her presence. Monika is open about her dedication:

> I want to sleep with you. I want to have children by you. I know I'm talking quite shamelessly. But why won't you look at me? Don't you find me attractive? I know these nurses' uniforms are hideous. (*She tears off her nurse's cap.*) I hate my profession! For five years I've been looking after sick people out of love for my fellow-beings. I never flinched; everyone could count on me: I sacrificed myself. But now I want to sacrifice myself for one person alone, to exist for one person alone, and not for everybody all the time. I want to exist for the man I love. For you. I will do anything you ask, work for you day and night: only you can't send me away! I have no one else in the world! I am as much alone as you [*The Physicists*, 52].

Möbius is shown trying to send her away at least three times. Monika's insistence became a motive for Möbius to kill her. Of course, Dürrenmatt does not justify murder, but he does explain it all too successfully after the manner of detective narratives. In and of itself, these explanations may be dismissed as part of the generic stock-in-trade, but the consistency of the portrayal of women as sacrifices, much fortified by the representation of Möbius's ex-wife, brings Dürrenmatt dangerously close to the physicists' point of view on this issue.

The theme of woman as votive offering is raised to new levels when the women become linchpins for the logic of the ego. Möbius and the other two swear to stay in the sanatorium in order to remain true to the exalted spirit of physics that has driven them to kill. A variant explanation might say that the presence of women itself was threatening to the physicists, especially intelligent and attractive women who desired them and saw through them. Each of the women had crept through the masks the men had worn.

The detective narrative links up neatly with the metaphysical. The revelations of Act II clarify not only motive but also identity. Dorothea Moser's assailant, perturbed by the dramatic changes in the asylum, divulges that he is not Newton, Einstein, or Beutler: he is Alec Jaspar Kilton, noted physicist. The nurses have been replaced by heavyweight and middleweight boxers. For Kilton and later for the other physicists, the boxers' dimensions and sizes provide a discomfiting change from the nurses. The physicists do not now control their lives. At this juncture, neither the audience nor the physicists know that von Zahnd maneuvers their existence. Because their moods and impulses have been respected to the point that they have got off scot-free after murder, they have been convinced that they were in control because of their manufactured madness. It is no coincidence that they feel that their freedom is threatened when males rather than females play the role of warders. Dürrenmatt exaggerates the physical prowess of the men, who are well known in international boxing circles. The introduction of the male warders also shows Dürrenmatt pushing a situation to its extremity in order to provoke thinking about the resolution of the problem. The stunning physical presence of these three giants, bizarre in this spectacle as they wait on the inmates, is the first indication that the sanatorium will turn into a prison.

Even before the revelation of the physicists' identities, the three men have bonded. Newton, for instance, was concerned about Ernesti and is now empathizing with Möbius because he cannot eat. For his part, Möbius almost grants Newton clemency by expressing his understanding of Newton's decision to do away with Moser. He reiterates his understanding when Einstein proclaims his identity and similarly rationalizes the murder of Irene Straub. Dürrenmatt has Einstein repeat verbatim what Newton said. Their bond perhaps makes intimacy with women difficult. The approval they get from each other makes general social accountability a matter of indifference. The echo mocks as it mimics because the mirroring effect divests each of them of singularity. They function for each other as the Lacanian mirror image might for the child during the mirror stage (Lacan 1977, 1–7). In the first stage, before their resolve to stay put, they do not know that they are seeing themselves but think that they are seeing someone else who belongs to the same genus. This is comparable to the child identifying the mirror image as a child, but not himself or herself. When they do acknowledge their likeness, the ego ideal, the sense of self, is strengthened by the reification of the mirror image. As with the child's méconnaissance of its reflection whereby it sees the image as more coordinated, they too enjoy more power and plenitude from the reflection. Like the world of Pirandello's *Henry IV*, their world too is one of sameness. Difference would jolt. In terms of their identities, Einstein/Eisler and Newton/Kilton have effectively ceased to be physicists and have become spies. Their perception of themselves has changed: Möbius's compact offers them an honorable version of the self.

Both Möbius and Newton claim to have been ordered by a higher authority. Newton/Kilton invokes the intelligence agency; Möbius has recourse to an even higher authority: Solomon or the divine tongue. Both sidestep the issue of personal/human responsibility. Möbius's argument is tawdry; it is inconceivable that both the men, one from the free trade sector, the other from a socialist economy, would be scandalized by the breakdown of the economic system. Nuclear destruction and the havoc it might cause are clearly a weapon to use for economic advancement in the capitalist and socialist worlds and hence imperial power. Although aware of underlying economic motives, Möbius is very much a prisoner of the "ideological state apparatus" that Dürrenmatt wished to demystify (Althusser 1971, 127–86). Knowledge colludes with power to maintain the status quo, to uphold the old pernicious ideology. Möbius emerges with a completely confused received ideology that claims to be above it but is actually under it.

The murders render the physicists criminal; ergo they must protect their secrets to protect humanity. Of course, the fact that they retreat on all their vows once Mathilde von Zahnd traps them in her little net calls their integrity into question.

If the structure of the play sets the three nurses up as impediments to the scientists' journey to save mankind, and if Frau Rose was a martyr because she succeeded in removing herself as one, Mathilde von Zahnd is the biggest impediment. Apparently, she initiated the love relationships between scientists and nurses. And she has started to use the inventions that the scientists had thought were safe from human beings.

Dürrenmatt creates a world of surfaces when he exposes Mathilde von Zahnd's machinations. She is a grotesque double to the physicists. She has outplanned and outmaneuvered them, and like them she has a secret agenda to hold the world hostage. Eerily, her logic mocks their rationale; both groups exult in power.

Von Zahnd is pictured as a hunchback, and many commentators liken her to Claire Zachanassien of *The Visit.* Mathilde emblematizes the grotesque as Claire does not, however. Claire has elements of the grotesque, but she also has a different dimension to her personality as the Fate that humanity must encounter. Moreover, a purely feminine articulation of destiny undergirds the eventual development of Claire as a figure of the fatal. The motivation in the play is feminine grief; Claire wants to get even with Ill for having rejected her for a wealthy woman.

Mathilde von Zahnd is not constructed as a realistic character. Rather she is a personification. Dürrenmatt makes her the only surviving heir of a wealthy in-bred family and uses the trope of idiocy to differentiate the physicists' craziness from her lunacy. She is, as it were, pathologically "abnormal." The logic of the play demands that the scientists be foiled, either to show up the impossibility of keeping knowledge free or the probability of it being perverted. In either case, the physicists emerge suspiciously heroic. They may be naive, even scatterbrained, but they are sane and concerned, despite their godlike pretensions that have to be curtailed.

The conclusion could appear mystifying in that the physicists reappear to restate their mythical identities. Reno claims that Möbius, for instance, "realizes at long last that he shares essential characteristics with the ancient king to whom he has so often referred; in a moment of deep insight, he comes to understand that what is true of Solomon is true also of himself" (Reno 1985, 73). Reno's discussion of Möbius's self-acknowledgment invites us to him as a tragic hero. Fickert insists that Möbius becomes humble and accepts a universe beyond human logic. Interestingly, Fickert places the time of recognition around Monika's murder: "the unavoidable murder of Monika proves the impossibility of achieving a peaceable society among men—his dream" (Fickert 1970, 44). Yet, for the female viewer, this view is inimical because Möbius's "sacrifice" annihilates the female while it restores his ego, dented as it is by Mathilde von Zahnd's clever trickery. Mathilde von Zahnd is constructed as the evil machinator who somehow gets to take the rap for the murders. She plans them to frame the physicists so that they can be her prisoners in perpetuity.

Clearly, knowledge has failed in the face of evil, sanity in the face of idiocy. While Mathilde von Zahnd's plans serve Dürrenmatt's purposes, the female reader is wary of the personification of the grotesque as female. A more "objective" viewer might advance the proposition that Mathilde von Zahnd's grotesquerie is intended to be gender neutral and to signify general monstrosity. Both von Zahnd and Einstein name her gender, however. It would appear that the choice of the female to signify the grotesque is highly suspect in the light of a traditional masculinist construction of the female monster in classical and medieval allegory, best exemplified by the choice of the female pronoun for Skylla in the *Odyssey*. While I do not wish to psychoanalyze the dramatist's fears of the female, I do aver that the play classically recasts the model of the man as voyager, the female as impediment; the man as sane, the female as insane.

Chapter 7

Woman as Nation: Hare's *Plenty*

Among 60s and post-60s British playwrights, David Hare has squarely earned the reputation of being a "committed," "political," or "left-wing" playwright. A self-described socialist, he clearly intended to intervene politically in an effective manner. The student revolts and the generally altered political consciousness of 1968 sustained the fringe theatre movement, and Hare, like David Edgar, Trevor Griffiths, and Howard Brenton, saw the theatre as a revolutionary weapon. In 1975 Hare adapted and directed *Fanshen,* which combined documentary and agit-prop, ignored psychological characterization, and worked with ideas of a self-conscious collective determined to build a revolutionary, utopian community. In 1980 Hare shifted his focus, partly because he had begun to doubt the efficacy of socialist theatre (Bigsby 1981, 31–32). He went back to the mainstream stage in an effort to reach a wider audience than agit-prop could command. Hare had started out by wanting to walk the fine line between agit-prop and the psychological theatre (Bull 1984, 70). He explicitly desired to wage war on the humanist dimension of socialist theatre (Innes 1992, 190). Commentators are intrigued by his combination of what may be termed the "political" and the "psychological." David Hare has critiqued the ruling class but has also been severely ironic about some progressive ideologies, including feminism. His double-pronged attacks do place his work in a space which opens itself to hostilities from both the left and right wings. He has come close to being dubbed the high poet of despair but has been able to elude the charge of being a disinterested nihilist (Bigsby 1981, 43–44). Ultimately, critics do acknowledge a political edge to his work even when they differ widely on how "political" may be interpreted. His early career with the Portable Theatre and his long collaboration with Howard Brenton render him a candidate for "political" theatre, while his sustained interest in character and specifically in what has been perceived to be "individuals" has suggested that he may be a liberal playwright with humanism's abiding interest in the ego, whether stable, or as in the case of David Hare's work, unstable.

The April 1978 production of *Plenty* at the National Theatre had mixed reviews. *The Sunday Times* thought the play had little to say, but the *Daily Telegraph* found that Hare had hit upon a new way of representing the generation's general anomie. Young, of the *Financial Times,* discussed Hare's direction, which emphasized the characters' angst (Lloyd Evans 1985, 229–30). Howard Kissel reported favorably on the New York debut and privileged the personal over the national in the play (Kissel 1982, 399). Another reviewer of the same production at the Public Theatre opined of Kate Nelligan's Susan Traherne that "The problem is that no man is a match for Susan" (Wilson 1982, 399). His comment is interesting in the light of the fact that his review sees the chief character as specifically female and identifies the critical flaw in the play as the absence of men.

Plenty exemplifies Hare's negotiation of the seeming opposition between the political and the psychological, the public and the personal. It could be argued that Hare saw the two as inextricably linked, following the women's liberation line on the personal being political, and that he attempted to show the spaces in which these links were soldered. Whether he had such an agenda is open to question. However, he did openly claim that he wanted to contextualize character to emphasize a sense of time over individual behavior. For Hare, history becomes a way of combating the fragmentation of modern life, of making sense of the individual (Rabey 1986, 166–67).

History as actor features prominently in David Hare's work, including *Plenty.* Whether his conception of history is idealist or Marxist is open to debate, however. C.W.E. Bigsby avers that the strongly antimaterial stance of *Plenty* shows the problems that Hare experiences with a strictly Marxist view (Bigsby 1981, 43). Hare himself says in the preface to *Fanshen* that William Hinton, whose book he adapted, had wanted to replace instances in the play where Hare had presented a liberal rather than optimistic or Marxist perspective on revolution (Hare 1986, ix). Although *Plenty* includes a scene set in 1968, it has been regarded as part of Hare's historical project because some of its early scenes are set in World War II. Hare's handling of history in this play is crucial to the treatment of character. The critical issue in the play circles around the characterization of *Plenty*'s female hero Susan. Emphasis on her character appears to lend weight to the notion that despite the apparatus of the new political theatre, Hare remains committed to articulating the impact of history on the individual rather than on society. Bigsby conjectures that Hare may be more intimately involved with moral dilemmas than other socialist writers who may have believed that the redistribution of wealth would solve the problem of modern society. Hare also does not attribute the entire problem to late capitalism, which many good socialists of the time were inclined to target as the enemy (Bigsby 1981, 41–44). Indeed, his plays set in the Third World clearly settled on European imperialism as one of the chief problems of the contemporary world.

Ronald Hayman's appraisal of *Plenty* as being caught midair between an "awkward division of focus between rotting psyche and rotten society" has been influential in readings of the play. Hayman further faults the play for the playwright's "ambivalent" attitude to Susan, which does not direct us to a preferred reading of the play (Hayman 1979, 80).

Hare, whose theatrical project is not avowedly Brechtian, is nevertheless indebted to Brecht in that he states that he wishes his audience to judge events and witness character. Thus he avoids the ideological maneuverings of agit-prop, including the idea of theatre as excessively pedagogical.

The content of *Plenty* is not radical, and the play is not experimental, although it is not modeled after the "well-made play" of the 50s. Hare does not use any specific alienation techniques in this play, nor does he break up the action abruptly. The action is fragmented to focus on Susan, a slightly different emphasis.

Hare tries to follow the postwar generation, but in a very restricted way. He concentrates entirely on the ruling class. The interest he takes in their dilemmas renders the implicit claim of the text to be about Britain both hollow and suspect. While it certainly would have been both naive and idealistic to depict a militant working class flared up by the Portable Theatre into rebellion against the ruling classes, it is disconcerting that a political playwright, one considered politically progressive, should have given the working classes or even the poor middle class so slight a role in the mapping of Britain. Bull states that the perspective of the play is "establishment rather than the shop-floor" and ventures the critique that "just as the lives of the characters are firmly rooted in the past, so are the explanations of continuity and decay" (Bull 1984, 77). One can accept the justice of such an estimation if one regards Hare's commentary as purely moral. However, his political critique of nostalgia as the desire for empire does advance a contemporary analysis. Perhaps the perspective Hare adopts is a function of his class background. As C.W.E. Bigsby pointedly reminds us, most of the playwrights and playgoers were of the privileged classes, in that education spelled class privilege in Britain (Bigsby 1981, 14).

The glaring absence of working class heroes, following the model of socialist realism or even capitalist realism after Arthur Miller, cannot pinion Hare into a content category that marked Terrence Rattigan rather than John Osborne. In fact, Colin Ludlow compares Susan's response to Britain to Jimmy Porter's anger in *Look Back in Anger* (Ludlow 1978, 76–78). However naggingly, Hare's milieus seem to hedge in his purview—whether the location is Saigon, Suez, France or Oxbridge. On the other hand, clearly the setting itself could be used as an element that indicts the world it houses. Indeed, the carefully decorated sets of *Plenty* did visually signal the corruption of the having classes, both at home and abroad.

Hare's historic journey into the past, especially through World War II, is problematic when considered from another angle. England went to war having the status of an empire. Susan says that they, the agents and foot soldiers, believed they were fighting for freedom. Whose freedom? England emerged from the war sans empire and was shamed by the Suez debacle. Does Hare underwrite Susan's vow that Britain had fought for freedom, does he withhold his judgment on that issue, or does he critique the nation's version of World War II history? Is Hare an official archivist, a "neutral" documentary maker, or is he a revisionist historian in the spirit of that model *Mother Courage and Her Children*? While Hayman criticizes Hare's ambivalence and others like Bigsby give him credit for not wearing ideological blinders, still others like Joan Fitzpatrick Dean admire him for what they perceive as an open invitation to the audience (Hayman 1979, 80; Bigsby 1981, 41–44; Dean 1990). My own sense of a way through these questions which are as significant as the ubiquitous "but is it good theatre?" is to work through these by understanding the places Hare assigns the traditional elements of stagecraft.

Ruby Cohn cites the move away from realism as a key feature of the drama of the 70s. Clearly, realism after the manner of Ibsen or even Osborne was not especially sacred to Hare, who nevertheless does use realism as a device within scenes. Strindberg, whose work he staged at the Portable, was more of an inspiration when it came to doublings and delusions (Cohn 1991, 128). Rogoff admires Hare's direction in the New York production of the play, especially his daring moves from warmth to coldness without having recourse to transitions (Rogoff 1987, 236). The well-made play did not hold much stock with Hare but neither did platform theatre. Yet Hare did not necessarily create a mixed form, nor did he actually import any of the more integral elements of filmmaking into structuring the play except for the all-important cut. Hare uses the edit function of film in a very simple and powerful way: to shift from scene to scene. Unlike the practice of continuity editing, he does not "suture" or stitch these scenes; unlike the political avant-garde, he does not employ it to intervene and direct. His scene breaks in *Plenty*, unlike the scene breaks in *Mother Courage*, which are framed by Brecht's stage directions that would be read out, are organized in order to force history to bear witness to human beings: to render up an accounting of why living in postwar Britain has turned out to be empty.

Hare's depiction of disillusionment in the naked set-up of the house, embellished only by a naked male body in the opening scene, pictures an ending of sorts. Both images, of course, are class-specific, and yet one is to understand that this emptiness is symbolic of England's lack. Ironically, Susan has divested the house of all its property while Brock, the middle-aged man covered in blood, is satiated with no less than 12 fingers of Scotch and the chosen drug of the times, Nembutal. Cave suggests that the bareness of the stage draws attention to setting in a manner that illusionist theatre with its penchant for producing a transparent reality construct did not. Further, the rapid shifts in scene would not have been possible if Hare had abided by "fourth wall realism," because he used truck stages and moved them down the stage floor. His strategy could be seen as a distancing effect, or at the very least a heightening of theatrical effect to call the reality of the stage into question (Cave 1988, 198).

Although the images have invariably been interpreted as a signature of the despair of postwar Britain, the tone is not elegiac, wistful, or demanding of sympathy for the situations of either Susan, her friend Alice, or her husband Brock. Rather it is a grabber, an invitation into their space and lives which is essentially a detour into World War II, Britain's role in it, and British politics after the war. Hare's strategy was to ensure that he showed a range of people and events. It is equally important to note that Susan reacts to the events that are occurring. She is one of several characters who are affected intimately by England's public demeanor, but Hare certainly does not present her as the only one. Scene II features a drop with young Susan and Lazar, Scene III the British ambassador's enterprising endeavor to rebuild Europe, Scene IV Susan's sense of stagnation and difference from Brock, who still works for the Foreign Office, Scene V the Festival of Britain and Susan's intent to have a child with Mick, Scene VI Susan's shooting of Mick. In other words, the impact of events is increasingly measured by showing a changing Susan. While the earlier scenes have a broader focus and seem to recount scenes from an earlier era, later scenes focus on Susan's various attempts to confront what is occurring to her.

Bull comments that Hare's characters do not reflect the reality they live in but combat it. This describes the terms of the discourse Hare engages (Bull 1984, 62). Susan may not reflect the status quo, but she participates in it, even while criticizing it. She resists the dominant ideology, but is nevertheless interpellated by its institutions, primary among them being the military apparatus and the diplomatic corps (Althusser 1971, 127–89).

Hare observed that Susan should be played with sympathy because there was plenty in the action that could distance the audience from her. The blending of subjective and objective perspectives, noted by Cave, sets up a spectatorial position that would be close to Susan and yet judge her. The objective purpose invites audience assessment of her reality in a socially progressive fashion (Cave 1988, 198). At the same time, Hare is persuaded that he is not looking for the alienation Brecht had sought as a way to political engagement.

Interestingly, Susan has had a fair amount of favorable press. Her disapproval of Britain's rule in the Suez, her general sharp distaste of diplomacy, her specific withdrawal from consumer capitalism, and her disgust about her advertising job have been read as signs of her resistance to consumer capitalism and the other maladies striking England. Cave admires Susan and characterizes her nostalgia as being "for a world she knew of richer spiritual opportunity" (Cave 1988, 201). He sees her as acting but also believes that she has the nerve to talk about ethics openly (Cave 1988, 199). In the light of the play's setting in the diplomatic enclave, Susan's frankness could well be a sign of her morality. If her contiguity with the diplomatic corps were to be established, her conflation of speech with action would be an indication of the great gap that separates the two. Both Susan and the diplomatic corps advertently expose the insufficiency of a liberal politics based on nationalism and imperialism.

Susan is often linked to Sarah of *Knuckle* and Isobel of *Secret Rapture*. Susan's idealism is foregrounded in these interpretations of her relationship to Britain. Susan's brand of idealism has been scrutinized by some other critics who find that Brock does have a glimpse of one side of the truth when he lashes out at Susan for hurting people around her in the name of some personal truth (Rabey 1986, 172). Even without passing judgment on whether Susan's personal truth is valid or not, one has to look at Susan's reaction to political events.

Susan serves with distinction, if with some tremors, as an agent in France. She goes to the fringes of possibility in the 70s in her aggressive pursuit of a father and shoots at the failed father Mick when he pesters her. She is contemptuous of English policy in the Suez and oblivious to material possessions. Yet Susan's view of the world is fairly status quo, if intolerant of greed and complacency in others. Susan helps to organize the Festival of Britain in 1951, that public exhibition of empire. Although she manifests her dislike of it, her rebellion does not make an impact on the establishment and only serves to draw Mick into a personal relationship with her. That she chooses to find a father for her child as part of a deal also reveals Hare's opinion of the radical feminist choice to parent children without traditional heterosexual involvement. Like the radical feminist "pregnant woman" in *Slag* who finds out that she is not pregnant after all, Susan too meets with little success. Hare's distrust or fear of nontraditional mothering is glaring in both plays, but especially so in *Slag,* in which the woman's child dissolves into a fart like her feminist pedagogy. Again, in *Plenty* Susan's decision is not presented as a mature, well-thought-out one but as one born of her frenetic disillusionment. Further, her rebellion against the patriarchal establishment results in hurting a workingclass boy, both physically and emotionally, by involving him in the luxury of a game he cannot afford.

Susan's world view is not very different from that of the antirevolutionary Darwin. He resigns over the Suez affair, which Susan does commend. He is fired with a sense of purpose when they first meet each other in Belgium after the war. His mission seems colonial in its rhetoric and scheme: the terrain has shifted slightly, but the tropes are constant. Susan is on the same energetic key: in January 1962 she is motivated by her remembrance of fighting for a viable ideal and in August 1944 she is driven by her optimism that the war would definitely change the English people. The terms of her protest of the Suez episode are damaging to the portrait of Susan as the idealist.

David Hare forestalls the audience from an oversimple view of Susan as tainted and hence one of the ruling classes by his psychological construction of her as deeply shattered. If Hare is ambivalent about how Susan's reactions should be read and what her role is in this history of the aftermath of World War II, he is very cut and dried about why Susan's life has become fraught with tension and why she behaves "unstably" or "irregularly." Postwar trauma would be a quasi-technical, definitive diagnostic term, but like R. D. Laing, Hare is more interested in the mad subject than in labeling her. Hare maintains that the disillusionment Susan suffered after World War II, when England became a seller's society and Susan sold both products and values, destroyed the sense of purpose she had during the war. Her nostalgia for World War II is particularly puzzling considering that Scene II covers a bungled agent drop, a supplies drop over which the British and French fight hostilely, and Susan's sudden emotional despair about Tony (the signal man with whom she has several affairs, the last one in 1947). Susan also deplores the lies that the British now package and sell as their contribution to the world. She does not object merely to the Suez fiasco but to diplomacy itself as a field because presumably there is no space for personal truth, personal integrity. Surely it could not have been accidental that Hare's opening postwar scene is built around Susan's lie that she is Tony's wife and her brazen request to Brock that he lie to Tony's wife on her behalf. A lie to cover up an escapade, however kindly the intention, is scarcely unconventional, nor is it a sign of rigorous personal standards.

Both Richard Allen Cave and Steven Gale suggest that Susan changes as a consequence of her environment. Cave views Susan as growing another layer of skin to preserve her inviolate self and says that if Susan becomes "selfish, brutish, unkind it is to protect the truth of that private vision" (Cave 1988, 201). Cave's explanation comes close to viewing Susan's madness as escape/protest, and Hare's pattern clearly bears out Cave's insight. Susan's jerkiness, distraughtness, and drugs remove her; her violence forces society to notice her. Hare then does not show Susan to be a character of contradictions such as Mother Courage might be. She is not constructed as mad exclusively by society. Her madness is not the basis of her actions; even Brock tells Darwin that she has reacted to Suez in the way she has because she feels so strongly about it. Hare's dialectic of movement—escape/protest—allows him to keep Susan on center-stage as one of the actors of history and simultaneously allows him to question her actions. The fact that she is moved to protest public events, albeit in a private fashion, makes her an agent, a subject of her own desires.

The shifts in her roles clearly have not been viewed simply as a function of her madness. Gale is completely convinced that Susan's "moral and psychological deterioration parallels her country's decline" (Gale 1985, 213). In this reading, Susan is her country's weathervane; her downfall follows that of her country. Gale is partly right to point out that this theme is conservative (Gale 1985, 213) because the implications are that with the loss of empire, the British government lost its stuffing and so did its people. Gale does not consider that Hare suggests this as a critique rather than as a swan song of his own. Ted Whitehead, in his review for the *Spectator* in 1978, was trenchant about the nostalgia for empire that permeated the production:

> Beneath the glacially witty dialogue of the play is a dangerous nostalgia and a deep sense of exhaustion, with a patrician-romantic distaste that is thoroughly English in tone. The National production is extremely sumptuous. What better place to hurl subsidized abuse at the ruling class? [Lloyd Evans 1985, 229–30].

Such an assessment would be accurate if the nostalgia that Susan experienced was one that Hare shared but did not scrutinize. It would make for a more challenging production if the authorial questioning of the nostalgia were also considered. Although Hare said he did not want distance from Susan, he does criticize Susan's behavior. Bull, for instance, argues that Hare shows the process by which Susan understands the falseness of her idealism (Bull 1984, 82). Hare separates himself from her by exposing this idealism. Since Susan is not exempt from behavior that would be viewed as ruling class and arrogant, as when she shoots at Mick, one can at least safely suggest that Susan is not so dramatically different from the other characters of the play, not just because she needs both Brock and Darwin but because having doubts about one's existence does not necessarily make one less hypocritical. Class privilege allows Susan luxuries that neither her friend Alice nor Mick has.

Plenty's historical dimension warrants a reading of Susan's fragility as a function of an inability to cope with peacetime, an inadequacy she shares with Lazar. The trope of the woman as mad or hysterical, however, was current at the moment partly because it allowed an angry generation to break down sexual taboos. Laing's classic thesis maintained that the women subjects of his study found living in their family situations absolutely hellish because of the contradictory demands made on femininity. The young women's morality was equated with their sexuality, placing a strain on their sense of self. The pressure to be sexual from popular and urban culture further made it difficult for them to accommodate family living with the constraints it placed on female sexuality. Although Laing did not specifically name patriarchal constructs of female sexuality as lying at the root of the women's disturbance, it was patent that the code seriously curbed the women's sexual freedom and sense of self (Laing 1965). Their craziness became a form of withdrawal from society. David Edgar's *Mary Barnes* dramatizes the value of liberal psychotherapy in integrating the women into society.

Hare's *Plenty* could also clearly be viewed as sounding some of these themes. Susan does not find monogamy or at any rate marriage to Brock attractive at all. One structuring motif of the play is the number of times she leaves Brock. The play opens with the image of the abandoned, bleeding Brock. If Susan's violence is placed in a feminist framework, her assault of Brock acquires different meanings altogether. At the most general level, her violence against Brock can be read as a breaking of the postwar silence. The violence can be viewed as speech. Cixous and Clément suggest that the hysteric's resistance to a cure "took the role of a resistant heroine: the one whom psychoanalytic treatment would never be able to reduce" (Cixous and Clément 1986, 9). Susan reemerges from her stint of complete passivity at the clinic and abroad to turn to activity. She combats her consignment into sequestration and silence. In this context, it is vital to recall that Susan is violent with Mick when she tries to escape from him and he tries to hold on to her. She shoots him out of anger at his imposition of traditional heterosexual convention, but finds that she has to turn to Brock to stay out of the institution. She buys her freedom out of confinement by walking into the prison-house of marriage. Her rage is also against men and the conditions they place on women. These experiences, measured against the relative sexual autonomy and freedom women like Susan had during World War II, enhance memories of that battle. Tony's role in Susan's story is of a piece with her memories of war; hence, she comes with him. Historically, of course, women were tremendously disillusioned that they had not gained more after World War II.

Hare's burial of the trope of sexuality curtails the play's perspective of Susan as the marginal in order to transpose an intense psychological gender-based dilemma on to the nation at large. Susan's distress and her responses are submerged by Hare's foregrounding of the asexual or emptying out of the sexual in the nation's self-construction. Hare models the image of Britain on categories that exclude the sexual, a picture that effectively erases the cultural tumult of the 60s (Parker and Russo et al. 1992, 1–21).

Hare's inclusion of the radical feminist moment in cultural life in the 70s is riddled by his own ideological contradictions. Speaking of *Slag* (1970), Hare's full-length dramatic exploration of utopian longing for a women's community, Michelene Wandor says: "Feminism is represented as ... something undesirable and repulsive, to be done violence to.... Feminism is shown to be muddled at best, tragic at worst, and usually somewhere in between: pathetic, brutal and abortive" (Wandor 1987, 111). A look at the representation of feminism and treatment of feminist issues in *Plenty* shows that the feminism Hare depicts is deeply flawed and lacks any real power to either change society or women's lives. Hare flirts with feminist issues, and fairly superficially.

Hare also never fully explores Susan's relationship with Alice although at one point Susan exchanges Brock for Alice as housemate. Of course, this does not necessarily entail a lesbian attraction but the substitution of the female for the male with the explanation that the female made her laugh would seem to insinuate some ambivalence of sexual feeling:

> BROCK: Are you going to let her live with you?
> SUSAN: I like her. She makes me laugh [*Plenty*, 37. All subsequent quotations are from *Plenty* (Garden City, N.Y.: Doubleday, 1978).].

Interestingly, Siemers posits that "sexual identity" and alienation are major themes in Hare's work, including *Plenty*, but he focuses on the lack of heterosexual intimacy (Siemers 1992, 100). Perhaps Susan is the male construction of a woman who is deeply dissatisfied with men, but has not abandoned them for women. Isobel of *Secret Rapture* gives up boyfriend and partner for a woman, her stepmother. Hare anesthetizes this dramatic and radical choice by ignoring the sexual and foregrounding the moral. Far from exploring these sexual ambivalences in *Plenty*, Hare removes Susan from this ambit by his rendition of her madness. Her madness alone would not exclude a sexually adventurous life, but the route Hare takes to extricate her from institutional life does. Brock rescues Susan, as it were, from institutional confinement, but also peculiarly enough from the kind of energy and change that marked Susan's life with Alice and her liaison with Mick. The rarefied upper classes whisk her away. The crisis itself is precipitated when Susan shoots Mick. Susan can shop for a man to father her baby and while this could be interpreted as a radical feminist gesture, shooting Mick can be read as an evasion of responsibility. In other words the gap between the rhetoric and the act is wide, a theme Hare loved to dramatize. A perfect example of such a gap is when Susan gives an entirely plausible reason for leaving Mick but then shoots him:

> SUSAN: I know what you think. You think I enjoy slumming around. Then why have I not looked for another father? Because the whole exploit has broken my heart. (Pause)

MICK: You think it's my fault....
SUSAN: Oh Lord is that all you're worried about?
MICK: You think it's something to do with me?
SUSAN: That was part of it, never to have to drag through this kind of idiot argument [*Plenty,* 56].

Susan refuses to make an adjustment to Mick's perspective and then fires four times. Hare uses Susan as a character function and as a psychological portrait. Rogoff, for instance, suggests that "Hare is studious about letting her acknowledge not that she loses control, but that she likes to lose control. Susan is the West sick of its privilege yet privileged to be sick" (Rogoff 1987, 235). Susan is unable to accommodate another perspective, notably a working-class one. The protests and escapes she traverses allow Hare to embody her as the nation.

Susan's failure to conceive with Mick and her failure to deal with the relationship in a less violent way undermine the earlier radical impulse to create a child without the traditional heterosexual bonds. That liberating moment is shown to be hysterical, ill-planned at best. Alice can do little to help Susan out, and Brock, cover-up man, has to be called to save the day. Judy Lee Oliva, curiously, finds that Alice is able to function in post–World War II Britain and also that she is far more adjusted than Susan (Oliva 1990, 85). Since Alice does get by, but quite the same way that Susan later does, by depending on friends and lovers, I can scarcely see her as a model for Susan. Also, Alice's causes revolve around women, certainly a very contemporary engagement. Hare compromises this by highlighting her dependence. Oliva falls prey to the compromise by insinuating that Alice does not analyze the causes behind women's activism. Hare's conflicted presentation of the relationship between Alice and Susan is further seen in the fact that ultimately it is Alice who warns Susan during Easter weekend not to tempt Brock into calling her doctors because of the threat of being placed in an institution again. At this juncture, Brock is savior turned jailer; very much the doctor/husband of Charlotte Perkins Gilman's "The Yellow Wallpaper." He uses his husbandly/ patriarchal authority to intimidate Susan into silence. Hare, while suggesting that a conventional heterosexual contract gags Susan, qualifies her feminist resistance to the institution by showing her as incapable of handling a relationship that does not have a paternalistic framework. In this context, it is important to note that she comes back to England for the funeral of the arch imperial patriarch Darwin. Darwin did speak up against Britain's role in the Suez but even during the scene in which he confesses to his disillusionment, his racist condescension to the nonwhite foreigners, along with his earlier dream of a peace-keeping Britain, is of a piece with the imperialist pretensions of Britain.

Susan's life with Brock is empty, replete with hollow voice and useless cardboard puzzles. Her earlier dissonance allowed for participation in the cultural revolution that was shaking the nation. Brock's protection of her accentuates Susan's need for a male authority figure and her own complicity with an upper-class diplomatic ideology. She succeeds in persuading herself that the working-class boy was unhurt, a falsehood she questions later. Hare uses the latter turn to critique Susan. His rendition of Susan as dependent on Brock refuses to acknowledge or develop a female figure who could be independent or rely on other women. Indeed, Hare fleshes out the picture of Susan's dependence on Brock by making Alice completely dependent on Susan. Alice has no financial resources and needs Brock's money, as do the other nameless women who surface. One uses Brock's money for an abortion; she needs it to retain control over her body. The rest of Brock's money will go to aiding single mothers. Had Susan become one, perhaps she would have shared the plight. Women seem largely unable to gain control over their bodies: witness Susan's futile effort to have a child. Such a portrayal insidiously conspires to place Susan with the ruling conservative upper classes and to reveal the flaws of her earlier feminist ideology. As an antimaterialist, she fares better, but the construction is no less conservative.

The psychological emphases lent to Susan's character make it difficult for us to conceive of her as bearing the burden of representing the nation. Yet her personal dilemmas are never really more than peripheral to the play. The play is able to end on an ironic and optimistic, if postmodern, note for Susan because the playwright has now rendered strict account of Britain's psyche in terms of time, place, and context. Britain is still mourning a war that took place during a time when it had access to the resources of the colonies and the world was not as complex as it was in the late 60s. And the stewards are still of the ruling class, hedging any chances the fledgling post–World War II nation might have of forgetting the hierarchical world.

Susan's characterization is complex in a fashion that medieval allegory is not. It does not sum up a single idea, but she is essentially an allegorical historical construction in that the character's action encompasses the complexity of a divided nation. Inevitably, both dramatist and audience are attracted to and repelled by her: attracted by her attempts to go forth in bold new directions such as the alliance with Mick and the return to England for Darwin's funeral, but repelled by the time-honored return to Brock, the rejection of the new, the return to a sealed fortress of the past and the active search for it in the cities of the world. It would be too easy to claim that Hare is repeating the cliché that England has gone crazy or that other favored theme that institutions such as foreign offices are prison-houses. In point of fact he does neither but offers a portrait of a country torn apart and ripping at the seams rather than one that has become corrupt and completely rotten. Ultimately his nuanced reconstruction of England views its major feature as nostalgia for a time of fighting Britishers during World War II, a notion that he shows to be destructive. Hare voices his distrust of such an England by exploring the mechanics of memory. His version of England's participation in the war in Scene II and the final scene is conclusive evidence of the glamorization of the war and indeed of the nationalist rewriting of history.

Hare's distance from the politics of nostalgia is made apparent by key flashback scenes which are presented either neutrally as in Scene I or exaggeratedly subjectively as in the final scene. Rabey and Ludlow find the final scene an ironic afterthought on Susan's war idealism (Rabey 1986, 173; Ludlow 1978, 77). Cardullo, tracing the pattern of lighting in the play, observes that the brilliant light that bathes the final flashback scene ruthlessly tears down the veil of darkness that shrouded the war scenes. Cardullo is persuaded that Susan has wound her way to knowledge about herself and England (Cardullo 1985, 63). Susan's deafness to the farmer's gripes and her own euphoria about the English learning to connect suggest that the moment is blindingly optimistic, but whether Susan sees that is open to question. Cave, discussing the 1978 production, also concurs that the final scene catches the unreal quality of Susan's nostalgia, which is almost certainly drug-induced (Cave 1988, 197). Hare's choice of Susan to embody the embattled nation hints at a tendency to idealize women, however, a tendency seen in his other plays such as *Knuckle* and *Secret Rapture*.

Hare's allegorical embodiment of Susan brings him dangerously close to idealizing both women and nation. Hare uses women as vehicles for his ideas and has openly said that he feels more comfortable using women rather then men for these roles. The result is that women are placed outside of time and history and are no longer actors but are manipulated. My objection is not that Susan is not a "real" woman hero but that her role as England gives her very few choices as an agent. Brock, Darwin, and Mick make choices and act to shape their own lives. Susan too acts, notably when she shoots Mickey and leaves Brock, but she is dependent on Lazar, Brock, and Darwin—England's sons. Predictably, Alice is dependent on her.

Susan is both a psychological and allegorical/historical construction. Such a pressure on the female character does not really give us a balanced picture of the female postwar citizens. Hare's dialectical mode of characterization moves us from Susan as woman to woman as nation. As nation, the flaws of the men accrue to her and she carries these wounds, an old emblem. As woman, she is able to stand on her own and is a victim of her own memory, of a nationalist vision of England, so that the pain of the loss devolves on her, an old burden. David Hare seriously compromises his revisionist critique of England by embodying Susan as a woman whom he cannot but idealize.

Part IV

Changing Sexualities and the Female Other

Chapter 8

Fetishizing the Female: Barnes's *The Ruling Class*

In England, theatre in the 60s, even when not specifically documentary, agit-prop, or Brechtian, did critique social systems in diffuse ways. The institution, represented by the madhouse as metaphor for society, became an important symbol of the failure of the liberal state apparatus. More generally, madness itself and its refusal to accommodate mainstream society linked the work of many contemporary playwrights such as Peter Barnes, David Edgar, David Storey, and Edward Bond. John Elsom observes that left-wing playwrights balked at attacking the Labour party, which was after all socialist. He contends that this reluctance resulted in a "lack of plays dealing with real, as opposed to spurious or diversionary, political issues." Elsom puts Peter Barnes with his "baroque" diction in this category (Elsom 1976, 180–81). Innes compares Barnes's comedy to Joe Orton's because of a shared "working class perspective" and a common purpose: waging class warfare. He suggests that Barnes "expose[s] the relationship between traditional values and repression" (Innes 1992, 298). I would add that Barnes derives much of his power from scrutinizing the collusion between political conservatism and sexual "repression" or "deviation."

Barnes's approach to theatre is exemplified by his first play, *The Ruling Class*. The *Observer*'s Ronald Bryden found *The Ruling Class* the best new British play of 1968, but John Wardle asked Barnes "to try again" (Lloyd Evans 1985, 161). Harold Hobson was extremely enthusiastic and said it "struck [him] as like a revelation" (Barnes 1969, vi). The overt connections that Barnes's text makes between politics and sexuality make it exemplary of a male version of sexual politics of the time. The play targets a vaguely defined ruling class and holds it up for scorn by exposing its madness.

Brecht used the "madness" of Shen Teh to critique the society that she lived in. Barnes too uses madness to illuminate social problems. Brecht dramatizes madness in terms of the split consciousness of Shen Teh, while Barnes represents madness in terms of the perversion of the Romantic conception. He uses laughter as a distancing technique to make us aware of social maladies. Laughter is produced by grotesquerie in Barnes's theatre. Peter Barnes uses a plurality of languages to create a theatre that mixes and melts genres to forge a new idiom, a new theatre, a new conscience. Madness is at the center of his world view, a sick madness that is pathological, ugly, depraved, evil. Indeed, his images of madness invoke arcane icons of madness that depict the mad as bestial. Barnes does not situate madness in the individual psyche but in the personages of authority. Barnes systematically attacks authority and attempts to dismantle the authority that the audience might fear by ridiculing it, by laying bare its festering sores. This attack is never all a joke, though, for it does try to change the ways in which we think of authority. Further, he unravels the modes by which we are subject to authority and disfranchises its mantle through a careful deconstruction of the component parts that make authority fearsome. The use people in power make of authority is quite simply sickly mad, according to the vision that *The Ruling Class* (1969) foregrounds. While the text insists that madness is a disease of body and mind, it also takes into consideration a more Romantic view of madness that suggests that the mad are more in tune with reality than the sane. Barnes destroys the Romantic notion, but only after he has set it up, and implies that it is a dream of monstrous stupidity and vacuousness. *The Ruling Class* repudiates all Romantic conceptions of madness and uses madness as a metaphor to depict the depravity, conservatism, and lunatic idiocy of the ruling classes. John Elsom objects to the focus of Barnes's critique, which he does not consider to be pointed because it is not pragmatic: "The problem with the House of Lords is not that peers are sadistic monsters, or even decadent aristocrats; but possibly that they can frustrate legislation from an elected government" (Elsom 1976, 91). *The Ruling Class* may well respond that psychic fractures intersect with the ruling of government and that at the literal level sexual politics undergirds many an important decision. Barnes suggests that the underclasses pay with their health for this sickness; the women and the lower classes are straitjacketed by the norm that the rattling cadavers of the British Empire clutch.

Jack, the protagonist, is initially constructed as the Other, who is mad, by the other characters in the play. Later, he is shown as mad, for he kills both Claire and Grace, the two chief female characters in the play. While Barnes presents Otherness as constructed, he also shows us that the protagonist is conditioned by the depraved ruling classes into accepting essentialist conceptions of gender. Jack cannot accept women as sexual beings. He constructs them as whores and prostitutes and hence feels that he has to rid the earth of these pestilential creatures.

Whether the playwright fetishizes the female is problematic to ascertain, but the male protagonist clearly does. A rage that should be directed against authority is vented on the women. The text describes a departure from the fetishism described by Freud, however. Freud talks about another object as substituting for the sexual object, such as a part of the body or an item of apparel (Freud 1989, 249). Fetishism also implies an overvaluation or misplaced valuation. Marx discussed fetishism as the obsessive valuation of the commodity in a capitalist society (Bottomore 1983, 165). Irigaray has argued that in a patriarchal society women are the prime commodities that are exchanged (Irigaray 1985b, 192–97). In such a reading, the female is fetishized as the most prized commodity. In *The Ruling Class,* the fetishization of the female is overdetermined by the sexual, material, and patriarchal.

The trajectory of the text shows that because the object of repressed sexual anger is obscure, the female functions as a fetish in that she is a token of that violent sexuality that needs to be expressed. Jack expresses his anger by sexual violence, by killing. The female is seen as fetish in that she stands for an aspect of the perversion of the self that seeks both sexual satisfaction and destruction of sexual desire. Barnes's later distance from his hero and his alignment of Jack with his father would indicate that he reflects a received version of male sexuality; he does not participate in it, nor does he construct it.

While the observation that women are victimized by the ruling class may be correct, Barnes portrays women from the ruling class's point of view, so that they emerge as romantic morons, helpless and irrevocably stupid. Although the women are not the focus of the play, they are crucial motivating devices in the plot of the play. The ruling class, whose prime interest is to perpetuate itself, can do so only through women; thus, the women become crucial to the development of the plot. Yet Barnes's women do not seem aware of their structural positions but are subsumed by the frightful, plaguey poxes that infect the weak. The insight that women are victimized by the murderous insanity of men is borne out by Büchner's *Woyzeck,* which moves toward a similar conclusion. In both cases the dementia of the ruling classes violates and destroys the women who are around them in one of two classic patterns: either because the male's sexuality demands redress when it is threatened, as in Büchner's *Woyzeck,* or literally because the male needs a woman to reproduce, as in Barnes's play.

The Ruling Class also explicitly makes a connection between the order of society and women's sexuality: the woman who transgresses the social norm and is sexually active outside marriage will be castigated for her wantonness. Indeed, in *The Ruling Class* the women, Claire and Grace, pay the price for the madness that the Gurneys exhibit. Barnes's parodic presentation of the upper class critiques the Britishness of the British and voices the discontent of those who are marginalized by it. It depicts a political system and a social order that poisons the land with its incurable sickness. A prologue staging the last hours of the 13th earl of Gurney, judge, keeper of the law, guardian of the family, frames the play and introduces the themes the play will dramatize. Barnes skillfully uses costume to underline the difference between the appearance of dignity and the reality of depravity. The earl's appearance at the banquet, his speech, his return home, and his request for a drink from the butler would all seem to be everyday acts, the staple of everyday life for the nobility. Barnes uncovers the vestiges in order to reveal that what is "normal" is in fact "perverse."

The earl fetishizes women in the Freudian sense. Barnes uses theatre or performance as an index of the Earl's fetishism. The earl's own costume and his actions serve as a fetish for the female.

The beginning of the prologue shows the earl at a banquet, resplendent in evening regalia. The end of the prologue has one of the most disturbing images contemporary theatre has crafted of the decay of a class. The earl comes home, pontificates on the tradition of the English nobility to his valet Tucker, gets into a white tutu ballet skirt, a three-cornered cocked hat, and long underwear and plays out a fantasy. A rope loosely wound around his neck, he writhes and twitches in an ecstasy that is both sexual and aggressive. He dashes his sword around at moments of real arousal. As he gets more excited about "juicy breasts, white thighs, red hair colour of rust," he feels that this is one of life's rarer pleasures. (*The Ruling Class*, 10. All subsequent references to the play are from *The Ruling Class,* in *Collected Plays* [London: Heinemann, 1981].) Note that the earl describes body parts, not the whole person. And of course the arousal is complicated by the image of the worm that destroys and brings death. Arousal as vengeance and vengeance for arousal. "A man must have his visions," he says as he wants to take another quick stab at his and gets caught up in the game.

Women themselves become fetish objects in the next stage of the earl's fantasy, which shows him using arousal for women as a way of battling the nation's enemies violently. Hence, the sword that cuts the heads of the subalterns, the natives of the Third World. He smashes the Mahdi and knocks off the stairs that keep his footing secure. In an effort to get free of the rope that is slowly strangling him, he twists, in a grotesque imitation of the earlier movement of pleasure. But the noose has got him, and he is dead when Tucker comes in with the late night constitutional.

The two images of the earl, in evening robes and white ballet skirt, clash violently; they visually express the dissonance between the word and the body, the name of England and the flesh of England, the ideal of England and the rotting core that is England. The scene blacks out as the earl, in skirt and hat, sways on the noose. England's shame is seen in terms of "sexual perversity," and it is linked with madness. Since Jack will become one of the Gurneys in his bestial madness which is expressed by sexual perversion, it seems that the same connection is being made, but in a subterranean way, with the 13th earl. The effect that the earl's evening dress produces—of a man who represents England's brightest and best—is undercut by the twitching, writhing man strung out on a noose, wearing a dancer's skirt. The earl's evening dress signifies that he is, as it were, the custodian of the law of the land and hence the liberty of the land, caretaker of England's best principles. The visual effect is further undermined by the verbal. The earl's opening toast, filched from Shakespeare's *Richard II*, catches the rising rhythms of the famous Gaunt speech that celebrates England, but mocks them. "This precious stone set in a silver sea" is directly quoted to set the tone, but England, far from being the womb of great kings who fight for right, is the seat of nobility who fight for privilege (*Richard II*, 2:1.46). What was a speech that celebrated a genuine spirit of greatness is a shadowy verse that upholds the status quo. It is swamped by a murky nostalgia for hierarchical ordering: "I say the fabric holds, though families fly apart" (*The Ruling Class*, 8).

That Barnes chooses to use the image of cross-dressing to dramatize decay speaks to a very pre-60s notion of sexual orientation. The earl may be reprehensible in being obsessed about his name and its continuation and in his studied investment in the nation as empire, but that Barnes should pillory him by invoking the trope of sexual ambiguity argues for a very conservative authorial notion of sexual politics. Granted, it exposes the pseudomasculine, pseudopatriotic facade, but begs the question of why the earl would be "perverse" because of his nocturnal change of clothes. Yet, because of conventional ideologies of respectability and sexuality, the earl's political corruption is relayed by his sexual disturbance. The equation between political corruption and non-macho sexualities is particularly frightening when one recalls that D. H. Lawrence used it in *Lady Chatterley's Lover* to express a similar hostility to the upper classes. In the novel, Clifford is impotent, while the gardener's famed virility stands for the important values of both nature and nurture. Such a critique comes close to maintaining that the upper class is sexually bankrupt, while the working-class men have it. The class-based critique, of course, does not signify a more progressive attitude toward women or feminism. Nevertheless Barnes's criticism of the earl's abuse of women is more to the point, because he is clear about how the ruling class views women, especially non-upper-class women like Grace.

It is for the family that the 13th earl decides to get married to a woman his brother Charles recommends. Women, in this prologue, are clearly established as creatures who are used, misused, and abused by the ruling class. The earl considers Grace Shelley "no one. But Charles recommends her as good breeding stock. Family foals well. Sires mostly. There's always room on the top for brains, money or a good pair of titties" (*The Ruling Class*, 9). Gurney breaks Grace down into body parts and the relevant reproductive entitlement. His half-brother Charles represents Gurney as finding sex with women displeasing. Charles's language exhibits nausea about women rather than desire. Barnes picks up the theme later and implicitly equates the functions Grace and Tucker have within the hierarchy. Both Grace and the valet Tucker are used by the Gurneys to uphold the family's position in society, but, their rights are never considered. Both are ultimately ruined because of their connection with the family.

If the prologue sets up the idea that madness and perversion are linked to a conservative political stand, the first act, which portrays the return of Jack, the 14th earl of Gurney, problematizes the idea, for Jack is loony, antiauthoritarian, and egalitarian. He enters the picture after the funeral oration and the reading of the will. The setting again emphasizes the dissonance between mask and face, appearance and reality. The funeral service and the family gathering after it are two stereotypical scenes drawn from English life. They are familiar, indeed, the staple of a long-dead English way of life and the setting of the "well-made" English middle-class play. Barnes parodies this fixture by the dissonance between setting and action, so that setting is foregrounded as in an antirealist play, rather than effaced as in the realist drama of the 50s. Structurally the two scenes emerge as tableaux that are enacted by the Gurney family and hence open to scrutiny. Barnes stresses the fact that members of the ruling class spend all the time they can spare from making money on keeping up appearances, or enacting the roles that have been defined for them by long, staunchly held traditions. Thus they keep up the tradition of the "stiff upper lip" till the terms of the will are read. The discrepancy between surface and depth becomes transparent at this point. No traditional belief in primogeniture restrains Charles, the dead earl's brother, from trying to get control of the money at once. Bishop Lampton's song worships goodness less than it does rigid class structures:

> All things bright and beautiful. All creatures great and small. All things wise and wonderful, the Lord God made them all. The rich man in his castle, the poor man at his gate, God made them high and lowly, and ordered their estate [*The Ruling Class*, 14].

Barnes associates the religious right with the conservatives; through the rest of the text, he discusses the question of whom this alliance oppresses and how.

Act I classes the mad Jack with the underprivileged—the women and the servants—and thus implies that Gentle Jack is saner than the Gurney family. While Barnes could seem to imply that Jack has been destroyed by his upbringing, he nevertheless makes it clear that Jack is very much part of the Gurney family. His rebellion against the Gurney family has led to his incarceration, but birthright ensures his freedom. Tucker, the butler, is sure that Jack is one of the Gurney lot. Bernard Dukore concurs with this opinion: "Although Jack is mad, he is not essentially different from the other peers. The play is named after his class, not after him. His skirt-and-sword wearing father is also looney" (Dukore 1981, 19).

Barnes dialectically traces both perspectives in order to undermine any Romantic notion one may glean of Jack's seemingly rebellious madness. Act II lumps Jack together with the rest of the Gurney family. Underneath Gentle Jack lurks Jack the Ripper. Whether it is the 13th or 14th earl, both want the juiciest meat cuts of female flesh. The 13th earl conjures up visions of sizzling sirloin; Jack goes straight out to butcher. The structure of Act I plays up the Gentle Jack image, while Act II shows that it has been built on Romantic myths. As Dukore comments, Jack's references to peace, love, and brotherhood alarm Sir Charles, who takes him to be a "Bolshie" (Dukore 1981, 15). Sir Charles is very much the pimp par elegance, par excellence. He convinces Grace, his mistress, to marry his brother, and when his brother dies, he persuades her to marry Jack. Further, he manipulates his wife, Claire, into seducing Jack's psychiatrist Dr. Herder in order to bias his judgment on the treatment. Jack is structurally contrasted with Charles, but they are both presented as patriarchs. Charles is the despotic patriarch, Jack the benevolent one. The bishop and Charles are ugly, while Jack shines with a mad innocence. His appeal is enhanced by the fact that he is seemingly harmless. His "strangeness," combined with his mad protestations for "love and understanding," lends him the aura of a Romantic hero (*The Ruling Class*, 21). He is the mad outsider, as it were, but he possesses the wisdom of folly. Jack's structural position in Act I recalls the traditional image of the intense, passionate hero who has come through the fires of madness to a new, more profound vision of the world. Typically, society is not ready for these insights:

> JACK: The monastic ideal isn't easy. I've had many broken nights. But I've come back refreshed. (He smiles) Though hardly equipped for society [*The Ruling Class*, 21].

Cast in an unworldly mold, Jack's innocence speaks of an easy grace that the others lack. His gestures seem more "sincere," more "heartfelt":

> JACK: We're all one family. Let's wash away the old sores. If the Bishop doesn't mind, I think we should pray.
>
> CHARLES: Pray?

JACK: For love and understanding. Surely you pray for love and understanding [*The Ruling Class*, 21].

Jack's madness glamorizes him because it creates the impression that he is making the Gurneys uncomfortable and thereby wresting power from them. His insistence on friendship and love implies that his madness is symptomatic of his alienation and distance from the Gurney family and their values. His mad chants—"EXPLODE only FEEL, LOVE, and sin no more. Most everything you see, touch and FEEL glorifies my love"—seem to signal his rejection of a world impervious to the exigencies of human desire (*The Ruling Class*, 25). Jack desires, and the desire is more "natural" and "human" than the money-grubbing ambitions of the Gurneys, for Jack neither barters people nor bludgeons them. His whole being is given up to expressing himself, verbally and physically. Thus he comes across as a rebel, an outsider, the Other who is more humane than the Gurneys. The fact that he lives in a world of his own and communes with Tim Leary and Buddha is a further sign of his desire for another world. The structure of oppositions set up between the Gurney family and him thus implies that his madness is a withdrawal from a civilization that repels him. It places him on the margin: a creature in pain, who protests helplessly and heedlessly against the dry aridity and injustice of the world. The Gurney family, in collusion with the social order, has caused his madness:

HERDER: He showed classic schizophrenic symptoms by withdrawing from the environment. Then, of course, he never forgot being brutally rejected by his mother and father at the age of eleven. They sent him away, alone, into a primitive community of licensed bullies and pederasts.

SIR CHARLES: You mean he went to Public School [*The Ruling Class*, 24].

Elsom regards the attack on the public school system the social critique of the play (Elsom 1976, 180–81). The public school system is here also being held responsible for Jack's trauma. Whether this is ironic or serious, it is problematic that of the two main problems attributed to the system, gay sex should be one. Its most ugly and stereotypical face is evoked: pederasty. Almost as though to confirm Herder's diagnosis, Jack mentions "sex changes" in crabs as though to signal the "insistence of the letter on the unconscious." He sees himself as the crab and mentions that Sacculina, a parasite, chews the crab out in imagery that is laden with nausea and fear. In this context, Jack could be referring to his retreat from Claire/female or the crab's retreat from Sacculina/female. Jack's fantasies also fall into place within this framework which pits the individual against society. He dreams of plenitude, an expansiveness of being, and an intensity of feeling that madness alone confers. He is everything. He incarnates the principle of creation and feels "like a river flowing over everything" (*The Ruling Class*, 26). He tells Claire:

> I pick up a newspaper and I'm everywhere, conducting a summit conference, dying of hunger in a Peruvian gutter, accepting the Nobel Prize for Literature, raping a nun in Sumatra [*The Ruling Class*, 26].

Jack experiences an expansiveness of feeling. He imagines liberation. The liberation depends on the production of desire, for when desire flows, it acts subversively and challenges the order of things. Jack's attempt to liberate himself and his "brothers" from social conventions that deflect them from fulfilling their desires illustrates the manner in which desire acts subversively. Unselfconsciously, he dances the "varsity drag" with the parish, as it were. Barnes's earlier alignment of cross-dressing with the corrupt upper class is given an interesting twist here because Jack's openness is liberating. Perhaps if Barnes had stopped here, one would consider the 13th earl's closetedness a critique of his repression, rather than his political corruption, and would consider the hero's behavior a signature of the more liberated generation. Jack himself says that "sexual perversion is no sin" when he startles Mrs. Piggot Jones by asking her how various parts of her body react when aroused. We are recalled to the trope of fetishism in no uncertain terms by the mention of blood, flesh, thighs, and heart. He destroys the county visit with his questions to Mrs. Treadwell: "Mrs. Pamela Treadwell, can you love? Can your blood bubble, flesh melt, thighs twitch, heart burst for love?" (*Ruling Class*, 36). After all, the 60s had called for a sexual liberation with a political one. However, Jack's later behavior renders his semblance to Gurney as "perverse" rather than liberated. Jack's desire also manifests itself as a protest against the oppressiveness of the hierarchical order. Jack wants to burn his coronation robes, a symbolic incineration of the marks of class distinction that keep him from mingling with the commoners:

> JACK: Burn 'em, Mr. Tucker. Burn em.
> SIR CHARLES: What? Great Scott, man, these are your coronation robes! Marks of our elevation.
> TUCKER: Lots of tradition here, your lordship.
> EARL: The axe must be laid to the root [*The Ruling Class*, 28].

Tucker's bitter criticism of the ruling class is sharper and more consistent than Jack's rhapsody, but Jack's criticism has more of an effect because he is more powerful. Charles needs Jack to sign the estate over. Charles has to abide by Jack's will because his own power stems from Jack's possessions and position. The very lineage from which Charles draws his eminence keeps Jack safe till such time as he is testified insane or till he produces an heir. Jack's madness is subversive to the family structure in that it threatens to topple it over, cause embarrassment and generally discredit the family. The family cannot afford repeats of the spectacle that the earl dramatizes for the worthy

Mrs. Treadwell and Mrs. Piggot Jones. The earl's speech on the British way of life would certainly not pass muster at the fête:

> Britain is an imaginary island off the continent of Europe, covering 93,982 square miles, with a population of over 52 million, lying in a westerly wind belt. A fly-blown speck in the North Sea, a country of cosmic unimportance in my sight. (Sadly at them.) You can't kick the natives in the back streets of Calcutta any more [*The Ruling Class*, 36].

The earl clearly seems more progressive in his politics than the county he is lord of. Since the only quality that distinguishes him from the others is his presumed madness, it appears that madness gives him a sharpness that the others lack. While the Gurney club is feudal in its mores and conservative in its politics, the earl is libertarian. His zest for the new ways classes him with contemporaries who are disillusioned with Britain and disgusted by its imperialist past and its present imperialist claims. Jack, then, is dynamic; the Gurneys static.

Barnes portrays Jack along these lines in a series of vivid confrontations between Jack and the Gurney family. At each turn, Jack volcanically erupts and commandeers the situation by virtue of his madness. His antics rivet the family, and he skewers the spatial arrangement of the house. He poses crucified on a cross and wears monk's garb; he acts the preacher, the vaudeville dancer, the singer. At the outset, his very appearance and existence disrupts the family gathering. He forces them to pay attention to him. He allies himself with Tucker and dragoons the guests into dancing with him. The energy of madness keeps him center stage. Jack dominates the action by the sheer virtuosity of his exuberant dialogue and movement. He controls the Gurneys subtly. They are compelled to watch him, for if they don't he will do something to jeopardize them. The fact that they are obsessed with him leaves him freer and more powerful than them. They, on the other hand, have their lives taken over by him. The line of action that builds the earl up as the subversive, rebellious, Romantic utopian is subverted in Act II when hippie Jack becomes happy strangler.

Jack's madness manifests itself in his distrust of the social order and also makes him impervious to their machinations. Tucker alone tries to warn him that there is a conspiracy afoot. Jack's social criticism is contrasted to Tucker's. When the family plans to have Jack certified, Tucker does some plain speaking:

> TUCKER: The family. I've seen 'em at work a'fore. They got the power and they made the rules. They're back there plotting against you like mad.
>
> GURNEY: Love cannot doubt nor faith the mustard seed, no more plotting, Mr. Tucker, please. It's negativism. Plotting's a word I put into my pressure-

> cooker, whrrr. It's gone. Feeling persecuted's one of the signs of paranoid schizophrenia. Many poor wretches in Dr. Herder's Dancing Academy suffered from same. But I am being watched they said. Everybody is against me they cried. (Shakes himself vigorously.) You've set up profound negative disturbances with your Kremlin plots, Mr. Tucker, I'm going in. (Turns abruptly and walks Upstage Centre.) Resist it, Mr. Tucker, that way madness lies [*The Ruling Class*, 30–31].

Barnes indicates that Jack's refusal to believe Tucker allies him with the pernicious Gurney family. Tucker associates him with them after this encounter: "He's the same as all the rest, what he doesn't want to be so just isn't so" (*The Ruling Class*, 31).

If Jack's madness is the measure of his difference from the Gurney family and hence his freedom from it, it also renders him vulnerable to the illusions they fabricate for him. Jack's disdain of them is undercut by his naive belief in goodness. One of the special effects the Gurneys design for Jack is the Lady of the Camellias, Marguerite Gautier. Jack's doctor, Dr. Herder, gets the credit for crafting this cardboard doll, for he sells his knowledge of Jack's condition for Claire's body and a huge research grant. In essence, he does not go beyond Tucker's succinct diagnosis: "Your nephew suffers from the delusion that the world we live in is based on the fact that God is love" (*The Ruling Class*, 40). The psychoanalyst is complicit in the crimes of the family and is part of the family at a subterranean level. In other words, he is less concerned with the patient than with the patron. Dr. Herder is incorporated into the family both because of the sexual and the economic imperative. A servant of the ruling class, just as much as Tucker is, Dr. Herder is yet another dupe of the Gurney family. Dr. Herder serves the Gurneys in the mission to make Jack one of them, knowingly and unknowingly. He succeeds in making Jack conform to the Gurney standard. His idea of sanity does not extend beyond conformity to social norms. Dr. Herder brings in the Electric Christ to battle for supremacy with the God of Love. The intended shock treatment is comparable to the shock treatment that Dr. Genoni proposes for the mad subject in *Henry IV.* Dr. Herder imagines that the cure will rank him with Freud and Breuer if Jack does cast off his divinity and finds his way back to his name. Barnes's criticism of the doctor forms part of the more extended critique of authority. Dr. Herder's defection serves to isolate Jack further until his marriage to Grace. Although Jack gives in to the Gurney scheme, he still retains the silhouette of a sympathetic character, if only because of his apparent obliviousness to the Gurney way of life. However, this perception changes as Jack gets increasingly entangled in church, family, and state. The scenes that mark the transition between Gentle Jack and Stiff Father are situated in the space between the farcical and the satirical. The wedding scene mimes the funeral scene. Jack quips continuously about his status as God; Tucker seems intent on rousing the rabble to protest the ceremony: "Load o' British jelly-meat whiskers! Stand up on your tea-soaked haunches and stop it. Piddling, half-dead helots" (*The Ruling Class*, 57). Jack interrupts the ceremony to question the legality or propriety of the marriage: "Certain R.C. knackers think I'm already married to the Virgin Mary" (*The Ruling Class*, 57). As in the funeral scene, the setting and costumes underscore the discrepancy between surface and depth. The organ, the bride's white dress, the photo collage of society weddings, the bishop, and the society audience render the scene artificial, i.e., more scenelike than naturalistic. The illusion of a naturalized production is broken as the scene draws attention to its theatrical qualities. The earl's beat-star-cum-Pan accoutrements enhance the fantastic quality of the setting by their very discordance. Tucker pulls out his false teeth, an act which only emphasizes the tremendous effort the Gurney family makes to keep the seams of the scene sewn together. Tucker and Jack pull the gags that get the laughs. Now the bishop is the butt of Barnes's satire. Earlier, the bishop had been seriously concerned about his nephew's marriage to a commoner. At the ceremony, he speeds through the service after having glossed over Jack's loony anxiety about his previous marriage with the Holy Virgin. Later, the bishop is distressed by the scandalous breach of propriety perpetrated by Grace's having worn white at the wedding. The small sequence of events is a caustic reminder of the unreality of the ruling class's concerns. The bishop is like the ostrich that buried its head so deeply in the sand that it never saw the light of day again. The Gurney coup—marriage for procreation and perpetuation—represents the grotesque and monumental stupidity of the upper class.

Grace functions as the prime fetish of the action of the play; completely overvalued for something else—the heir—and completely undervalued for herself. This is the clearest instance of woman as the fetish. Sir Charles repeatedly talks in misogynistic terms about marriage in general being disastrous, but both he and Claire insist on Grace's body being used as a conduit for the Gurney heir, a conception of motherhood that radical feminist Mary Daly discusses. Daly contends that a patriarchal culture views the female body as a passageway and thus robs women of the privilege of maternity (Daly 1978). One only has to remember that classical Western precedent established by Apollo in the *Oresteia* when he exonerates Orestes of matricide because the woman has no rights over the seed. The role of woman as channel in *The Ruling Class* is overlaid by her representation as "maternal fetish" and "sexual fetish."

The women could conceivably have access to some power because both of them are essential to the male Gurney scheme to regain control of the estate, but they play the roles of pawns within the well-calculated game plan to have the earl certified. The structure of the plot indicates that they do not have an independent existence; their lives are linked to Charles's and Jack's. Claire sleeps with Dr. Herder to retain her position in the family. Grace, of course, is absolutely essential to the plan. Her motive for associating with the Gurney family is as comprehensible as Tucker's. Now Grace can be queen of Harrod's instead of charlady. Both women reject Charles, the master tactician but are drawn to Jack, the body of love, especially after he has been proven sane. Act II describes the extent to which the women have been victimized. If Act I shows that women are the linchpins of the domestic familial order, Act II extends the concept to suggest that the conservative order ricochets viciously against them. Barnes insists that the women and members of the lower class are slaves of the upper class. This dynamic is drawn after the earl is "cured." Thus Barnes implies that the women were deluded by the Romantic notion of madness. Since Jack becomes violent when he is most a Gurney, the women's folly in hoping to get something out of the Gurney connection is even more glaring. When Jack is "healed," he assumes his role as Gurney, earl, marshal of law, police of sexual morality. Innes concurs that the play's assumption is that Jack's violence makes him one of the ruling class (Innes 1992, 299). Act I ends with Jack proclaiming his name and identity. Act II is what the name is all about.

The earl's opening lines in Act II are "Call me Jack" (*The Ruling Class*, 78). The emphasis on the name refers to the Gurney name, which signifies the decadence of the upper class. Jack's clothes in Act II show that he has been restored to the upper echelons. The dark suit and waistcoat point dramatically to his changed state of mind. Interestingly, Jack is aware of the fact that sanity is about regulation. After a few random words on Nijinsky in his old manner, he controls himself and says: "Be patient, I'll learn the rules of the game" (*The Ruling Class*, 79).

The setting reflects the "progress" he makes in mastering the rules. The cozy Victorian bric-a-brac that accumulates in the drawing room highlights his return to conservative "normalcy," which for Barnes spells insane idiocy. The point is underlined by Kelso Truscott's verdict on Jack. The Master in Lunacy only has to listen to the old Etonian refrain to decide that Jack, like other old Etonians, is "perfectly adjusted to society" (*The Ruling Class*, 87). In the light of Dr. Herder's observation about the role Eton played in the earl's madness, the scene appears edged with an irony that subtly claims that the pathological is considered normal. The pathological is further defined as the conservative in Barnesian terms that oppose the Truscott verdict. If Truscott needed any persuasion of the earl's sanity, the earl's speech which defends the queen and every one of the conservative mores against "perversion" wins Truscott over.

Truscott's decision changes the family setup. Both Claire and Grace want to exchange the oppressive patriarch for a benevolent one who will be more malleable to their desires. Sir Charles loses credibility and authority when his plan is foiled by Truscott. Symbolically, Charles has been replaced by Jack, and Jack has become a Gurney. While the women want to ally themselves with the legitimate patriarch, they also imagine that the new regime will not be so authoritarian. Claire's conversation with Dr. Herder illustrates this belief: "I'm always on the lookout for new men" (*The Ruling Class*, 88). She dreams of enchantment with the new man:

> HERDER: Your nephew needs very delicate handling at this stage. And if possible, a little love.
> CLAIRE: That shouldn't be too difficult.
> HERDER: You helped Sir Charles crucify him.
> CLAIRE: Jack's changed. He's strong now.
> HERDER: What about us?
> CLAIRE: We're too much alike. Ice on ice. I wanna' feel alive.
> HERDER: And you think Jack'll perform that miracle?
> CLAIRE: Oh, rats to you [*The Ruling Class*, 89].

If Claire fantasizes a new life, it is not because Jack is now a chip off the old block but because Jack the Loon had been intense about his feelings. She imagines that now that he is "sane," the intensity has remained while the craziness has vanished. Grace too envisions a new way, one where she will be her own mistress by virtue of Jack's position. Without further ado, she shakes Charles off:

> Right? I've had enough of your right. You've stuck your aristocratic schnozzle into my affairs for the last time. Right? Jack's changed. Right? Everything's changed—you, me, us, them. It's a new deal all round. Right? You know what I mean. Right? Right! [*The Ruling Class*, 88].

The pace of the play shifts in the next scene, in which Barnes exposes the fallacies inherent in the Romantic conception of madness to which Claire and Grace subscribe. Jack soliloquizes:

> She betrayed you. Lust muscles tighten over plexus. guilty, guilty, guilty. The punishment is death.... I knew I was Jack. Hats off. I said Jack. I'm Jack, cunning Jack, quiet Jack, Jack's my name. (Produces knife, flicks it open.) Jack whose sword never sleeps. Hats off I'm Jack, not the Good Shepherd, not the Prince of Peace. I'm Red Jack, Springheeled Jack, Saucy Jack, Jack from Hell, trade-name Jack the Ripper!... Mary, Annie, Elizabeth, Catherine, Marie Kelly. (Sings.) "Six little whores glad to be alive, one sidles up to Jack, then there were five" [*The Ruling Class*, 90].

The repetition of the name serves to connect Jack's vile perversion with the Gurneys, for Jack's "recovery" has hinged on his being able to establish himself as a Gurney. It also has the resonance of the Union Jack of which Jack ultimately becomes emblematic. The chant of the women's names implies that Jack's murders are impelled by moral motives saturated by the sexual. He justifies his acts by invoking sexual mores that keep women chaste. By virtue of their sexual freedom, Claire and Grace are no different from whores who betray all men all the time because they are never faithful to any single male. In Jack's mind, Claire and Grace are whores. By a brilliant superimposition of dialogue and scenery that invokes Jack the Ripper and a nineteenth-century setting and situation, Barnes conveys Jack's interior in purely exterior terms. Although Jack has metamorphosed into Jack the Ripper, Barnes does not simplistically hint that Jack was acceptable before he was "cured." While he may not have been murderous, his association with the Gurneys did render him culpable. Despite his forays against the establishment, Jack was not successful in either liberating himself or Tucker. On the contrary, he was in the process of developing into a homicidal maniac. Thus Barnes relentlessly destroys the image of the Romantic Outsider. If Act I suggested that the Romantic madman's protest was flawed, Act II suggests that madness is a sickness that cannot masquerade as a marginal manifestation of protest. Rather, it would be more accurate to claim that madness metaphorically epitomizes the ruling class's rage against its tools, the women and the lower classes. By extension, it becomes a comment on the questionable role of the madman as rebel.

Barnes insinuates that the anger against women results from their sexuality. Jack the Ripper did seek to kill prostitutes, and it is this guise that Barnes projects on Jack Gurney. Barnes explicitly connects sexual perversion with madness. Ironically, Mrs. Treadwell picks up on this idea on her second visit to the Gurneys: "He's so like his father. He gets more like him every day, it's frightening" (*The Ruling Class*, 95). Scene 5 of Act II, which dramatizes this visit, parallels Scene 6 of Act I and emphasizes Jack's transformation. Not only is the setting completely Victorian, but also the tone. Jack exhibits the Victorian nausea toward sexuality, a reversion from his earlier liberalism and sexual openness. He finds sex distasteful and chair legs disturbing but obsessively holds forth on "orgasms and erotic tongueings." He later acknowledges that it was an uncensored slip. Jack is covering up the sexual as he wants the chair legs covered up, to evade disturbing images of his desire. Ultimately the women become fetish objects of his drive to sanity and "righteousness"; they become the objects of displacement of his conservatism.

Act II systematically reverses Act I. The sexual repression is matched by a repressiveness in politics. Where Jack had sealed his friendship with Tucker, he betrays him now and makes him the scapegoat. Structurally, this couples Tucker with Claire, for Claire too falls victim to Jack's rage. The love rhetoric has degenerated into lust for femocide, killing of women. The setting functions as an objective correlative of Jack's interiority in the scene that depicts the murder of Claire. It portrays a nineteenth-century slum street and casts Jack in the role of buck, Claire in the role of prostitute. The religious maniac is filled with opprobrium for Claire, the "slut": "Orgasm, coitus, copulation, fornication. Gangrened shoulder of sex. If it offends. (Softly into her ear.) Tear. Tear. Spill the seed, gut-slime" (*The Ruling Class*, 98). The tempo of violence increases with each sexual move that Claire makes. Barnes visually presents the perverse murderousness of the ruling class. As Claire seduces him, the earl whips out a knife and kills her. A visually shocking scene, it twines sexuality with death, for Claire writhes, not in the throes of sexual pleasure, but in the grip of death. Jack implicates Tucker in the murder and neatly does away with both agitator and prostitute. To the law, Tucker's innocuous association with a left-wing group proves his culpability. Tucker's comment articulates the logic of the situation. Tucker has to absorb the filth that the earl projects on him: "Upper-class excrement, you wanna' do me dirt 'cause I know too much. I know one percent of the population owns half the property in England. That vomity 'one per cent' needs kosher killing, hung up so the blue blood drains out slow and easy" (*The Ruling Class*, 107).

The earl perfects his upper-class act and performs splendidly at the House of Lords, where he consolidates his conservative position. Charles has become the shadow of his former self, and Dr. Herder has gone mad. Dr. Herder's subservience to the Gurney family has cost him his authority over his patient and his control over his mind.

The Epilogue visually emphasizes the sickness of the ruling class. Innes correctly notes that the violence of the epilogue in particular, and the play in general, casts the audience as voyeurs. He states that "although the implied demand is for action instead of (the conventional) passive acceptance of the dramatic situation, insults are defused by comedy" (Innes 1992, 307). Not only is the audience's anger lulled, but I would venture that a portion is titillated rather than "attacked," as Innes would have it. Of course, there are no reception histories recording arousal in "high brow" theatre, so I base my suggestion on the sales of films that deal exclusively with sexual violence. The sensationalism of the violence of *The Ruling Class* is almost comparable to the shock value/arousal of the snuff film. The very verbally graphic killings themselves disturb in that they *visually* and *verbally* play out a fantasy of sexual violence that has the potential of reifying male sexual arousal patterns revolving around women as victims of sexual violence. I am aware, of course, that the porn flick shows the woman as being aroused by the violence, which Barnes does not. However, both Claire and Grace want Jack. The female viewer, like the female actor on stage, is extinguished. Male speaks to male.

Jack kills again. One of the Gurneys at last, Jack of England and St.

George swathes Grace into his parliamentary robes and knifes her. She serves as fetish, object of his hatred of immorality, object of sexual desire and the need to suppress it. Her cry of agony signals the decline of the country. Barnes dramatizes the family life of one of England's noble families to depict the violence and depravity of the body politic. Jack's madness, as does his father's, metaphorically suggests the sickness of the ruling classes. The savagery of the disease is inflicted on Tucker, Grace, and Claire. When sick, murderous conservatism is the rule of law, the underclass is victimized and the women of the underclass pay a heavy price. Barnes's account of the fetishization of the female is split by his characterization of them as fetish objects.

Chapter 9

The Sexual Menace: Pinter's *The Hothouse*

Harold Pinter, one of the most influential of modern dramatists, scarcely had a reputation for being a political dramatist in the 50s and 60s. He is exhaustively documented as declaring that he could not write out of a sense of politics (Merritt 1990, 129–61). The "Pinter problem," as his veiled theatre of lacunae has been called, has been interpreted in radically divergent ways, including symbolically, existentially, and as a unique variation on the spare, bleak theatre of Samuel Beckett. Perhaps the most germane and useful of these approaches is offered by Stephen Gale, who has traced the development of menace in Pinter's work (Gale 1977). Critics believe that the effectiveness of plays like *The Caretaker* (1960) is due to results from the internal menace, which is not completely articulated but is instead left to be ominously threatening to both character and audience (Gillen 1983, 86–96; Dukore 1990, 23–35). Micheline Wandor's interpretation of menace in a Pinter play such as *The Room* (1957) or *The Birthday Party* (1958) is more concrete. She argues that the unnamed danger is the state which is manifested in the victimization of the women and in the incoherence of the men's lives. The men, however, retain authority over the domestic space, although the familial may erroneously appear to be the site of the female (Wandor 1987, 33).

Among these early plays, *The Hothouse*, written in 1958 but not produced until 1980, has been considered less than successful partly because of its overt politics and its fully thematized critique of institutions. It was directed by Pinter himself in 1982 in a televised production. The set was fairly elaborate, and the television version was chilling (Hinchcliffe 1986, 159). Robert Cushman of the *Observer*, for instance, in a 1980 review of the play finds that the critique of state institutional terror is not very "intersting" and that the "author is clearly more hooked on the mechanics anyway" (Hinchcliffe 1986, 159). Ronald Knowles has difficulty with the structure of the play because of its inclination towards theatrical sensationalism and startling devices. He judged the play to be "a little more than a series of unassimilated sketch materials" (Knowles 1985, 138). Pinter had, after all, been trained in the revue circuit. Martin Esslin, who had taken up the cudgels in Pinter's defense in a big way, thought *The Hothouse* was excessively steeped in the Pinteresque (Esslin 1970, 208). Even critics who are favorably inclined see the play only as a clearing house for some of Pinter's themes and a point of departure for some of his typical characterizations. Pinter's own early negative assessment of the play as not being appealing because of its absolute satirical focus has contributed to the relegation of the play to the sidelines of Pinter criticism (Stamm 1981, 290).

Set in a mental asylum, the play uses a crucial metaphor of the 60s and 70s playwrights to dramatize the failure of the institutions of the welfare state. Pinter's mode differs from that of other British dramatists such as Orton, Hare, and Barnes, who later also staged madness. While the play has been compared to Pirandello's *Henry IV*, it is only faintly reminiscent of Pirandello's extended meditation on the relationship between madness and sanity. Unlike Pirandello, who disturbs viewers by making them doubt the definition of madness, Pinter's play specifies the concrete repercussions of madness. Indeed, the playwright leaves the condition of madness or even psychic disturbances to the margins of his text and concentrates on the effects of power, whether absolute or limited, on a group of individuals charged with running an insane asylum.

Pinter veils the inmates themselves; we never see any of the "mad" characters on stage. Theatrically, this technique works to produce multiple effects. Pinter himself, for instance, was later able to suggest that the play was intuitively implying that psychiatric wards were being used to hold political prisoners (Merritt 1990, 137). It is clear that for a 70s audience and a contemporary one, the absence of the inmates indicates the banishment of the socially unacceptable. The invisibility of the mad expresses society's effacement of difference visually, while the language of the text reinforces the theme.

The insight that the marginal individual is obliterated or even reconfigured is not new to the plays of the time. Familiar notions of the haunted, modern individual alienated from the self couple neatly with generalized renditions of the hollow modern. Pinter, of course, like Frisch and Dürrenmatt among others, was more interested in the intruder as challenger of received history, bourgeois domesticity, and the complacent nation-state. *The Hothouse* complicates patterns of inside/outside by completely avoiding constructing a character whom one can understand in a psychological or realistic sense. While critics, including the author, view the absence of a point of identification in *The Hothouse* as a major drawback, I find the work theatrically extraordinary among Pinter's plays in that it distances the viewer. The play works as though it were alienation theatre because it demands a political rather then an emotional response. Instead of terrifying us with an unnameable menace, it awakens us to it. Instead of mystifying us, it demystifies us on the uses to which power is put.

The "angry" note, or the antiauthoritarian bar, is struck in a characteristically Pinteresque fashion in the opening scene. Roote, the man in charge, is in conference with his second in command, Gibbs. Critics have pointed out that the dialogue between the two reflects the power struggle between them, and this is the central conflict of the play. They add, however, that this thematic focus is lost by the inclusion of other elements (Knowles 1985, 138).

The dialogue between Roote and Gibbs does highlight each man's stake in power and position, but it also reveals their abuse of power in so striking a manner that interest aroused by the power struggle is diminished. Their conversation also shows that Gibbs will dominate soon, so that the deposition of Roote is anticipated as inevitable. The play, however, takes its twist in the "how dun it": in how Gibbs comes to control the institution and what this means for society at large.

In the opening scene of Act I, Roote and Gibbs exchange words sparingly on institutional business. Their conversation clearly covers over what they are really talking about: the psychic and sexual lives of the staff, specifically Roote and Gibbs. Although they purport to be talking about the inmates, Roote does not know them and Gibbs uses his knowledge to intimidate Roote. Critics have enumerated the number of sophisticated subterranean uses Pinter's dialogue involves, including the struggle for mastery of discourse (Gale 1977; Almansi 1987, 89–105; Esslin 1970). In this instance, Gibbs' accuracy of information threatens Roote and puts him on notice that his hours as chief are numbered.

Roote gets patients 6457 and 6459 mixed up. The patient numbering system is yet another way by which Pinter screens the mad. On the one hand, the essential obliteration of identity is foregrounded; on the other, the patients' selves remain secret, unexposed to the vigilance of the authorities. Pinter, then, veers away from setting up binary oppositions such as sane/insane; he also refuses to exploit the spectacle of mad folk. Rather, the sane folk are on display, not as crazy folk, but as murderous, callow, corrupt, petty bureaucrats.

The Hothouse is a play set in an asylum, but there are no mad folk on stage; at least there is no one who acts visibly mad. The logic of the discourse also insists that Gibbs's action of killing the entire staff derives from the system in place. Shockingly, considering his character, his actions are not aberrations. On the theatrical surface, no one is mad. Below the surface, Gibbs's acts seem disturbed. Madness lurks below the surface, but Pinter does not attribute madness as a motive for action of the plot. Gibbs's and Roote's power drives run the machine of the play.

Gibbs's comments are unctuous and his servility to Roote suspect. Roote, in the exchange quoted below, could be played as a man who really has lost control and cannot decipher his handwriting to tell the difference between 6457 (dead man) and 6459 (the woman he has interviewed). Alternately, he could be played as a man who is shrewd enough to cover his tracks and is trying to silence Gibbs by masking any personal knowledge of either inmate. Gibbs's refusal to follow suit edges Roote closer to the brink. The pace of the questions and answers slackens when Roote launches into long talks on the mission of the institution or its mode of operation. Both subjects become signs of genuine perplexity: Roote is not secure of his power. More importantly, he figures out that the absurd reproduction of hierarchy both ensures and threatens his position. After Roote and Gibbs have ascertained that they call the patients by numbers because it used to be the practice, they grapple with their own relationship.

> ROOTE: I was standing where you're standing now. I can tell you that. Saying yes sir, no sir and certainly sir. Just as you are now. I didn't bribe anyone to get where I am. I worked my way up. When my predecessor ... retired ... I was invited to take over his position. And have you any idea why you call me sir now?
> GIBBS: Yes, sir.
> ROOTE: Why?
> GIBBS: Because you called him sir then, sir.
> ROOTE: Right! [*The Hothouse*, 21. All subsequent references are from *The Hothouse: A Play* (New York: Grove, 1980).]

The pause suggests that Roote usurped his authority and fears that Gibbs will do the same.

Critics have looked at the characters in *The Hothouse* as grotesque caricatures (Stamm 1981, 290; Esslin 1970, 103–5). They are clearly not psychological, realistic portrayals. They do have a lot in common with Ionesco's characters: both sets of characters are unaware that they are comics playing with a straight face. Ionesco's surfaces do not yield, Pinter's do.

If the Roote and Gibbs interchange rehearsed a power struggle without openly playing it out, Roote and Lush's interaction skillfully dresses up their strong erotic attraction to each other. This aspect of *The Hothouse* is as characteristic of the Pinteresque elements as is the power struggle. Indeed the famed opacity of conversation and gaps in meaning can be squarely attributed to the welling-up of imperfectly submerged gay sexuality and taboo heterosexuality. The plays that were written before the censorship ban was lifted clearly bear the imprint of this tension. *The Hothouse* (1958) is metaphoric of the hot, simmering passions that break the surface of institutional life at the asylum.

Alan Sinfield's account of the gay theatre–going public during the 50s and early to mid 60s explains the importance of Pinter to the gay public. Their attraction to Pinter was less an appropriation of his plays than a response to a specific call pattern. The outsider motif struck a chord with closet gays of the middle and upper classes, who were the sexual interlopers in heterosexual society. Sinfield's thesis is that "Pinter's version of outlaw-intruder was apposite to homosexuality at this time: both were imagined as mysterious and violent, lying in wait in the silences, explicitly nowhere but, by so much potentially everywhere" (Sinfield 1992, 171–72). He continues by making a point crucial to our understanding of *The Hothouse.* He states that to insist that the Pinter canon dealt with intense male relationships, as indeed it does, is not to "out" the play as being a gay play, because homosexuality in the 50s was neither completely formulated nor in deliberate hiding. Sinfield concludes by suggesting that "oblique homosexual representation should be studied for the *process* that constitutes it so, and for the social reasons that demand such a process" (Sinfield 1992, 172). My understanding of Sinfield's thinking is that Pinter played a role in the construction of homosexuality by engaging with dominant ideas of it as threatening to the social fabric, but did not necessarily wish to or know how to name it as such because of his own imbrication in the dominant ideology. Joe Orton too picked up on Pinter's tortured formulations and decided, without any of Sinfield's demurrals, that Pinter's texts presented "lots of opportunities for sexual ambiguities" (Orton 1986, 64).

Sex and violence form the basis of all the interchanges in *The Hothouse.* The opening cleverly almost blends the two with its play on Roote's "forgetting" of 6459 and 6457. Number 6459 has had a child, but the father is unknown because the entire staff had sexual relations with her. Unlike Strindberg's *The Father*, none of the men involved claim the child for fear of institutional reprisal. Roote's assessment of the problem is bizarre and becomes signatory of the placement of the women in the institution. He is chirpily comfortable with the sexual use of the female inmate(s), human beings the institution supposedly protects.

> ROOTE: And you say a number of the staff have had relations with this woman, do you?
>
> GIBBS: Apparently, sir.
>
> ROOTE: (standing) Well one of them's slipped up, hasn't he? One of them's not been using his head! His know-how! Common or garden horsesense! I don't mind the men dipping their wicks on occasion. It can't be avoided. It's got to go somewhere. Besides that, it's in the interest of science. If a member

> of the staff decides that for the good of a female patient some degree of copulation is necessary then two birds are killed with one stone! It does no harm to either party. At least, that's how I've found it in my experience. (With emphasis.) But we all know the rule! Never ride barebacked. Always take precautions. Otherwise complications set in. Never ride barebacked and always send in a report. After all, the reactions of the patient have to be tabulated, compared with others, filed, stamped and if possible verified! It stands to reason. (Grimly.) Well, I can tell you something, Gibbs, one thing is blatantly clear to me. *Someone* hasn't been sending in his report! [*The Hothouse*, 43].

Illogic governs the institution. The status quo permits the staff to have sex with women inmates as long as it is surveyed and tabulated. The myth of scientific rationality has to be preserved. The sinister dimension of this revelation implicates them in institutionalized rape; quite literally members of the staff can have their way with the women. Matters of consent are not even raised.

To verify 6459's identity, Roote and Gibbs go through a long session of questions and answers similar to the one they have on 6457. Both times Roote wavers between knowing the inmate and not knowing him or her, and in both cases it is clear that his pretense at lack of knowledge distances him from the crimes and any culpability he may have. His transparent maneuver is exposed, again giving Gibbs the upper hand.

> ROOTE: Quite a sensual sort of face?
> GIBBS: Quite sensual, yes, sir.
> ROOTE: Yes. [*Pause.*] Yes, she's got a sensual sort of face, hasn't she?
> GIBBS: I should say it was sensual, sir, yes.
> ROOTE: Wobbles when she walks?
> GIBBS: Oh, possibly a trifle, sir.
> ROOTE: Yes, she wobbles. She wobbles in her left buttock.
> GIBBS: Her left, sir?
> ROOTE: Well, one of them. I'm sure of it.
> GIBBS: Yes, she has a slight wobble, sir.
> ROOTE: Yes, of course she has. [*Pause*] She's got a slight wobble. Whenever she walks anywhere ... she wobbles. Likes eating toffees, too ... when she can get any.
> GIBBS: Quite true, sir. [*Pause.*]
> ROOTE: No—I don't think I know her [*The Hothouse*, 41].

Almansi argues that discourse in Pinter is riddled with lies and that Pinter's "idiom" is a "human" one because of the lies (Almansi 1987, 89–105). If Roote can get Gibbs to go along with his lies, Roote has proof of his mastery over the situation. This particular scenario is repeated later with Lush. Roote's later conversation with Ms. Cutts, the drama instructor at the asylum, seems to suggest that he has been lying about 6459:

ROOTE: You remind me of someone.
CUTTS: In my new nightie? Who?
ROOTE: Where did you get that thing?
CUTTS: It's a gift. Who do I remind you of?
ROOTE: Where did you get it?
CUTTS: From a friend. Do you like it? She just gave it to me. I had tea with her today. She's a nursing mother. She doesn't need it. She insisted I should have it. She's so sweet, and she's got such a bonny baby. I said to her, now we're friends, I can't go on calling you 6459, can I? What's your name? Do you know, she wouldn't tell me? Well, what does your lover call you? I said, what little nickname? She blushed to the roots of her hair. I must say I'm very curious. What could he have called her? She's sweet, but she said the baby misses his Daddy. Babies do miss Daddy, you know. Archie, can't the baby see his Daddy, just for a little while, just to say hello?
ROOTE: (quietly) No. Daddy will stay where he is [*The Hothouse*, 139].

The register of the language is puerile and views sexuality and parenting in infantile terms, almost as though 6459 were playing at being mother, a game Cutts would like to play. The search for the father becomes caught up in the resonances of menace now because the father's part has breached institutional discipline, not because he had sex with a powerless inmate, but because he did not turn in a report. Gibbs's efficiency also does not permit Roote to forget the whole matter because his continued authority is firmly tied to the identity of the father of 6459's baby. Gibbs too could perhaps be the child's father. Roote insinuates as much in a scene that is hilariously double-edged. On the one hand, Roote's comments seem patently absurd; on the other, they carry a vitriolic male argument about the feelings of father(s) vs. mother.

GIBBS: Don't you think the mother might miss the baby, sir?
ROOTE: I won't miss it. Will you miss it?
GIBBS: No, sir. I won't miss it.
ROOTE: Then why should the mother miss it? [*The Hothouse*, 46].

The mother has no rights whatsoever; the fathers/male staff control both body and mind. Elizabeth Sakellaridou argues that 6459 is another example of Pinter's "absent mothers." Number 6459's erasure as mother, her victimizations as woman, and her obliteration as individual are representative of woman's place in the institutional hierarchy and in society. Sakellaridou makes a claim for Pinter's progressiveness. She states that he challenges conventional assumptions of maternity (Sakellaridou 1988, 50). While Sakellaridou is accurate about Pinter parodying extreme aspects of masculine glorification of motherhood, he nevertheless structures his play around the power of the maternal, thereby revealing his own contradictory participation in the culture's androcentric valorization of the maternal. Wandor's insight that sexuality is "fraught" in Pinter and that he "explores further a displaced Oedipal relationship in which the 'mother' figure is given a precarious compensatory moment of sexual power over the 'son,' functioning also as a fantasy figure for him," is borne out by the trope of maternity in *The Hothouse* (Wandor 1987, 33).

The hothouse atmosphere of the setting, which is intensified by the heat emanating from the radiators in Act II in some productions, lends itself to infantile regressions in the case of the four men. Number 6459's recent motherhood, with its obvious suggestions of sex, fecundity, fertility, and security, triggers some pathetic posturing on the part of Roote. His infantilism is further proof of his diminishing power:

> GIBBS: What shall I do about the baby, sir?
> ROOTE: Get rid of it.
> GIBBS: The mother would have to go with it, sir.
> ROOTE: Why?
> GIBBS: Can't live without the mother.
> ROOTE: Why not?
> GIBBS: The mother feeds it.
> ROOTE: I know that! Do you think I'm an idiot? My mother fed me, didn't she?
> GIBBS: Mine fed me.
> ROOTE: But mine fed me! (Pause.) I remember [*The Hothouse*, 44–45].

Gibbs's insistence about such puerile points gives him the upper hand. Roote's sharp reaction betrays a basic infantile lack of assurance. Pinter succeeds in connecting the thematics of power with psychic equilibrium by bringing up the "archetypal" female figure: the mother.

This attachment to the memory of the maternal body, while in and of itself surely not reprehensible, is presented by Pinter in the most unsavory light. Two middle-aged men have recourse to the maternal trope to verify their sense of authority and self to themselves and the other. While the dramatist mocks them as he obliterates 6459, he nevertheless betrays a certain queasiness about female flesh, a shrinking. Elizabeth Sakellaridou states that the later Pinter overcomes this stage, which she calls the "archetypical." In this stage, he shows his terror of female sexuality and projects that male fear on female characters (Sakellaridou 1988, 13). In this play, Pinter does not only represent that male fear, he participates in it, which subtly puts on trial his own critique of the two men.

The men obsessively return to the mother in Act II when once again they talk about the problem of the inquiries that 6457's mother has made about him. Number 6457 is the patient whom Gibbs hints Roote has murdered.

> ROOTE: How do you know she was his mother?
> LUSH: She said so.
> ROOTE: She was a liar!
> LUSH: No, she wasn't.
> ROOTE: How do you know?
> LUSH: She looked like a mother.
> ROOTE: How do you know what mothers look like?
> LUSH: I had one myself.
> ROOTE: Do you think that I didn't?
> LUSH: (pointing at Gibbs) He didn't.
> GIBBS: Oh yes, I did, damn you!
> ROOTE: I was fed, Mr. Cleverboots, at my mother's breast.
> GIBBS: So was I.
> LUSH: Me too.
> (Sudden silence.)
> ROOTE: *WELL? AND WHAT ABOUT IT?* [*The Hothouse*, 106].

This other mother, 6457's concerned mother, is also absent. Lush manages to fob her off with some jargon on convalescence and rest. If 6459 cannot direct the destiny of her son, in fact cannot suckle the infant, neither does 6457's mother have any real command over her son living or dying.

Sexual and erotic tension between the men partly accounts for the diminished presence of the women. The women are no less significant because of their dwarfed roles, however. Sexual unease and gender anxiety inform discourse and act in the play. Unmanageable and unselfconscious impulses toward power in sex and power in the institution motivate each staff member. Pinter, like Strindberg, does show that sexual/psychic contradictions undergird institutional politics and formulate authority structures.

Adler places Pinter in a category apart from Strindberg (Adler 1981, 385). He regards the pattern of the "domineering wife or mother" that he believes describes Laura of *The Father* to be fairly routine in modern dramatic texts. However, he believes Pinter to be working with an unusual theme whereby "the man willingly chooses to relinquish his own position to permit the woman to flower, acquiescing to the female's needs to help her attain complete fulfillment as woman" (Adler 1981, 377). Pinter is here presented as concerned with the female self and the constitution of female subjectivity. Adler argues his case by using *The Homecoming* (1964), where he believes that Teddy, Ruth's husband, "gives her up" to enable her to come to selfhood. Of course, the sinister resonances of the dialogue between the men of the family speak to the exchange of Ruth between the men. That Ruth consents to staying behind in England in this male ménage suggests that she will have more power in the sexual space than in the domestic enclave in the U.S. Pinter, then, cannot easily be assimilated as a profeminist dramatist. The difference between the Strindbergian Laura and the Pinteresque Ruth is that Ruth agrees to an exchange of her body and self and derives subversive power; Laura acts autonomously to emerge powerful. Further, the men in *The Hothouse* do not appear to have any idea that women have selves that need to be nurtured. Roote asks Cutts if she is happy with *him*, but there is no amplification of either female desire or the female self through the text.

Cutts, the drama instructor, expresses some of the sexual ambiguities that trouble the staff. She is the only woman character we see on stage. Elizabeth Sakellaridou finds that she "becomes the bearer of all the archetypal features that men attribute to women" (Sakellaridou 1988, 47). Cutts is not a real woman, but neither are the men real. Cutts does play a role in the power struggle between the two men, initially perhaps to gain power but maybe later to survive the aftermath of the battle. She is mistress to both Gibbs and Roote. While Sakellaridou attributes Cutts's servility and flattery of the men to her "avidity to satisfy her feminine vanity and satiate her sexual hunger," it would be more accurate to see her as a male projection of a woman who also uses sex to gain power, in a situation where she has very little (Sakellaridou 1988, 49). Sakellaridou is incorrect in her assumption that Cutts becomes a figure to fear because of her voracious appetite; on the contrary, Cutts takes a lot of trouble to reemphasize femininity as weakness. Were she to be like Circe or the Sirens, emblematic of pure femininity, she would be irresistible because men would want to be with her to prove their masculinity. Cutts's female "essence" is fraught with fear, and an effort to be "feminine," yielding, pleading, coveting, is the most stereotypical way possible to mask her own bid for power. Cutts poses no threat to the men, unlike patient 6459 and the mother of patient 6457. Sakellaridou is of a different opinion and views Cutts as a surrogate mother to Lamb and as incarnating the principle of the "great Mother." She suggests: "One might also detect Strindbergian undertones in Ms. Cutts' deadly embraces, which threaten the men she comes in contact with" (Sakellaridou 1988, 51). Laura in Strindberg's *The Father*, for instance, has more agency, literally more visibility on stage, and is at least as important a character as the father. At the structural level, Cutts is definitely not as significant as either of the two invisible mothers. Sakellaridou does, however, pick up on the theme of Cutts subtly eroding male authority (Sakellaridou 1988, 49). I read such a supplement to her sexuality as a consequence of the male playwright's construction of female sexuality. Pinter does not invest Cutts with sufficient self-consciousness to enable me to suggest that the attrition of male authority is in any way a concerted, conscious onslaught. The want of such a balance between male and female not only separates Pinter's *The Hothouse* from Strindberg's *The Father*, but also makes *The Hothouse* a play that completely excludes a female perspective, even a distorted female point of view.

Cutts does not erode male authority because her mode is patently opportunistic and because neither man apparently lets his guard down with her. Pinter salvages Cutts as victim by portraying her as eager for both power and survival. Her opportunism exonerates her from Sakellaridou's charge that she is totally stupid. Neither Roote nor Gibbs confides in her, and Gibbs purposely keeps his plans from her. Cutts's extraneousness to the power play, despite her push to it, draws attention to the homosexual compact between the men.

The homoerotic connection that I speak of does not refer only to physical sexual bonding between men, but also considers Irigaray's concept of the homosexual economy that makes women units of exchange between men who enjoy the primary relationship. Irigaray theorizes that patriarchal societies are founded on the exchange of women and that culture as we know it is rendered possible through the circulation of female bodies. She regards the institution of such an economy "ho(m)mo-sexual monopoly" because all production of materials and symbols refers back to the male (Irigaray 1985b, 172). Her analysis of how homosexuality maintains the heterosexual law is instructive and relevant to *The Hothouse*:

> The use of and traffic in women subtend and uphold the reign of masculine hom(m)o-sexuality in speculations, mirror games, identifications and more or less rivalrous appropriations, which defer its real practice. Reigning everywhere, although prohibited in practice, hom(m)o-sexuality is played out through the bodies of women, matter or sign, and heterosexuality has been up to now just an alibi for the smooth working of man's relations with himself, of relations among men [Irigaray 1985b, 172].

Irigaray's emphasis on the cardinal relationship in society, whether material or symbolic, as being between men is salutary. Heterosexuality becomes a convenient norm because it facilitates the exchange of women as commodities and only serves to reify sameness, repress difference, and reinstate men as both subjects and objects of desire. My own sense is that Roote and Gibbs are exemplary of that mirrored sameness in their bid for power, which is shortcircuited apparently by female sexuality as exhibited in the play. In other words, the smoothness of the male relationships is wrecked by the intrusion of women. Yet Pinter's play does not become subversive: the male power line gets reestablished by Gibbs and the minister, while the women are completely effaced. It is clear that women's bodies have underwritten this exchange through the emphasis on the women's maternity or more specifically their production of the commodity, or item of value: the child. Both 6457's mother and 6459 are blanked out because they spell the physical, which is essential to the material base of the economy through the reproduction of children. Their reproductive function is much feared, but seemingly valorized in this text in which male initiative and energy are directed towards repressing the maternal.

The play pursues the trope of sameness among men by referring to the ground or terrain on which they exercise control—women. Roote and Gibbs definitely share Cutts and possibly 6459. Gibbs and Roote presumably vie for power: not merely in competition over the institution but also in a more personal rivalry over women. The typical heterosexual motif is warped by both men's relative indifference towards Cutts and is matched by their greater absorption in each other. Whether this interest is only due to their fear of each other is open to question. The symmetry of their positions situates them as mirror images of each other: Gibbs will become Roote, Gibbs is now what Roote once was. Pinter takes care to show that both men are aware of their similitude (*The Hothouse*, 21).

The involvement of Roote and Gibbs with each other is overdetermined by the nature of their struggle; the menacing element is Gibbs's violence, which emerges because of Roote's disdain of Gibbs. Both men resemble each other; both are narcissistic. The conflict between them is further sharpened by their attempts to wipe out a displeasing mirror image.

Gibbs's complex emotions towards Roote are alluded to opaquely in his conversation with Cutts. The introduction of Lush forces Gibbs to reveal his emotions. Gibbs loathes Lush, who forms part of the triangle. Sakellaridou argues that the triangle is formed by the two men and Cutts, but in actual point of fact it is not Cutts, but Lush who takes the place of the "other lover." Lush plays a more libidinally aware Gibbs. He challenges Gibbs's authority in the 6457 matter and subtly provokes Gibbs by having information that Gibbs does not, and he dances around with it much as Gibbs does with Roote. Gibbs dislikes Lush, and his fear of him is twofold: that Lush will take his place with Roote and that Lush can actually usurp his power. Gibbs is vituperative about Roote and Lush.

Gibbs envies Lush his intimacy with Roote and asks that Lush leave the room when he tells Roote that Lamb is the father of 6459's child. He also tells Cutts, "That old fool in there, he sees nothing, getting drunk with that ... bitch" (*Hothouse*, 122). The pause before "bitch" could imply that Gibbs was going to use another word. The choice of the slang "bitch" suggests that Lush is definitely not masculine and perhaps even plays the role of woman with Roote. The homosexual resonances that run through the text disarticulate the basic binary opposition masculine/feminine. In other words, when a man crosses the outer bound of heterosexuality and makes his similitude with other men visible, his masculinity or gender identification is up for grabs.

Lush, like Gibbs, confronts Roote, but even more directly. Pinter dramatizes a tense but intimate relationship between Lush and Roote. When Roote confides in Lush that he is given up visiting the patients, Lush steers the conversation to a more explosive question.

> LUSH: Why have you given up visiting the patients?
> ROOTE: I've given up, that's all.
> LUSH: But I thought you were getting results?
> ROOTE: (staring at him) Cheers.
> LUSH: Weren't you getting results?
> ROOTE: (staring at him) Drink your whiskey.
> LUSH: But surely you achieved results with one patient very recently. What was the number? 6459, I think. (Roote throws his whiskey in Lush's face. Lush wipes his face.) [*The Hothouse*, 88–89].

Later Roote also takes physical liberties with Lush and beats him when he (Roote) claims that he has been delegated by a higher authority. Lush presents him with an exploding cigar, but their interaction has a rehearsed quality that crops up each time Roote tells Lush not to call him colonel. Further, Lush is an invited guest; Gibbs an intruder.

In this triangle, the women outside on the periphery seem to have very extrinsic but crucial roles to play. Cutts and 6459 are presumably there to reassure Roote of his masculinity. Cutts plays on Roote's anxieties and Gibbs's apprehensions, probably with greater success with Roote. Sakellaridou sees Cutts as obsessed with her own femininity. While Cutts may require reassurance on that score, she also appears to use it as a weapon to secure her position with both men, a move that brings her into the drama rather than one that leaves her watching it.

> CUTTS: Perhaps if I were more feminine you wouldn't want me to go out in the cold.
> ROOTE: I don't want you to go out. I want you to stay.
> CUTTS: Or perhaps ... perhaps it's because you think you're not masculine enough.
> ROOTE: I am.
> CUTTS: Perhaps you're not.
> ROOTE: You can't want me to be *more* masculine?
> CUTTS: (urgently) It's not what I want. It's what *you* really *think*. It's what you really *deeply* think and *feel*. It's what *you* want, it's what you truly *are*, can't you see that, Archie? I mean, if you're suddenly worried that you're not masculine enough—I mean, that I'm not feminine enough and that you're too feminine—well, it's not going to work, is it? [*The Hothouse,* 142].

Roote's hesitation reveals his sexual ambivalences. Cutts, the drama teacher, appears at least to be able to carry off the "feminine" role. She is clearly indifferent to Roote and believes that her position will be secure because of her association with Gibbs. Cutts's notion of masculinity as being overbearing is dependent on cultural fantasies about sexually aggressive men. In part, her femininity also relies on a similar stereotype of the female as passive and sexually aroused by such aggression. Her calling Roote on his masculinity is a clear sign of waning power. Pinter links the masquerade of masculinity with the trappings of power. Whether it is because Roote has lost his authority or because he is not sufficiently aggressive and expresses his insecurities to her, Cutts insinuates that he is "too feminine" (*Hothouse*, 142). Her reference to Roote's excessive femininity reminds us that Lush has also been termed female. In this instance, we are forcefully recalled not only to the trope of homosexuality but also to the norm of compulsory heterosexual masculinity. Roote falls short of the latter according to Cutts. He seems to have difficulty with his gender identification.

Cutts's own gender identification is not as firm as she would ideally like. She starts off by seemingly asking for reassurances that she is sufficiently feminine but concludes on an oddly discomfiting note that almost speaks of a gender reversal. The disarticulation of masculine/feminine, with its concomitant sexual attachments and power values, is complete. Roote's awareness of the loss of power and masculinity is signaled by his abrupt announcement to the staff—a withdrawal into public discourse.

The resolution of the play is shockingly without transition. We come out of the cauldron to find that Gibbs has slaughtered the entire staff and saved Lamb, lock tester and participant in neural testing, for the role of scapegoat. The mad have still not spoken, but Gibbs and the ministry attribute these killings to them. The only sound we have heard from them marks the transition from the asylum to the ministry office. Gibbs gets promoted for his killing. The conclusion is Pinter's ironic indictment of authority. More telling is the insight that the sexual difficulties of the authorities are compensated for by the very real power they have over the silent, marginal mad. Within the framework of such a dramatization, Pinter portrays a world without women, but a world where women, because of their sexuality, can make men appear insufficient or shake their confidence in their own masculinity. Yet women are not the menaces. Women exert too little power directly in the play, but by tapping on male sexuality and fear of heterosexual insufficiency, they end up threatening a man's masculinity. The disturbances created to the stability of male gender identification prevent male bonding from reaching its sexual conclusion. Roote falls because of 6457's mother and 6459. The mystery surrounding 6457's death is never solved, but that mother is not the comforting mother of cultural memory, neither apparently is 6459 or Cutts, who perhaps may not be feminine enough because Roote is not masculine enough.

Finally, *The Hothouse* is a space that has vanquished women, a world without women. And when women do surface, there is trouble because they destroy the order. But Pinter does not celebrate their destruction of the murderous order because they are powerless to effect any real change. His portrait of the male establishment as sexually disturbed, "sane," and in power becomes a devastating, if oblique, critique of heterosexual relationships. Yet his critique is subtly skewed in that women play a role in tilting power relationships only behind the scene, not onstage.

Chapter 10

Phallic Fun: Orton's *What the Butler Saw*

Joe Orton's theatre, starting with, but finally veering away from, tired proclamations of Pinteresque betrayal and menace, appeared at first to construct new versions of marginality and identity. Sinfield puts it well when he says that Orton lent meaning to the Pinteresque by naming homosexuality (Sinfield 1992, 173). A gay playwright, one who had openly explored relationships in *Entertaining Mr. Sloane* (1964) and *The Ruffian at the Stair* (1967), could be expected to work with alternate models of sexuality and sexual identity. Indeed, in one way or another, Orton's work does speak to these issues, although not perhaps from a specifically gay platform. Succinctly summarizing Foucault, Terry Woods observes that gay sexuality introduces disorder into the ordered institution of marriage and the laws of desire (Woods 1990, 151). Although not working with a prescribed model of gay identity, Orton's work does refigure heterosexual desire in such disconcerting ways that his articulation has an impact on the audience's preconceived, stereotypical views of gays. In a 1967 interview with Giles Gordon, Joe Orton insisted that he wanted to get away from stereotypes of "queers" (Gordon 1967, 95). Referring to *Sloane*, he said that he wanted to show an "ordinary" man who liked men.

While Joe Orton did not think of himself as the spokesperson for gays and indeed was astonishingly indifferent to theatre censorship on gay material and gay rights generally, his personal and theatrical frames of reference were clearly influenced by the physicality of the underground gay subculture presented in John Lahr's edition of Orton's diary (Orton 1986). The Tangier entries also reveal his intense involvement with sex, drugs, theatre, and rock 'n' roll. These entries, of course, may have been meant for public consumption; his agent Peggy Ramsay had given him the idea. In his correspondence, Orton did seem to enjoy shocking or sensationalizing his audience, especially the middle brow, middle class, as evinced by the pseudonym he assumed, Mrs.

Edna Welthorpe, to give vent to feelings of moral outrage. Martin Esslin, comparing Orton's desire to shock to the satirist Swift's, finds that Orton has no corrective vision:

> Orton's rage is purely negative, it is unrelated to any positive creed, philosophy or programme of social reform. And it is this aspect of it, which, in my opinion, makes Orton's *oeuvre* so significant for an understanding of the social situation in Britain, and no doubt many other countries, in his lifetime and up to the present: for he articulates, in a form of astonishing elegance and eloquence, the same rage and helpless resentment which manifests itself in the wrecked trains of football supporters, the mangled and vandalised telephone kiosks and the obscene graffiti on lavatory walls [Esslin 1984, 96].

C.W.E. Bigsby, on the other hand, views Orton's philandering with the genre in a more subversive light. He argues that "For Orton, farce became both an expression of anarchy and its only antidote. In his play, role playing is not a series of false surfaces concealing a real self; it is the total meaning or unmeaning of protagonists who survive by refusing all substance" (Bigsby 1982, 17). While Innes agrees that politics for Orton were "irrelevant," he makes the provocative observation that Orton waged class warfare through farce (Innes 1992, 270–71). On the other hand, several followers of the alternate theatre find that Orton did not, in fact, succeed in shocking anyone's sensibilities and that he did not explore marginal sexualities with any seriousness (Sinfield 1992, 170–86). Sinfield argues that Orton "exploited and contributed to the process through which homosexuality became publicly speakable" (Sinfield 1992, 171). Sinfield's point is that the framing of the issues around homosexuality constrained Orton and his sexual/cultural politics.

Entertaining Mr. Sloane edged on the socially unacceptable because of the brother/sister pair's willingness to acquiesce to the murder of their father by Sloane in return for equal shares of Sloane's body. That it is the male body rather than the female one that is coveted makes Orton's comedy more risky than traditional bedroom farce, which retains strictly patriarchal rules of exchange: men exchange women. In a slight twist of this originary formulation, women resist exchange in *What the Butler Saw* (1969). While not able to do the exchanging themselves, their resistance to exchange results in some bizarre versions of male and female subjectivity that the farceur works.

What the Butler Saw, posthumously produced, refers to the seaside peepshows that apparently titillated butlers. The image of the title is visual and unpleasantly suggests that the spectator will be the voyeur. The mediation between the viewer and the spectacle enables the playwright to highlight sexualities that are not public currency in a heterosexual world. To some extent, Sinfield is correct in his estimation that Joe Orton is always addressing himself to Edna Welthorpe. For instance, Orton wanted the setting of the play to be as conventional as possible so that the audience would be dumbstruck by the unconventionality of the action, especially the sex, which he predicted would have them in hysterics (Sinfield 1992, 179, and Orton 1986, 125). Christopher Innes concurs that "its [sex's] primary function is to arouse the most violent reactions possible in the average (by definition bourgeois) audience" (Innes 1992, 269). Orton pitched his stuff to Edna through the use of innuendo, obliquity, and indirection, so that what is finally expressed directly gets buried under the weight of such archness, which is based on two entirely different sexual worlds: heterosexual and homosexual.

The voyeur, if viewed as classically male, is punished by having his visual privilege fractured. Unlike Mulvey's voyeur, whose male identity would be resecured by the male looks in the diegesis or the world of the narrative onstage, the male viewer of the play may find his spectatorial position discomfiting (Mulvey 1975, 6–18). In terms of the narrative model, the male viewer would, however, emerge safe, for his role as active, as "bearer of the look" and power, is left intact. The female viewer, however, does not find her positioning any more validating than she does in the classic male Hollywood film or the male canonical dramatic text, where she would find that identifying with the female would be a masochistic pleasure at best. The female may well find that whatever agency she can dredge out of the play would ironically be by struggling to regain a position not inherently powerful.

The play also invites a voyeur of a different sort: the sane viewer who watches the mad, sexually distraught characters. That the characters are mad because they are sexually distraught is never open to question. Orton himself maintained that there was not "a lunatic in sight—just the doctors and nurses" (Orton 1986, 115). Set in a psychiatric asylum, the play does not get involved with the characteristic set of questions that asylum plays pose. It is only very peripherally concerned with the twentieth-century individual trapped in an institution. While other critics commend Orton on his critiques of the welfare state, only *The Good and Faithful Servant* (1970) really fills this bill. *What the Butler Saw*, far from celebrating "polymorphous perversity" (Charney 1982, 498) or even the politically current notion that sexual identities are not stable, uses these amenable tropes to critique the dark underside of heterosexuality, specifically the heterosexual family unit. This critique is severely compromised by Joe Orton's "out," the overlay of madness that obscures the exposure.

Orton's disarrayal of family values extends to England's iconic heroes, including Winston Churchill. The most "visible" prop of the play is a penis from Churchill's statue that gets accidentally embedded in Geraldine's stepmother (Geraldine is the female hero). This accident causes the stepmother's death. Towards the end of the play, the missing penis is returned to Sir Winston's statue. Esslin regards this as the "restoration of the nation's fertility symbol to its rightful place" (Esslin 1984, 106). Whether Orton fragments Churchill's penis to mock the man or does it to enshrine his phallus or does it merely to pun on what a prick he was remains open to debate. Smith suggests that the emblem of the phallus is the central thematic of the play and that the trope itself is borrowed from the dionysiac ritual of the *Bacchae.* He places the trope in the context of Orton's privileging of the site of the dream. In his diaries, Orton notes his attraction to the dionysiac and plans to tighten the delirious state and reframe it with Apollonian aspects. Orton's glide into the dream state at moments in the text is clearly not open to dispute, nor can it be debated that the phallus is the primary supplement of the dream state (Smith 1989, 129). The censorship board apparently did consider these explicit references lèse-majesté (Orton 1986, 256). Orton did tell Oscar LeMenstein that *What the Butler Saw* says that Churchill "had a big prick." Beehler, however, thinks that the phallus is not the prick, that it is "more like Lacan's symbolic phallus" (Beehler 1982, 96). My own inclination would be to view the action around Churchill's penis as a constant symbolic reference to the penis and its central importance in defining the desire of the play. While Beehler may be correct in drawing the tired distinction between the phallus and the penis, it may be more relevant to the thematic of the play to remember that whatever you may call it, a prick remains one. In this sense, then, Churchill's resurrected penis embedded in Geraldine's stepmother acknowledges only male desire. Joe Orton's distribution of the sexual energy of the cast is intimately connected to his construction of maleness, femaleness, and madness.

Some critics, including Joe Orton himself, have conspired to create the illusion that Orton actually "[broke] down all the sexual compartments that people have" (Gordon, 1967, 96). Leslie Smith is the most generous when he says, "It [Orton's work] needs, I think, to be seen as part of a wider celebration of sexuality in all its manifestations" (Smith 1989, 126). *What the Butler Saw* obviously has its fair share of naked bodies, but sexual compartments, as in male/female or heterosexual/gay/lesbian, far from being broken down, are reassembled. Orton uses the trope of madness to indicate that these characters are marginal, not straight; but in so doing, he also denies their positions any legitimacy. Further, even in its most risqué moments, *What the Butler Saw* does not have a sexual overture that is *not* heterosexual. Although the characters change clothes, that is all they do. Even the role-play is restricted to a heterosexual domain. Madness for Orton is wildness, or *wilding*: license to do what one may not do on a daily basis. Orton does not respect the everyday sanctities. Indeed, he says that they are quite simply beastly. He definitely does not privilege normalcy over madness. Nevertheless, Orton's "realism" forced him always to bring the play back to the viciousness of normalcy. Orton did not dichotomize madness and sanity. He did, however, dichotomize sexuality in a fairly traditional patriarchal format.

Maurice Charney makes a serious charge against Orton's traditionalism. He states that "the intensely homosexual misogyny that runs through the play [*Entertaining Mr. Sloane*] is a controlling theme in Orton, whose women are either slovenly matriarchs, like Kath of *Entertaining Mr. Sloane* or coldly bossy phallic temptresses like Nurse Fay in *Loot* or Mrs. Vealfoy in *The Good and Faithful Servant*" (Charney 1984, 2). It is debatable whether the misogyny is specifically homosexual, but, on the whole, one would agree with Charney, except perhaps to add that these women are primarily characterized by their relationships to men. What makes Charney's comment startling is his assurance later in the essay that Orton is a poet of transition states in human beings and that he celebrates the exchange of identities (Charney 1984, 25). How is it possible to effect a change of identities, let alone an exchange, while continuing to portray women from a stereotypical male perspective? Clearly, Charney, like other favorably inclined critics, is prepared to celebrate sex changes without structural changes.

John Bull and Frances Gray take Orton to task for his treatment of female characters: "Never very attractively presented, [they] became in subsequent plays the victims of a no longer thinly disguised sexual disgust on Orton's part" (Bull and Gray 1981, 79). Orton's "disgust" or attitude toward the female body is rendered apparent in *What the Butler Saw,* where the women's bodies, initially desirable, are completely undesirable by the conclusion. Women's desires are also completely insignificant, irrelevant, or unattractive. Sexual jokes on women are crude, not particularly subversive, and very definitely stereotypical. Dr. Prentice plays on the old hoary myth of the frigid woman, "Despite all appearances to the contrary Mrs. Prentice is harder to get into than the reading room at the British museum" (*Butler,* 311. All subsequent references to the play are from *What the Butler Saw,* in *Joe Orton: The Complete Plays* [London: Grove Press, 1986].). Dr. Prentice's response when Nick tells him that he has failed to rape Mrs. Prentice makes this a moment of homosocial bonding that is based on a male perception of the woman, at her expense. The conversation unwittingly uncovers the homosexual compact between the men and enables Joe Orton to place pseudo rapist/son at the same level as rapist/husband. We do not know that Nick and Prentice are son and father, but the moment of understanding between them clearly reverses the old Oedipal triangle with a vengeance. Nick's reply to Dr. Prentice's joke concerns the mistress of the schoolgirls. Having been disappointed by Mrs. Prentice,

Nick seduces some underage schoolgirls. According to Nick, the schoolmistress complains to the police because he did not molest her. Here Nick plays on yet another stereotype flattering to men: women get mad at men when men don't desire them sexually. Male desire of *women* becomes absurd but remains powerful because it is linked with desire for power.

Male desire, articulated conventionally in farce, opens the play. Dr. Prentice, a psychiatrist who is in the process of hiring a secretary, interviews Geraldine by trying to seduce her. The lines are ribald and swift but fairly typical, despite the seeming outrageousness of the doctor's propositions. He "tests" her by testing body parts. The characterization of Geraldine is rather odd in comparison to Orton's other plays. While *Loot*'s Fay was in control, as was *Entertaining Mr. Sloane*'s Kath, Geraldine is not in control. Peculiarly enough, she starts off by resisting the doctor, asks for a female chaperone, and then succumbs completely because Prentice complains about his wife's "nymphomania" (*Butler*, 289). Geraldine's shift is characteristic of Orton's disdain of psychological characterization. Within the farcical framework, Geraldine's lack of knowledge about Prentice's motives is going to set her up as the patsy, the girl who knows nothing. Geraldine is not as helpless as Peter Barnes's women characters are. They invite exploitation; Geraldine plays along with the doctor, but interestingly enough the play does not fulfill his sexual desire. Indeed, during the course of the play, no one has sex with anyone, even offstage. Geraldine's manipulability ultimately becomes a condition of her relationship with Prentice who is her biological father. More problematically, Prentice becomes the focus of the play as he tries to retain his control over the situation, a mastery he loses the minute his wife walks in on him attempting to seduce Geraldine. Since Prentice is the man who is trying to evade exposure, events are plotted by his perspective. While we understand what Geraldine and the other characters experience and feel, the shape of events and the way they appear are influenced by Prentice's predicament and position in the dilemma. He cannot control them, however. Rance, the inspector of mental asylums, and Prentice's wife vie for control and both try to wrest power away from Prentice. In an almost paradigmatic pattern, Prentice, who has already lost authority, regains it only when he assumes the paternal role, which he clearly abuses by his unsavory scufflings with Geraldine.

Geraldine's portrayal may be recuperable by viewing her as the "straight girl" in farce, the one who is the moral center, who urges us to root for a return to normalcy. John Russell Taylor points out, however, that Orton does not afford us that luxury of focusing on a straight role (Taylor 1971, 136). Geraldine's plight does invite sympathy, but more because she is assaulted and does not know it. Her situation then is potentially more dangerous than one that is merely uncomfortable. Further, when the straight world does reappear at the conclusion, the news that Prentice is her father can hardly reassure us. Orton's straight world is more unsafe and unpleasant than his farcical world; his sane world, similarly, is more dangerous and repugnant than his "insane" world. In this way, Orton manages to have the traditional organizing scheme for a conclusion, but he mocks it. In making the difference between the two worlds apparent, however, he merely attempts to reverse the values attached to them; he does not actually muddy these values.

Too often Joe Orton's work is presented as espousing no valid social critique at all; however, Orton inverts values conventionally attributed to the world of farce/straight world. He indicts the family but leaves issues of sexual preference and difference largely where he found them. Jonathan Dollimore considers that Joe Orton's use of "black camp," a determined rejection of true essence, authenticity, and depth, identifies his work as toppling normative sexualities and behaviors. He defines a specific mode of camp that could well describe Orton's own theatrical practice:

> This kind of camp undermines the depth model of identity from inside, being a kind of parody and mimicry which hollows out from within, making depth recede into its surfaces. Rather than a direct repudiation of depth, there is a performance of it to excess: depth is undermined by being taken to and beyond its own limits [Dollimore 1991, 310–11].

Sinfield, in opposition to Dollimore, maintains that the avoidance of any depth skirts serious issues of identity and that this is a weakness in this play and Orton's other work. Sinfield's rebuttal of Dollimore's praise of postmodern shine as total rebellion appears politically more powerful to me.

What the Butler Saw does empty out all traditional meaning from the heterosexual compact, especially because of Prentice's desire for his daughter Geraldine and because of the sheer violence that engenders the relationship between Mr. and Mrs. Prentice. Rape and incest subtend the thematic, bringing heterosexuality to the fore, emphasizing it, allowing it to play itself out to its conclusion, which emerges as the heterosexual family unit.

For Dr. Prentice, it is business as usual when he attempts to seduce Geraldine. His emphasis on Geraldine's absent father is ironic; he is Geraldine's father. Characteristically, he thinks that it reflects on Geraldine's character that she does not have a father. Dr. Prentice's maneuvers and Geraldine's stock responses are laced with some witty gibes on the absurdity of the roles both characters play, but Dr. Prentice's virtual power does not become apparent until he begins to construct Geraldine as mad: "What I see upon the couch isn't a lovely and desirable girl. It's a sick mind in need of psychiatric treatment. The body is of no interest to a man of my stamp" [*Butler,* 287].

These overtures denote an ugly desire for power, and a total one, but since Prentice never accomplishes his goal and suffers from dire stress, he is not credited with too much power. Rather, he is mocked. After all, his role-playing with Geraldine entails a familiar male fantasy: male prowess "healing" female sickness. But the female viewer does not take satisfaction in Prentice's being ridiculed. Geraldine is ridiculed to an even greater extent for playing along with Prentice's fantasy and is punished far more severely. Prentice's "sexual cure" threatens to place Geraldine in a straitjacket for life. In the presence of Dr. Rance, the inspector, Geraldine not only assumes the role of Prentice's patient at the level of the farce that Geraldine and Prentice perform, she is the only "mental" patient in the asylum and is blissfully unaware of it. Prentice's victimization of Geraldine is only paralleled by Orton's own victimization of the female hero. She offers no resistance at all.

The fact that Prentice himself comes under the surveillance of Dr. Rance after he has failed to cover up satisfactorily does not vitiate Geraldine's utter helplessness. Prentice stays in the game of talk/double talk, dress/double dress, play/double play almost throughout the action of the play. The few moments that he is not scheming to stay in control result in his actually gaining control because he finds out that he is the Father and therefore totally vindicated, totally powerful. Curiously, the play does not follow the scheme outlined in Orton's other work, where the "representatives of middle class moral standards are father figures, the conventional symbol of authority. Their removal, clearing the way for a celebration of a new (dis)order, projects the destruction of restrictive social norms that Orton hoped to achieve through his drama" (Innes 1992, 272). Far from removing the Father, *What the Butler Saw* reestablishes his authority doubly: both as Geraldine's father and psychiatrist. Geraldine has no moves through the entire play. The only speech that she is allowed through the action of the play occurs when she answers questions posed by either Prentice or Rance. When she speaks of her own volition and tells Rance she is a woman, her words are totally disregarded. She does not initiate any action, does not resolve any problem on her own. Geraldine is not just the stock hapless dupe of farce, she is a stereotypically passive female. Orton was not much given to using this type of female character, however. Indeed, when women have significant roles in his plays, they are almost always cast after Fay, the nurse in *Loot*, a powerful murderer who also breaks the compact between men. Indeed, Fay is the woman as predator, Geraldine the woman as prey.

Geraldine is shorn of her hair, put into a padded cell, and then strapped into a straitjacket. Her helplessness is particularly visible. The others appear to be enjoying themselves in an abandoned, if harrowed, fashion. Mrs. Prentice too is straitjacketed because of "hallucinations" of naked men. Prentice's gun fends the straitjacket off so that he regains some phallic authority. Even

Mrs. Prentice wields a gun at key moments, displaying the power the "phallic" woman has. And although Nick is comparable to Geraldine in his sex changes, he is immediately believed when he reasserts his identity as the chamberboy at the Station Hotel.

What the Butler Saw introduces a different sexual ethos with the entrance of Mrs. Prentice. She has been referred to as a "nymphomaniac" and the "holy grail" before she arrives at the doctor's office. Unlike Fay, Mrs. Prentice is also manipulated, but unlike Geraldine, she wields power in advancing the action of the play. In fact, in paradigmatic, if farcical, relationship to Strindberg's *The Father*, Mrs. Prentice accuses Dr. Prentice of madness and is almost successful in having him committed. Mrs. Prentice has the aura of marginality around her. She is said to belong to a "coven," later named a lesbian coven. She also says that the only reason she is allowed in the membership is because Prentice is considered a female. A political lesbian, a sexual nymphomaniac? In keeping with the tone of the farce, the lesbian coven seems to be coming apart because of the defection of one of its members. The peripheral references to lesbian sexuality, linked to Mrs. Prentice (who is heterosexually pursuing her husband, has written on the clitoral orgasm, and accuses Prentice of not paying her sexual attention), seem to make the politics of sexual preference an irrelevant and fashionable bisexual sport set up to titillate the butler at the keyhole. Mrs. Prentice dabbles with the marginal, but she herself is enmeshed in institutions: heterosexuality, mental asylums. Her sexual identification is fairly secure throughout the text, but her voracious sexual appetite is open to question. While Prentice gets some sympathy from Geraldine because of Mrs. Prentice's "nymphomania," Mrs. Prentice herself insists that Dr. Prentice hardly ever has sex. Mrs. Prentice's desires, even if hypothetically excessive, could hardly be extraordinary in a bacchanalian revel. Yet her desire strengthens Dr. Prentice's desire and indeed becomes Dr. Prentice's justification of his attraction toward Geraldine. Orton reinscribes this stock scenario not to mock the incapable husband or question his masculinity or even his heterosexuality but to emphasize the unattractiveness of the hunting female. Mrs. Prentice's sexual aggressiveness, conflated with feminism and lesbianism, renders the most conventional character, Prentice, the scamp/hero of the farce and the most sexually transgressive character, Mrs. Prentice, the outsider.

The stereotypical equation of a sexually aggressive woman with a lesbian shows Orton's insensitivity to women desiring women. Mrs. Prentice's casting as castrating *and* lesbian suggests the play's reluctance to consider a female desire not cast in traditional terms. It expresses the fear of male exclusion, fear of a "female planet." If Prentice manifests the frozen paranoia of a man unable to desire an aggressive female, Orton does not pause to query the relationship. Through Nick, he claims that this equation between cannibalizing sexually aggressive woman and heterosexually nauseated male is the condition of heterosexuality and the family: "My parents were divorced, sir. I missed the warmth of a happy family atmosphere" (*Butler*, 292).

The homosexual motif is not altogether abandoned by the playwright. It surfaces again as part of the stock-in-trade of the farceur. This is, of course, a variation on old heterosexual bedroom farce, but how radical a variation? Nick confesses to having been molested by men; Prentice is implicated because he remembers the fee for such a pleasure; Match is afraid he is going to be molested and is warned that if he resists, he will never experience the pleasure. Geraldine's brother Nick is not gay. He takes equal pleasure in women. He tries to rape Mrs. Prentice and has his way with some underage schoolgirls. Perhaps Orton's real boldness lay in talking about underage sex. None of the characters is even dimly aware of a gay political identity or a politics based on sexuality/sexual preference. Orton does, however, broach the dangerous in articulating the relationship between sexual pleasure and violence. Smith recognizes the aggression inherent in Orton's construction of sexualities and views it as falling within a British tradition of challenging authority through sexuality (Smith 1988, 130). Unlike Fassbinder's *Querelle,* which forbids the heterosexual eye from participating in the gay scene, Orton's *What the Butler Saw* accommodates the heterosexual gaze. Orton flicks over the repression and aggression structurally but succeeds in speaking about the pleasure of forced sex. The violence is not coterminous with a rebellion against authority; such an analysis overlooks the pleasure of the body, and it is in this region that Orton is the most disturbing. That Prentice and Mrs. Prentice get back together and recommemorate a rape with pleasure is to speak of a politically incorrect pleasure. Orton's viewpoint may be bold, but it also makes phallic violence/pleasure inherent to the heterosexual relationship. While some feminist viewers may critique Orton for not engaging in a dialogue with women on female pleasure or even for not attempting to articulate female subjectivity, his placement of violence as central to male heterosexual pleasure performs a radical critique. By showing the woman as enjoying sex to the extent that she only wants to have it in a closet, site of the originary rape, Orton on a permanent basis critiques women for accepting the male framing of desire, perhaps, but he also leaves them voiceless and desireless and definitely leaves female desire in the closet.

Nick, the Prentices' son, replicates the pursuit of phallic pleasure. He attempts to rape Mrs. Prentice in symmetrical mirroring of Prentice's attempt with Geraldine. The critique of heterosexuality recedes as the accretion of pleasure in phallic fun continues. Joe Orton's exposé of heterosexuality gets splintered by the production of farcical comedy through phallic pleasuring.

Orton touches on a taboo topic and then abandons it to move on to another taboo, but he does not develop the relationship between society, the taboo, and individuals breaking it.

Cross-dressing, a motif used in the *Bacchae*, a model for Orton, touches on these taboos. Jonathan Dollimore reminds us that cross-dressing has the ability to challenge seemingly unalterable gender binaries (Dollimore 1991, 289). Geraldine, Nick, Match, and Mrs. Prentice all change clothes at least once. All of them are naked at least once. Geraldine is stripped early in the play and later shorn of her hair. She does not get her dress back; the only clothing she is offered is the straitjacket. Nick wears a dress through a small portion of the play, and Match is in a state of undress for another small portion. Mrs. Prentice wears a slip and a coat till she divests Dr. Prentice of Geraldine's dress. Beehler interprets the role of unclothing in this text as part of a move on the part of Orton against clothing as an index of gender (Beehler 1982, 91). He makes a case for the deliberate heterogeneity of gender: "In *What the Butler Saw* the unclothing of bodies reveals not a natural state of sexual determinacy, but rather a dizzying confusion of sexual heterogeneity that can be closed only by the return to the artifice of clothing itself" (Beehler 1982, 91).

Beehler's contention that both sexuality and sanity are by-products of clothing credits Joe Orton with a sophisticated, nonessentializing conception of gender. Dollimore also suggests that the play becomes "an orgy of confused and *refused* gender identities" (Dollimore 1991, 316). Orton's clothing effects depended on the *natural body* for their shock value. If Rance gets taken in by the clothing effect, it is because he is the ultimate dupe, the psychiatrist. Geraldine's insistence that she is a woman in the face of Rance's rejection would not carry either pathos or humor if the audience did not know that Geraldine was biologically a girl. The joke is on both of them, but not on the audience. Orton's farcical play with bodies/clothing remains safe because the audience always knows what gender each person is assigned and is also perfectly familiar with farcical conventions that dictate pseudo sex changes.

Leslie Smith also indicates that the exchange of clothes speaks to a Strindbergian splitting of identities, a loss of the old, coherent, stable identity because of a switch between the subject and object of desire (Smith 1989, 128). A transversal could cause gender trouble, as it does in the case of the *Bacchae,* an Ur text for Orton, where Pentheus dons women's clothes. John Bowen's *The Disorderly Women,* for instance, convinces us that the monarch in drag truly reinscribes gender codes and pays the price for it by his grisly disemboweling. *What the Butler Saw* does not effect such a transversal. Prentice does not wear women's clothes, and neither does Rance. Geraldine, Nick, and the bumbling cop, Match, do change clothes. Prentice is twice accused of transvestism, once when he is holding Geraldine's dress and once when he claims her shoe. Garber advances the intriguing proposition that "The cultural effect of transvestism is to destabilise all [such] binaries: not only "male" and "female," but also "gay" and "straight," and "sex" and "gender." This is the sense—the radical sense—in which transvestism is a "third" (Garber 1992, 133).

Orton does call upon the idea of the "third sex" when Rance brings it up as an improbable fantasy. Of the characters in the text, male characters appear to have that fluidity rather than Geraldine, of whom Rance makes the comment. Prentice's masculinity, already impugned by Mrs. Prentice because of his sexual inadequacies, is further assailed by the charge of transvestism. His attraction to Geraldine also acquires the shades of same-sex contact. In the action of the play, transvestism is viewed as so extremely "other" that Prentice's sanity, his core identity, is threatened, a pointer to the connection between sexual orientation and identity. Sexual preference and identity are perhaps more intimately sewn together in the text than gender and identity.

The mention of transvestism brings on the cry of madness and becomes instrumental in Mrs. Prentice's alliance with Rance. Despite Prentice's seeming loss of control, his dressing Nick in drag takes him out of trouble. The whole deception is arranged to convince Rance that Nick is Geraldine or that he is the missing female secretary. The cross-dressing scheme works on an old theatrical practice, the belief that clothes disguise men and women onstage and give rise to comedy. Orton could possibly be playing with the old fear that a male who is not fully dressed as such is not one; his heterosexual masculine identification is definitely jeopardized. Nick, for instance, openly asks why a male/male relationship is unnatural. If masculinity is clearly only on one side of male/female, then Prentice's, Nick's, and Match's masculinities are under erasure. The old convention, nevertheless, does play with the implicitly subversive momentum of transvestism, which definitely challenges an audience's gender expectations. Further, as Dollimore might say, the maintenance of gender difference after such elaborate gestures towards transgression perhaps indicates the extent of repression. In Joe Orton's case, the journey back would not be to biological gender differences but perhaps their glittering illusion. Interestingly, neither Geraldine nor Nick is charged with transvestism.

Geraldine in men's clothes comes close to threatening Prentice's viability, not necessarily because she gains power in the symbolic as a male, as Shen Teh does in Brecht's *Good Person.* As Nicholas Beckett (Nick), a guise Geraldine has accepted out of sheer naked desperation, she tells Match that Prentice has made advances to her. Match reconsiders Prentice's respectability, but only briefly. Prentice turns the tables on Geraldine by referring to Beckett's exploits with the underage schoolgirls. Geraldine finds herself once again powerless because she cannot claim her identity without her gender and vice versa. Her complete lack of power is tantamount to inability to claim her gender and frames her as mad. The two elements come together to lay siege on her sanity. While it is not in the interests of the comic effects of farce to suggest that she may actually be crazy, Orton comes close to suggesting that the mismatch between gender and identity has created mental trouble. Geraldine has reached a point where she no longer understands when people are speaking of her. Her sense of her identity is at odds with society's. She has had difficulty with references to herself for some time but has idealistically believed that she could reclaim her gender/identity. The assault on her sanity makes her fear for her freedom. Orton's farcical derailment is intimidating at this juncture. The loss of gender affiliation is perceived as the loss of sanity. Gender derailment is mental derailment.

That gender becomes equivalent to a specific identity and the reverse suggests that Orton does not offer plural conceptions of identity or gender. Dramatic confusion of identity cannot signify an epistemic challenge to anatomical gender/essentialized conceptions of gender. Orton, however, does draw our attention to the fact that Prentice is most threatened when he is supposed to have made advances to a male. Since he has not, his authority is recuperated. Paradoxically, Rance, who looks at Prentice askance because of a whiff of transvestism, takes gay sex in his stride. Orton implies that Rance himself may have a gay leaning and thereby suggests that all the men in the text (except for the oblivious Match) are imbricated in a gay episode. Rance wants to "examine" Nick and Match. In the light of Prentice having examined Geraldine, Rance's professionalism seems to be tinged with specific homoerotic motives. Rance's "desires" contrast with his lectures on behavior, further allowing Orton to knock authority, but reveal its desire. Indeed, Orton's edge lies in showing that heterosexual male desire for women is neither natural or inevitable. Even Rance questions "compulsory heterosexuality" twice.

> GERALDINE: I must be a boy. I like girls.
> RANCE: I can't quite follow the reasoning there [*Butler*, 325].

Peculiarly, Geraldine is confessing to a liking of women; a subtlety that once again intrigues without transgressing. Rance also derides Prentice when he intones on his "heterosexuality." Geraldine's lack of clothes invests her with two identities: Geraldine Barclay the secretary and Geraldine Barclay the madwoman. Rance jumps to the conclusion that Geraldine's nakedness is a sign of her madness. In his book, there are only aberrations from propriety, no enjoyment of the body. For him, Geraldine's nakedness spells desire for the father. The father's assault is quickly transformed into a Romantic version of illicit and forbidden passion: "The vehemence of her denials is proof positive of her guilt. It's a text-book case! A man beyond innocence, a girl aching for experience. The beauty, confusion and urgency of their passion driving them on" (*Butler*, 301).

Orton explores Rance's fantasy with the concluding sentences, "The Church, true to Her ancient tradition, counsels chastity. The result—madness" (*Butler*, 301). Later, Rance will beg for a chance to cure Geraldine, a very transparent portrayal of the psychiatrist as fantasy sex doctor. In other words, the woman's "madness" credits him with authority and sexual potency. Orton's spoof of Rance is in keeping with his ideas, which were closer to R. D. Laing's more liberal versions of women's psychic disorders and indeed more advanced in that he does not return to an inner self or a more natural order (Dollimore 1991, 317).

The genre of farce itself has to deny its seriousness in order to be taken seriously. That Joe Orton presented all his inversions as running gags to provoke hysterical laughter is a measure of his understanding of the psychology of farce. Psychoanalyzing farce, Freedman suggests that "a strategic denial and displacement of meaning is intrinsic to the genre and essential to the human acceptance of normally unacceptable aggression which it allows" (Freedman 1980, 234). Yet within this generic mode of making light of, or making to seem absurd, disruptive actions such as breaking the legal, social, and sexual norms—indeed all the characters except Rance seem to do so—Orton does break the generic pattern in one significant way. Unlike other farceurs, he does not punish the transgressors. He may withhold pleasure to the sexual reprobates, but he does not channel the plot toward the archetypical punishment scenario. Instead, he retains the register of fantasy. Charney believes that the concluding tableau celebrates "sexual fulfillment"; if so, it can only be a very ironic feast because many of the celebrants' object choices were incestuous, definitely not the model either for hetero or gay coupling (Charney 1984, 24). Ostensibly liberating, the redrawing of the heterosexual family unit contains the straining of male sexual identities. The very glittery concluding pastiche obviously parodies family resettlement but succeeds in rendering gay sexuality invisible yet again. Perhaps the very implausibility of the reunion signifies the importance of the sexual trouble experienced. Moreover, the generic conclusion does demand this resolution, and while Orton shatters the genre from within, he does not appropriate it completely, nor does he rewrite it.

Smith notices the dark side of the conclusion, which he views as "morally anarchic" (Smith 1989, 135). Sinfield does not find that "incest between consenting adults" would be so shocking in 1969, but I am inclined to object to the phraseology if applied to father/son/daughter or mother/daughter/son incest because "consent" is almost impossible to ascertain when power/authority on the one side and fear on the other constitute the relationship (Sinfield 1992, 180). Bigsby states that the chief image of sexuality in Orton's plays is a "fundamental dissonance" and that incest as norm works as "redemptive volatility" in the later plays (Bigsby 1982, 30–31). That the norm of incest undergirds the order of heterosexuality, where it is *not* perceived as dissonant, becomes the disturbing feature of Orton's world view. Further, that rape is the element that maintains heterosexual desire becomes inimical to this female viewer who watches Geraldine almost raped, hears of Mrs. Prentice raped once by a stranger turned husband and almost raped again by a stranger turned son, and notes that Mrs. Prentice will relive the rape over and over again as a moment of carnal pleasure that arouses desire. Katherine Worth suggests that Orton gives us a great "id-releasing" experience and succeeds in controlling it (Worth 1984, 84). The resolution is so completely clear about *naming unspeakable* incestuous relationships and in *specifying* desire commingled with violence that I find the "return" to reality frightening, especially now that the conventional generic triggers have been pulled and have left rape and incest at the core of the family unit, heterosexual relationships, and same sex desire.

For some (heterosexual and lesbian) female viewers the conclusion brings with it the disquieting equation between the sane world and the heterosexual world, constituted above all by sexual violence. The play enshrines the penile eye. It burns the female eye to open it, but it ultimately blocks female vision.

Conclusion

The imaging of women in the modernist canon appears to be a superimposition: figures discernible under the surface that cannot be brought to light. The female figure is the ground on which the male text is imprinted. The terrain is marked in different ways that shape the lighted surface. When we "look through" to the ground, the female figure becomes visible, but if she is heard, it is only through the male echo.

Male figuration of femininity dramatizes many versions. Familiar tropes through the plays are of the female as mirror image, as spectacle, as body. The physical is symptomatic of the female, the intellectual the male. Above all, despite the tremendous difficulty in attempting to generalize about texts that span a hundred and fifty years, one framework remains intact: the male network of references.

Male desire enacts itself on stage and text regardless of the character on stage. Relayed through women characters, male desire assumes distortions that widen the gaps in the text. In those plays that do acknowledge a different desire, contradictory articulations circumscribe female desire. These plays, Brecht's *The Good Person* and Hare's *Plenty,* are more readily appropriated for feminist ends.

Considering that the possibilities of plural readings of any given text are endless, even granted there are limits, the male canon could have greater possibilities for other female readers/viewers. Feminists of another time period may well see different patterns than the ones I have seen. And even within our own period, feminists in performance would interpret these texts more concretely. Lesbian feminist readings may also be more sensitive to sexual likeness and hence foreground an alternative sexual politics.

My sense is that, in general, modernist plays have more feminist possibilities as productions. Some would, I believe, resist feminist takeoffs, although most would be amenable to some change because of gaps in the text. It would be difficult to imagine a production of *Woyzeck* that did not shackle female sexuality, unless Woyzeck's madness/marginality were eliminated. *The*

Father definitely has more potential, especially if female points of view are foregrounded through uses of the mise-en-scène.

Curiously, the seemingly more metacritical theatre of Pirandello is recalcitrant to a revisionist production because the script on the female is so intricately arranged. One displacement could highlight Henry IV as a regressive child, but it would return us to male fantasies of cannibalizing women. Even more difficult to attach to a feminist platform is the very successful *Marat/ Sade*, perhaps because of its conventional emphasis on that most contaminated of cultural icons, the female body. Perhaps the route that some dramatists and filmmakers have taken of not displaying the female body at all is one way out of the cultural impasse.

Plays in the canon that have "strong female roles," such as Brecht's *The Good Person* or Hare's *Plenty,* would seem to be more hospitable to women actors and viewers. Shen Teh's desire for autonomy and Susan's sexual desire could be evoked quite powerfully. The costuming of Brecht's Shen Teh and her body itself as the site of cultural contradictions have the greatest scope for dramatizing femininity under trial. Backed up by a resoundingly patriarchal crew to play the gods, the parable could illustrate the female breaking many codes. Bisexuality could be insinuated in the performance to lend the character a greater mobility than Yvette, the prostitute in *Mother Courage.* The pregnancy, which has stopped Brecht's feminist readers, could be dramatized in such a manner that cultural contradictions about maternity are highlighted. We could see a Shen Teh mother-to-be, but with the same sexual and social desire. My own qualification of the last would be that the production be registered as utopian, for if Shen Teh were seen to celebrate a pregnancy that was not economically viable, audience response could again be distressed. *Good Person* can accommodate a feminist viewer until the controversial pregnancy.

Plenty could almost be played as a lesbian text, but once again, dragging the text away from its manifest level creates problems. If the performance is not discreet about the male characters, the text could seem to cast a negative light on lesbian relationships. The radical aspects of Susan's wish to be a single mother and its curtailment could be played up. Whether the imperialist motif of the text and Susan's role in imperialism would be critiqued could present a difficulty. The play could be sketched, however, to make a progressive point about how the left wing is fairly conservative about the Third World.

Dürrenmatt's *The Physicists* perhaps expresses the more violent, because more buried, forms of sexism. It could be played in a progressive way only by deconstructing male fantasy. A female observer could be attracted if the whole were pictured through very visible male points of view in terms of stylized self-projections, mirror imagings, and delusions of monster females. The trope of the female as monster just cannot be negotiated in this text.

The Hothouse and *What the Butler Saw* refuse feminist interpolations, primarily because of the extraordinarily stable male reference points and the vagueness of female characterization. In both cases, the ground seems to have receded from the male figure. No doubt *The Hothouse* could be converted to a gay text, but the representation of gays would then be in jeopardy. Similarly, Orton's *What the Butler Saw* can only be depicted as a dizzying sexual romp. Too many elements of the play would have to be truncated to begin to clear the space for a feminist production.

Theatrically, Barnes's *The Ruling Class* could focus on male crossovers in a positive light, but the representation of women makes it impossible to graft the play to feminist notions.

Many of the texts are hostile to the female reader unless she assumes a male viewpoint. Women in the text have very little power. What power the woman has is invariably delineated as a rebellion contained. The most pleasurable texts are the ones where the rebellion erupts through the surface: Brecht's *The Good Person*, Hare's *Plenty* and, ignoring other difficulties, Weiss's *Marat/Sade.*

As there is no universal viewer, so is there, in point of fact, no female viewer, only female viewers. I use the term cautiously to create a space or a positioning for women in texts that do have clearly etched male positionings in terms of identification, power, knowledge, and pleasure.

B. Ruby Rich's promise that the female viewer's rereading empowers her is validated, but not entirely (Rich 1990, 268–88). Mulvey's diagnosis that the female viewer's pleasure in identifying with the female turns masochistic and painful has been borne out sharply by instances in each of the plays (Mulvey 1975, 6–18). Is there a woman in this play? Or is there a play on the woman? In many situations, the female reader has to let go of her gender identification in order to enjoy the pleasure of the text, more specifically, the presentation of the marginal perspective.

For much of the time, the female reader has been suspended. She has oscillated, has shifted. However oblivious to real female presence the texts are, the insistence on regarding male representation of women serves to draw the female reader out of contradictory postures. She can free herself from the male positioning the text enjoins by turning her eye to the female figure.

Weaving out, the female reader squints in order to be able to see the female figure under the male surface. The grounding has remained female, however, because the male subject is constituted strictly in relationship to the female/the female body. And male theatre has been performed through the female image.

Annotated Bibliography

Abicht, Ludo. "Peter Weiss: Exile, Resistance, Aesthetics." In *Exile and Enlightenment: Studies in German and Comparative Literature*, ed. Uwe Faulhaber, Jerry Glenn, Edward P. Harris, and Hans-George Richert. Detroit: Wayne State University Press, 1987. A good general essay on the central significance of progressive aesthetics to progressive politics in Weiss's work, especially *Aesthetics of Resistance.*

Adler, Thomas. "Notes toward the Archetypal Pinter Woman." *Theatre Journal* 33, no. 3(1981): 377–86. Adler comments that Pinter provides the male characters willing to make accommodations to woman in her search for personal fulfillment. Uncritical of Pinter's portrayal.

Almansi, Guido. "Harold Pinter's Idiom of Lies." In *Harold Pinter*, ed. Harold Bloom, 89–105 New York: Chelsea House, 1987. A well-written essay on Pinter's use of dialogue as creating a web of lies. Almansi discusses the innovativeness of Pinter's approach against the backdrop of Western theatre history.

Althusser, Louis. "Ideology and Ideological State Apparatuses (Notes Towards an Investigation)." In *Lenin and Philosophy and Other Essays*, trans. Ben Brewster, 127–89. London: Monthly Review Press, 1971. Enormously influential essay that discusses the interpellation of the subject and the modes by which various organizations reproduce dominant ideology withal securing the consent of the subject. In other words, he shows how the subject willingly participated in the dominant ideology.

Artaud, Antonin. *The Theatre and Its Double*. New York: Grove, 1958. Influential practitioner and theorist of drama. Artaud propounds the idea of a visceral theatre of cruelty.

Attar, Samar. *The Intruder in Modern Drama*. Frankfurt am Main: P. D. Laing, 1981. Attar says *The Good Person of Szechwan* is a parable about how the world needs to be changed.

Barnes, Peter. *The Ruling Class*. New York: Grove, 1969. Contains Hobson's introduction.

Bartram, Graham, and Anthony Waine, eds. *Brecht: A Perspective*. London: Longman, 1982. The editors make the useful point that the West has split Brecht into politician and playwright and tends to elevate the playwright while downgrading the politician.

Beehler, Michael. "Joe Orton and the Heterogeneity of the Book." *Sub/Stance* 33/34, 11, no. 1(1982): 84–98. Beehler uses Orton's defacement of library books to discuss his articulation of the "natural" and "unnatural" book. He suggests that the book is used as a figure for the body. The essay tackles *What the Butler Saw, The Boy Hairdresser, Head to Toe, Funeral Games,* and *Entertaining Mr. Sloane.*

Belsey, Catherine. *Critical Practice*. London: Methuen, 1980. Accessible text on twentieth-century critical practices that favors the ideological, feminist approach.

Bentley, Eric. *The Brecht Commentaries: 1943–1980*. New York: Grove, 1981. Commentary by one of Brecht's most ardent admirers in the Western world. Bentley's thesis is that *The Good Person of Szechwan* is about the impossibility of being good in a rotten world.

_____. "Strindberg, the One and the Many." In *Strindberg: A Collection of Critical Essays*, ed. Otto Reinert, 97–104. Englewood Cliffs: Prentice-Hall, 1971. Interesting essay on Strindberg's techniques.

_____. *Theatre of War: Comments on 32 Occasions*. New York: Viking, 1972. Bentley considers that madness completely imprisons Henry IV in Pirandello's *Henry IV.*

Bersani, Leo. *A Future for Astyanax: Character and Desire in Literature*. Boston: Little, Brown, 1976. Shows the connection between male sexual desire and sexual violence in fiction.

Best, Otto. *Peter Weiss: Vom existentialistischen Drama zum marxistischen Welttheater*. Bern: Francke Verlag, 1971. Best says the two protagonists of *Marat/Sade* are alter egos. He finds that Weiss makes use of illusion in a way that Brecht does not. Useful breakdown of the structure of the play. He sees the play as a high point that announces the changes in the dramatist's work.

Bigsby, C.W.E. *Joe Orton*. London: Methuen, 1982. Bigsby considers Orton a postmodern practitioner of anarchic art. He views Orton's use of sexuality as a subversive weapon and regards Orton as an antiauthoritarian playwright. He looks at Orton's themes throughout the work and stresses the absence of traditional characterization and conventional plotting of farce.

_____. "The Language of Crisis in British Theatre: The Drama of Cultural Pathology." In *Contemporary English Drama*, ed. C.W.E. Bigsby, 12–51. London: Edward Arnold, 1981. Bigsby traces the beginnings of new drama and speculates on the reasons for the relative dearth of women dramatists. This essay also considers whether the 50s drama was truly radical. Finally, Bigsby discusses the relationship of several new dramatists to language, which he finds as important as their relationship to society.

_____. "The Politics of Anxiety: Contemporary Socialist Theatre in England." In *Modern British Dramatists: New Perspectives*, ed. John Russell Brown, 161–76. Englewood Cliffs: Prentice-Hall, 1984. Discusses some of the canonized playwrights since 1950 and debates what "political" has come to mean to playwrights from Osborne to Hare and Edgar.

Binion, Rudolf. "The Play as Replay." In *Soundings: Psychohistorical and Psycholiterary*. New York: Psychohistory Press, 1981. Binion almost diagnoses Pirandello's psychic health. He asserts that *Henry IV* also has shades of the troubled, triangular relationship or "complex" that the dramatist had with wife and daughter. Binion supplies personal references for the characters of the play.

Blonsky, Marshall, ed. *Signs*. Baltimore: Johns Hopkins University Press, 1975. Diverse contributions on the cultural interventions possible through semiotics.

Bloom, Harold. Introduction to *Harold Pinter*, ed. Harold Bloom. New York: Chelsea House, 1987. A comparison with Beckett and a brief comment on Pinter's world view and his Jewishness.

Boal, Augusto. *Theatre of the Oppressed*. New York: Theatre Communication Group, 1985. A masterly critique of the Aristotelean theatre and its basis in purgation. Boal maintains that the voiding is of elements that do not belong with the norm. Accordingly, he finds the system overly manipulative and unwilling to accommodate diverse spectatorial positions. Well worth reading.

Bottomore, Tom, ed. *A Dictionary of Marxist Thought*. Cambridge: Harvard University Press, 1983. Well-researched entries on key concepts by some of the most reputable Marxist scholars.

Breuer, Joseph, and Sigmund Freud. *Studies on Hysteria*. Vol. 2 of *Complete Works of Sigmund*

Freud. London: Hogarth Press, 1955. Reprint. New York: Basic Books, n.d. Case studies of female patients, including the case of Dora. Fascinating reading that allows us to see how Freud theorized, based on case studies.

Brown, John Russell. Introduction to *Modern British Dramatists: New Perspectives*, ed. John Russell Brown. Englewood Cliffs: Prentice-Hall, 1984. A familiar but useful overview of developments in British drama from the 50s through the 80s.

Brustein, Robert Sanford. *The Theatre of Revolt: An Approach to the Modern Drama.* Boston: Little, Brown, 1964. Brustein's influential pronouncements on *The Father* by Strindberg gave the play low priority in the Strindberg canon. Brustein's book remained a standard text on modern drama until well into the mid-eighties.

Bryant-Bertail, Sarah. "Women, Space, Ideology: *Mutter Courage und ihre Kinder.*" *The Brecht Yearbook* 12(1983): 38–61. Bryant-Bertail makes the provocative statement that Brecht's situation as outsider in both capitalist and Stalinist states is clearly revealed in his portrayal of women characters.

Buck, Stratton. "The Uses of Madness." *Tennessee Studies in Literature* 3(1958):63–71. Buck focuses on Balzac's Louis Lambert and touches on schizophrenia and mysticism.

Bucknill, Charles. *The Mad Folk of Shakespeare.* London: Macmillan, 1867. Among the earliest studies of madness in the theatre. A physician, Bucknill attempts to trace the pathology of Shakespearean characters.

Bull, John. "David Hare: The State of the Nation." In *New British Political Dramatists*, 60–94. London: Macmillan, 1984. An insightful essay that uncovers Hare's notion of the political. Bull also explores the historical and its relevance to political theatre.

______, and Frances Gray. "Joe Orton." In *Essays on Contemporary British Drama*, eds. Hedwig Bock and Albert Wertheim, 71–96. Munich: Max Hueber Verlag, 1981. This essay links Joe Orton's life to his work. There are also extended comparisons with the theatre of the absurd. A detailed discussion on characters' use of language and its connections to Joe Orton's world view concludes this analysis.

Butler, Judith. *Gender Trouble.* New York: Routledge, 1990. Theoretically fascinating book on the constitution of gender in non-essentialistic ways. Butler also talks about the relationship between heterosexuality and homosexuality. Performance, as an integral part of gender identities, is central to her thinking.

Cardullo, Bert. "Hare's *Plenty.*" *Explicator* 43, no. 2(1985):62–63. Interesting explication of lighting and music effects of the play.

Carlson, Harry G. *Strindberg and the Poetry of Myth.* Berkeley: University of California Press, 1982. A myth-based approach, the book is pleasurable reading and more amenable to culling feminist readings than other Strindberg criticism.

Sue-Ellen. "Brecht and Women: Homosexuality and the Mother." *The Brecht Yearbook* 12(1983):65–73. Case comments that mothers are crucial to plays that distance themselves from a politicized sexuality and concentrate on desexualized politics.

______. *Feminism and Theatre.* New York: Methuen, 1988. Influential book that serves as a framework for feminists in theatre, whether they work with men's or women's texts. Very well written and also has many insights on the general relationship between feminism and art forms. Sensitive to lesbian issues.

Cave, Richard Allen. *New British Drama in Performance on the London Stage, 1970–1985.* New York: St. Martin's Press, 1988. Essential reading on performances of the plays, with especially useful chapters on the staging of Pinter's and Hare's plays.

Charney, Maurice. *Joe Orton.* London: Macmillan, 1984. Useful book that has a brief sketch of his life and chapters on the plays and novels, with a final summation of the Ortonesque.

_____. "What Did the Butler See in Orton's *What the Butler Saw*?" *Modern Drama* 25, no. 4(1982): 496–504. Charney discusses the assumptions of Orton's farce. He argues that Orton's farces are very different from Plautus's New Comedy. He pays special attention to Orton's discomfiting endings.

Chaudhuri, Una. "The Spectator in Drama/Drama in the Spectator." *Modern Drama* 27, no. 3(1984): 281–98. Poststructuralist approach to drama, text, and spectator.

Cixous, Hélène, and Catherine Clément. *The Newly Born Woman.* Trans. Betsy Wing. Minneapolis: University of Minnesota Press, 1986. Dialogue between the two women on the status of the hysteric in society. Much of the work concerns the difficulty of women coming to speech. Cixous suggests that women write out of their bodies, speak through them. The hysteric is symptomatic of the woman in patriarchy in this respect. Clément disagrees. The whole is written in an evocative and poetic way. Interesting theorizations on the bisexual and her relationship to hysteric and sorceress.

Cohn, Ruby. "*Marat/Sade*: An Education in Theatre." *Educational Theatre Journal* 19, no. 4(1967):478–86. A good general essay on the play. Makes some provocative points about coupling in the play.

_____. *Retreats from Realism in Recent English Drama.* Cambridge: Cambridge University Press, 1991. Overview of antirealist conventions in drama. Cohn also shows the emphasis on the divided psyche in the work of 80s playwrights. She argues that they are interested in the "workings of the unconscious."

Daly, Mary. *Gyn/Ecology: The Metaethics of Radical Feminism.* Boston: Beacon Press, 1978. Radical feminist text from a divinity scholar who looks at religious imagery. Daly also argues for a new women's language. She has been much criticized for her lack of cultural sensitivity. Lesbian framework.

Dean, Joan Fitzpatrick. *David Hare.* Boston: Twayne, 1990. The book deals with Hare's work for theatre, film, and television. Sections discuss themes, background, characters. Dean says *Plenty* is a composite of characteristic Hare themes.

Deleuze, Gilles, and Felix Guattari. *Anti-Oedipus: Capitalism and Schizophrenia.* Trans. by Robert Hurley, Mark Seem, and Helen R. Lane. Minneapolis: University of Minnesota Press, 1983. Classic analysis of the relationship between desire, the body, and schizophrenia. Comes up with "schizo-analysis." Widely perceived as having some accurate responses to Lacanian themes.

Derrida, Jacques. "Cogito and the History of Madness." In *Writing and Difference*, trans. by Alan Bass. Chicago: University of Chicago Press, 1978. Derrida suggests that the sane cannot speak from the site of insanity, for they inflect the language of the mad with their own speech patterns, which are ultimately coherent. Derrida finds that Foucault's project fails to articulate the language of the mad but succeeds in rendering the poetics of the mad viewed from the vantage point of the sane.

Diamond, Elin. "Parody Play in Pinter." In *Harold Pinter*, ed. Harold Bloom. New York: Chelsea House, 1987. Diamond shows how Pinter's professional training in theatre may have influenced his ironic treatment of certain dramatic devices.

Dolan, Jill. *The Feminist Spectator as Critic.* Ann Arbor: U.M.I. Press, 1988. Clearly written text on the feminist viewer's role in male- and female-authored American drama. Useful for drama students interested in audience studies.

Dollimore, Jonathan. "The Challenge of Sexuality." In *Society and Literature: 1945–1970*, ed. Alan Sinfield, 51–85. New York: Holmes and Meier, 1983. A crucial essay that covers a lot of ground on public and private discourses on sexuality. It also discusses literary and critical texts that were important to understanding changing perceptions of sexuality.

_____. "Orton's Black Camp." In *Sexual Dissidence: Augustine to Wilde, Freud to Foucault,* 315–18. Oxford: Clarendon Press, 1991. Dollimore suggests that Orton challenges the norms through the use of stylized postmodern parody. Exciting book on gay strategies.

Dörner, Klaus. *Madmen and the Bourgeoisie.* Trans. by Joachim Neugroschel and Jean Steinberg. Oxford: Basil Blackwell, 1981. Dörner describes and documents the historical construction of madness in Western Europe.

Dosenheimer, Elise. *Das deutsche Soziale Drama von Lessing bis Sternheim.* Konstanz: Südverlag, 1949. Dosenheimer examines the economic situation that confronts Büchner's Woyzeck. She suggests that the inevitability of his financial situation lends the text an aura of tragedy comparable to a Greek tragedy.

Drandt, Manfred. "Comic, Tragic or Absurd? On Some Parallels between the Farces of Joe Orton and Seventeenth Century Tragedy." *English Studies* 59, no. 3(1978): 202–17. Exhaustive comparisons between Orton's plays and several Jacobean plays that stress similarities of incident, especially in *Loot* and *The Revenger's Tragedy.*

Dukore, Bernard. *The Theatre of Peter Barnes.* London: Heinemann, 1981. Full-length study of the playwright's work.

_____. "'Violent Families': *A Whistle in the Dark* and *The Homecoming.*" *Twentieth Century Literature* 36, no. 1(1990): 23–35.A comparison of *The Homecoming* with Tom Murphy's play, the essay is perceptive about the possibilities for violence in Pinter's family structures. Although he does not explicitly state it, Dukore describes the simmering sexual violence just beneath the surface of *The Homecoming.*

Dunne, Kerry. "Woyzeck's Marie 'Ein schlecht Mensch'? The Construction of Female Sexuality in Büchner's *Woyzeck.*" *Seminar: A Journal of Germanic Studies* 26, no. 4(1990): 294–309.

Eagleton, Terry. "Brecht and Rhetoric." *New Literary History* 16, no. 3(1985): 633–37. Discusses the importance of alienated acting, the fascination of both simultaneous presence and absence.

Elam, Keir. *The Semiotics of Theatre and Drama.* London: Methuen, 1980. Essential reading for students of theatre interested in semiotics. Provides a good introduction to the field.

Elsom, John. *Post-War British Theatre.* Boston: Routledge and Kegan Paul, 1976. Useful survey.

Eskelund, Jakob. "Wahnsinn in Georg Büchners Werken: Fatalismus oder gesellschaftliche Determination." *Augias* 6(1982):27–51. Eskelund discusses Büchner's responses to Johann Christian Woyzeck's trial. He finds that the dramatist's sympathies lay with the murderer in that, though he considered Woyzeck guilty, he believed that there were extenuating circumstances.

Esslin, Martin. "Joe Orton: The Comedy of (Ill) Manners." In *Contemporary English Drama,* ed. C.W.E. Bigsby, 95–107. London: Edward Arnold, 1984. Although Esslin finds Orton's work "symptomatic and significant," he believes Orton lacks the moral vision necessary for great satirists. He compares Orton with Pinter.

_____. *The Peopled Wound: The Work of Harold Pinter.* Garden City, N.Y.: Doubleday, 1970. The book has a useful chronology of Pinter's early work, a background chapter studded with relevant quotations from Pinter's own thoughts on theatre, analyses of the major works, and a chapter that interprets linguistic tropes and silences in Pinter's plays.

_____. *The Theatre of the Absurd.* Garden City, N.Y.: Doubleday, 1961. Classic text propounding the elements of the absurd. Since then the "absurd" has become one of the basic descriptors of the drama of Beckett, Ionesco, etc.

Ewen, Frederick. *Bertolt Brecht: His Life, His Art, and His Times.* New York: Citadel, 1969. Ewen sees the dualism of good and evil in Shen Teh. Also considers that according to Brecht, goodness is natural, evil unnatural.

Farocki, Harun. "Gespräch mit Peter Weiss." In *Peter Weiss*, ed. Rainer Gerlach. Frankfurt am Main: Suhrkamp, 1984. Weiss talks mainly about his career in film but also about his surrealistic and psychoanalytic phases.

Feder, Lilian. *Madness and Literature*. Princeton: Princeton University Press, 1980. Feder is interested in the revelations of the mind and in tracing the development of civilization. She describes the study of madness as the study of the mind itself. Her approach is primarily Freudian. She analyzes drama as Dionysian frenzy and emphasizes the mental processes involved in the formation of myths. Feder interprets madness and irrationality in both the *Bacchae* and *Ajax* as the sign of struggle within the consciousness of a people to transcend the bestial and attain the civilized. She also discusses the difference between ancient and Rennaissance views of madness. A well-written book that balances itself persuasively between literary and psychoanalytic study.

Fickert, Kurt J. "The Curtain Speech in Dürrenmatt's *The Physicists*." *Modern Drama* 13, no. 1(1970):40–46. Fickert argues that the conclusion of this play is in keeping with the playwright's pattern of the hero returning to a sense of the ineluctable.

_____. *To Heaven and Back: The New Morality of the Plays of Friedrich Dürrenmatt*. Lexington: University of Kentucky Press, 1972. Fickert outlines Dürrenmatt's indebtedness to theories of relativity and the playwright's moral conception in his plays.

Foucault, Michel. *Madness and Civilization: A History of Insanity in the Age of Reason*. Trans. by Richard Howard. New York: Vintage Books, 1973. Foucault attempts to "speak the mad" without speaking for them. The book traces a genealogy of madness. Foucault contends that the creation of the institution in 1657 signaled a radical bifurcation of the sane from the insane. Madness was experienced in an undifferentiated fashion before the Hôpital Générale made it possible for the administration to sequester, observe, and supervise the insane. The sane now control and inspect the mad and view the mad as the Other, the non-self, who paradoxically guarantees or reassures the self of its own sanity. Classic text on the construction of the Other.

_____. "The History of Sexuality." In *Power/Knowledge: Selected Interviews and Other Writings 1972–77*. Trans. Colin Gordon, Leo Marshall et al., 183–94. New York: Pantheon, 1980. Interview with Lucette Finas. Makes accessible some of Foucault's more intricate ideas on sexuality and madness.

_____. *The History of Sexuality*, vol. 1. Trans. by Robert Hurley. New York: Pantheon, 1978. The introduction to Foucault's massive project on sexuality in the Western world. Establishes some general parameters.

_____, ed. *I, Pierre Rivière*. Trans. by Frank Jellinek. New York: Pantheon, 1975. A case book of readings on Rivière's notes. Helpful in understanding Foucault's idea of discourse.

_____. "Panopticism." In *Discipline and Punish: The Birth of the Prison*. Trans. Alan Sheridan, 195–231. New York: Random House, 1979. Influential chapter on surveillance and the gaze as forms of coercion and punishment.

Freedman, Barbara. "Errors in Comedy: A Psychoanalytic Theory of Farce." In *Shakespearean Comedy*, ed. Maurice Charney. New York: New York Literary Forum, 1980. Absolutely fascinating article on New Comedy and Shakespeare's *The Comedy of Errors*. Theorizes on the psychological investments of characters in farces.

Freud, Sigmund. "Three Essays on the Theory of Sexuality." In *The Freud Reader*, ed. Peter Gay, 239–93. New York: Norton, 1989. Essential reading for those who are interested in psychoanalytic versions of sexuality, normal or otherwise.

Fuegi, John. "The Alienated Woman: Brecht's *The Good Person of Szechwan*." In *Essays on Brecht: Theatre and Politics*, eds. Mews, Siegfried, and Herbert Knust. Chapel Hill: University of North Carolina Press, 1974. Fuegi speaks about the development of the protagonist as a person. He also makes the important point that Shen Teh has to be covered if the town is to be uncovered.

_____. *The Essential Brecht.* Los Angeles: Hennessey and Ingalls, 1972. Fuegi argues that *The Good Person of Szechwan* is not epic because the scenes develop. He reads it as an Aristotelean play and speaks of us drawing toward Shen Teh in sympathy and away in fear.

_____ et al., eds. *Brecht: Women and Politics.* Special edition of *The Brecht Yearbook* 12(1983). Important compilation of feminist essays on various aspects of Brecht's work.

Gaggi, Silvio. "Brecht, Pirandello and Two Traditions of Self-Critical Art." *Theatre Quarterly* 7, no. 32(1979):42–47. Gaggi sets Brecht and Pirandello up as opposites. Emphasizes Brecht's concern with process as well as with content and uses Brecht's self-referentiality to prove his points.

Gale, Stephen. *Butter's Going Up: A Critical Analysis of Harold Pinter's Work.* Durham: Duke University Press, 1977. A study of Pinter's thematic and technical development. Follows a chronological outline. Has a good chapter on language.

Gale, Steven H. "Sex and Politics in David Hare's *Plenty.*" In *Drama, Sex and Politics*, ed. James Redmond, 213–20. Cambridge: Cambridge University Press, 1985. Gale makes the argument that Hare links the loss of empire to loss of morality and leadership in postwar Britain.

Gallop, Jane. *The Daughter's Seduction: Feminism and Psychoanalysis.* Ithaca: Cornell University Press, 1982. Rhetorical and deconstructive detailed readings of feminist psychoanalysts, including Luce Irigaray, and their complex relationship to the Ur-texts of Lacan.

Garber, Marjorie. "Breaking the Code: Transvestism and Gay Identity." In *Vested Interests: Cross-Dressing and Cultural Anxiety*, 128–65. New York: Routledge, Chapman and Hall, 1992. Garber works through the modes by which transvestism is definitely of "another" gender that cannot be subsumed by "male" or "female."

Gilbert, Sandra, and Susan Gubar. *The Madwoman in the Attic.* New Haven: Yale University Press, 1979. Influential feminist critical text on the female artist and the lack of a female tradition. Discusses the divided nature of the female artist in patriarchy by invoking the figure of Bertha in Charlotte Brontë's *Jane Eyre.*

Gillen, Francis. "Nowhere to Go: Society and the Individual in Harold Pinter's *The Hothouse.*" *Twentieth Century Literature* 29, no. 1(1983):86–96. Gillen argues that the play is about the cost society extracts from the individual.

Gilman, Sander. *Difference and Pathology.* Ithaca: Cornell University Press, 1985. Gilman exemplifies the pathologization of different groups such as Jews and blacks. These groups become projections of what the dominant group fears. Finally, they are cast in the light of the abnormal.

Gordon, Giles. "Joe Orton." *Transatlantic Review* 24(1967):93–100. Interview with Orton, who talks abut his views on theatre, playwrights he admires, his life. He spends some time on his prison episode and his defacement of library books.

Gould, Thomas. "The Uses of Violence in Drama." In *Violence in Drama*, ed. James Redmond. Cambridge: Cambridge University Press, 1991. The author differentiates among kinds of violence exhibited throughout the history of drama and concentrates on tragedy and melodrama.

Gray, Ronald. *Brecht, the Dramatist.* Cambridge: Cambridge University Press, 1976. Gray views *The Good Person of Szechwan* as a parable. He also suggests that Wang is demanding less idealistic, more practical standards. He reiterates the theme that goodness is difficult in an evil world.

Hare, David. *The Asian Plays.* London: Faber and Faber, 1986. Part of Faber's project to collect Hare's works and group them as Asian plays, history plays, etc. Contains *Saigon, Year of the Cat* on Vietnam, *Fanshen* on China, and *A Map of the World,* set in Bombay. Hare tries to deal with Eurocentrism in these plays.

Hartigan, Karelisa. "Herakles in a Technological World: An Ancient Myth Transformed." *Classical and Modern Literature* 5, no. 1(1984):33–38. Hartigan discusses the hero as "monster killer" and Dürrenmatt's focus on how the power of knowledge is used.

Hauser, Ronald. *Georg Büchner.* New York: Twayne, 1974. Hauser bases his argument on Büchner's frequently pessimistic letters. He contends that the play is about the universal human being's encounter with a cruel and blind destiny. Hauser insists that Büchner's advice was to allow nature to set one free.

Hayman, Ronald. *British Theatre Since 1955: A Reassessment.* Oxford: Oxford University Press, 1979. Hayman finds *Plenty* is Hare's best effort but faults it for not being clear about its focus. He discusses other playwrights roughly of the same generation and political bent.

______. *Bertolt Brecht: The Plays.* Totowa, N.J.: Barnes and Noble, 1984. Hayman claims that Brecht wanted to show that human beings need to take the initiative.

Hayse, Joseph. *Madness on Stage: The History of a Tradition in Drama.* Ph.D. diss., University of Wisconsin, 1976. Hayse traces the convention of madness in drama and proves that later modern representations draw from an established tradition. An exhaustive typology of mad characters on stage.

Hesson, Lizabeth. "Revolution, Art and Politics: Peter Weiss." *Neohelicon* 14, no. 2(1987): 275–85. Hesson argues that the dramatist's exile made him identify with the underprivileged. Profile of Weiss as the Wandering Jew.

Hilton, Ian. *Peter Weiss: A Search for Affinities.* London: Oswald Wolff, 1970. A useful introduction to the life and work. Emphasizes the hybridity of *Marat/Sade.*

Hinchcliffe, Arnold P. "A Progress Report." In *Harold Pinter: Critical Approaches,* ed. Steven H. Gale, 153–63. Rutherford, N.J.: Fairleigh Dickinson, 1986. A discussion of Pinter's plays after *The Betrayal.* Debates the proposition that Pinter's style changed with this play.

Hinderer, Walter. "Deutsches Theater der Französischen Revolution." *The German Quarterly* 64, no. 2(1991):207–19. Using Büchner's *Danton's Death* as a point of departure, Hinderer examines several plays from different epochs on the topic. He considers Weiss's play different because of its "phantasmagoric" quality. He believes that the historical contradictions of the past and present are evoked by the play.

Holland, Peter. "Brecht Bond Gaskill and the Practice of Political Theater." *Theatre Quarterly* 7, no. 30(1978):24–36. Holland discusses the split in England between Brecht as an exemplar of stagecraft and Brecht as a political dramatist. He states that Brecht's emphasis on theatrical practice rather than on what he was saying was seen when the Berliner ensemble went to Britain in 1956.

Horn, Gisela, and Haike Wirrmann. "Der Weibliche Widerstand." In *Wissenschaftliche Zeitschrift der Friedrich Schiller (Jena)* 36 Heft 3(1987):383–88. Weiss's *Die Ästhetik des Widerstands* proffers criticism of socialist power structures from a feminist angle and envisions a new kind of relationship between the sexes.

Hornby, Richard. "Performance Patterns in *Woyzeck.*" *Literature in Performance* 42(1984): 46–54. Hornby recounts the difficulties in staging an "unfinished script."

Innes, Christopher. *Modern British Drama: 1890–1990.* Cambridge: Cambridge University Press, 1992. The book is comprehensive and covers British drama from a historical and social perspective from Pinero and Shaw. Innes sees Orton's work as privileging anarchy. He studies all of Orton's oeuvre from the standpoint of Orton's critique of society. Innes is also excellent on Hare's political interventions and provides a theatrical and social context for his work.

______. *Modern German Drama: A Study in Form.* Cambridge: Cambridge University Press, 1979. Absolutely indispensable to the student of theatrical ideas and forms of the work of canonical twentieth-century dramatists, including Grass, Brecht, Frisch, Dürrenmatt, Weiss, Handke.

Irigaray, Luce. *Speculum of the Other Woman.* Trans. Gillian C. Gill. Ithaca: Cornell University Press, 1985. Irigaray's rereading of metaphysics, including Freud and Plato. Argues that no theory of representation has ever represented the woman. Says that the male sees the female as a mirror image. Also argues for a women's language. Influential feminist theorist, who has become even more attractive to feminists after critics showed that she was not essentialist.

______. *This Sex Which Is Not One.* Trans. Catherine Porter with Carolyn Burke. Ithaca: Cornell University Press, 1985b. Series of essays, including an illuminating and accessible interview. Has the controversial "When our lips speak together." Irigaray writes of lesbian sexuality in a poetic way. She systematically rebuts previous psychoanalysts on female sexuality. Very original on female sexuality, motherhood, and female subjectivity. There is a sharp political and feminist edge to her work.

Johnson, Walter. *August Strindberg.* Boston: Twayne, 1976. Johnson considers *The Father* an unambiguous tale of a woman who drives a man mad.

Karnick, Manfred. *Rollenspiel und Welttheater.* München: Fink, 1980. A solid overview of some "world" texts, especially German. Mentions that economics and society work with the inflexibility of natural law.

Keller, Oskar. *Friedrich Dürrenmatt: Die Physiker.* Munich: R. Oldenbourg Verlag, 1970. Consists of detailed portraits of the characters' Weltanschauung and brief comparisons with *Galileo* and *In der Sache J. Robert Oppenheimer.*

Keyssar, Helene. *Feminist Theatre.* New York: Grove, 1985. On women's theatre from the 60s. Keyssar discusses Shange, Churchill, Wandor, Gems, to name a few.

Kissel, Howard. "*Plenty.*" *New York Theatre Critics Review*, 1983. Positively glowing tribute to Kate Nelligan's performance as Susan Traherne.

Knopf, Jan. *Brecht's Gute Mensch von Sezuan.* Frankfurt am Main: Suhrkamp, 1982. Knopf sees the play as a thinly veiled Chinese work. Also has compilations of theatre reviews. Useful for reception history. Interesting information on the first production of the play from Ginsburg, Ott, and Diebold. The Swiss Communists did not like it; Carl Seelig found the Doppelleben interesting; Ott thinks the moral is that God helps those who help themselves.

Knowles, Ronald. "*The Hothouse* and the Epiphany of Harold Pinter." *Journal of Beckett Studies* 10(1985):134–44. Knowles shows how the play consists of revue sketches and how they were the basis of Pinter's art.

Kowsar, Mohammed. "Analytics of Schizophrenia. A Deleuze Guattarian Consideration of Büchner's *Danton's Death* and Weiss's *Marat/Sade. Modern Drama* 27, no. 3 (1984): 361–82. Minute display of these themes in the text.

Krause, Egon. *Woyzeck: Texte und Dokumente.* Frankfurt am Main: Insel, 1969. Useful information on the material surrounding the text. H1, H2, H3, H4—the different versions of the text—are compiled.

Kuhn, Annette. *Women's Pictures: Feminism and Cinema.* London: Routledge and Kegan Paul, 1982. Primarily of interest to students of film, the book theorizes the position of the female viewer, discusses Hollywood and alternative cinema. Excellent book, of interest to feminists, especially poststructuralist feminists.

Kvam, Kela. "Strindberg and the Roles of the Sexes." In *Strindberg on Stage: Report from the Symposium in Stockholm May 18–22, 1981*, ed. Donald K. Weaver. Stockholm: Swedish Centre of the ITI, 1983. Biographical approach. Kvam believes that *The Father* is a "regression" on the playwright's part and indicates that the dramatist underwent difficulties defining his sexual identity because of the new women's liberation movements. Kvam correctly sees the play as figuring the conflict between patriarchy and matriarchy. Kvam is also sympathetic to Laura's subversions and compares them to the strategies of a slave.

Lacan, Jacques. "The Mirror Stage as Formative of the Function of the I as Revealed in Psychoanalytic Experience." In *Ecrits: A Selection,* trans. Alan Sheridan, 1–7. London: Tavistock, 1977. Influential and much cited essay on the constitution of subjectivity. Disputed by feminists, notably Mary Ann Doane in her brilliant clarification that Lacan talks only about the *boy* child. See Doane, "Women's Stake: Filming the Female Body." *October* 17 (Summer 1981): 22–36.

Laing, R. D. *The Divided Self.* Harmondsworth: Penguin, 1965. Very popular in the 60s. Case studies of women who are disturbed. Lends itself to progressive use. Laing tries to avoid normative labeling.

Lennox, Sara. "Women in Brecht's Work." *New German Critique* 14 (Spring 1978): 83–89. Essay that deals with Brecht's relationship with the Communist party and his changing representation of women according to their ideology.

Levenson, Jill. "Dramatists at (Meta) Play: Shakespeare's *Hamlet,* II, ii and Pirandello's *Henry IV.*" *Modern Drama* 24, no. 3(1981):330–37. In Pirandello's world, play acting and reality are blurred.

Lloyd Evans, Gareth, and Barbara Lloyd Evans, eds. *Plays in Review 1956–1980.* New York: Methuen, 1985. Useful excerpts of reviews on various productions. Important for reception history.

Löb, Ladislaus. "Peter Weiss's *Marat/Sade*: A Portrait of the Artist in Bourgeois Society." *Modern Language Review* 76, no. 2(1981):383–96. Löb argues that the play is about the difficulty of pursuing art in a bourgeois society. Biographical sketch of Weiss as an artist.

Ludlow, Colin. "Hare and Others." *London Magazine,* July 1978, 76–78. Ludlow believes that the English lack of affect is the main theme of *Plenty.*

Lukács, Georg. *Deutsche Realisten des 19.Jahrhunderts.* Berne: A. Francke AG Verlag, 1951. The socialist critic takes issue with the critical insistence on the importance of psychology. He criticizes Büchner for not emphasizing the dramatist's revolutionary works.

Madsen, Borge. *Strindberg's Naturalistic Theatre.* Copenhagen: Munksgard, 1962. Madsen focuses on the naturalistic period. He says that *The Father* appears to follow a bold and simple line of action.

Mairs, Nancy. *Plaintext.* Tucson: University of Arizona Press, 1986. Autobiographical essays on the woman's role in society. Reflections on women's relationship to madness and space. Lyrically and thoughtfully written.

Malkin, Jeanette. "Gagged by Language: Verbal Domination and Subjugation." In *Verbal Violence in Contemporary Drama from Handke to Shepard,* 38–102. Cambridge: Cambridge University Press, 1992. Malkin argues the specific significance of language as an actor, an able communicator of violence; she traces the violence as the movement from speech to speechlessness.

Matthaei, Renate. *Luigi Pirandello.* New York: Frederick Ungar, 1973. Matthaei discusses the playwright in the context of his times. She views the chief character as a victim of society and implies that the unnamed is a portrayal of the tendencies that fascism unleashes.

Matthews, Jill. *Good and Mad Women: The Historical Construction of Femininity in Twentieth Century Australia.* Sydney: Allen and Unwin, 1984. Matthews is explicit about the connections between the failure to be the good woman and resulting madness. She is post–Laingian in that she theorizes that female expectation, especially of sexuality, drives the women "crazy." She also claims that there is a "gender order" that creates ideas of good men and good women. She assumes that it is impossible to be feminine and that mad women are only extreme in that perpetual continuum of failure. A fascinating book.

Meier, Albert. *Georg Büchner: Woyzeck.* München: Wilhelm Fink Verlag, 1980. Very useful book on the background. Meier makes a lot of references to contemporary cases and has an interesting interpretation of Woyzeck's isolation.

Merritt, Susan Hollis. "Pinter and Politics." In *Harold Pinter: A Casebook*, ed. Lois Gordon, 129–61. New York: Garland, 1990. A critical survey of major critical positions on Pinter's politics and his own changing relationship to political drama.

Morgan, Margery. *August Strindberg.* Houndmills: Macmillan, 1985. Morgan sees the death of Adolf in *The Father* as the demise of male domination. She considers the play a demystification of marriage and also studies its mythic dimensions.

Morley, Michael. *Brecht: A Study.* Totowa, N.J.: Rowman and Littlefield, 1977. Morley views *The Good Person* as expressing the battle between love of self and the social.

______. "Dürrenmatt's Dialogue with Brecht: A Thematic Analysis of *Die Physiker.*" *Modern Drama* 14, no. 2(1971):232–42. A generally sympathetic reading of the play that sees its resemblances to *Galileo.*

Mulvey, Laura. "Visual Pleasure and Narrative Cinema." *Screen* 16, no. 3(1975):6–18. The essay dominated film studies for a decade. It is now influential in certain brands of feminist drama criticism.

Murdoch, Brian. "Dürrenmatt's *Physicists* and the Tragic Tradition." *Modern Drama* 13, no. 3(1970):270–75. Murdoch takes the elements of the tragic and assesses the text against them.

Nightingale, Benedict. "Harold Pinter/Politics." In *Around the Absurd: Essays on Modern and Postmodern Drama*, ed. Enoch Brater and Ruby Cohn, 129–55. Ann Arbor: University of Michigan Press, 1990. Nightingale queries the connections between Pinter's overtly political later plays and his earlier plays. A glimpse into Pinter's political concerns.

O'Brien-Moore, Ainsworth. *Madness in Ancient Literature.* Weimar: Wagner und Sohn, 1924. O'Brien-Moore focuses on the way in which Greek and Roman drama reflects dominant ideas on madness that the society of the time may hold. He argues that representations of madness in literature of high seriousness corresponded to popular conceptions of madness, but that as poets became mere epigones, the depiction of madness became virtually a literary convention.

Oliva, Judy Lee. *Theatricalizing Politics.* Ann Arbor: UMI, 1990. A chronological look at Hare's work, film, radio plays, and theatre, organized according to Hare's overall thematic focus for that time period. Useful information on theatre reviews.

Oliver, Roger. *Dreams of Passion: The Theatre of Luigi Pirandello.* New York: New York University Press, 1979. Oliver believes that the unnamed in *Henry IV* chose madness.

Oliver, William. "*Marat/Sade* in Santiago." *Educational Theatre Journal* 19, no. 4(1967): 486–502. Oliver talks about the differences between Brook's production and his own. Interesting insights into Roux and the Herald in *Marat/Sade.*

Orton, Joe. *The Orton Diaries.* Ed. John Lahr. New York: Harper and Row, 1986. Indispensable work that records Orton's running progress on the drafts of the plays, his life with Halliwell, and his attitudes toward gay identity.

Otten, Terry. "Woyzeck and Othello: The Dimensions of Melodrama." *Comparative Drama* 12, no. 2(1978):123–37. Otten suggests that both Othello and Woyzeck were frustrated outsiders who allowed their irrational instincts to overpower their rational faculties.

Paolucci, Anne. *Pirandello's Theatre: The Recovery of the Modern Stage for Dramatic Art*. Carbondale: Southern Illinois University Press, 1974. Paolucci assumes that Henry IV of *Henry IV* is a creative mask or persona for Pirandello. Her ideas on Pirandello's masks became widely accepted in Pirandello criticism.

Parker, Andrew, Mary Russo et al. *Nationalisms and Sexualities*. New York: Routledge, 1992. Essays on the relationship between the construction of the national and sexual identities in a variety of international texts. Provocative interventions with reference to gay and lesbian sexuality. Some attention to film, three essays on drama.

Patterson, Michael. "A 'Laingian' Reading of Pirandello's Henry IV." *Modern Drama* 27, no. 4(1984):637–45. Patterson concentrates on psychoanalyzing the character on stage and diagnosing his problem.

Paulson, Arvid, ed. *The Father*. In *The Strindberg Reader*, 437–49. New York: Phaedra, 1968. Very useful for the history of the reception of the various productions of the play.

Poore, Carol. "Mother Earth, Melancholia, and Mnemosyne: Women in Peter Weiss's *Die Asthetik des Widerstands*." *The German Quarterly* 58, no. 1(1984):68–87. Poore claims that Weiss was becoming increasingly interested in incorporating feminism in his work and that he was not content with just critiquing patriarchal socialism, but also came up with a utopian alternative.

Proser, Matthew. "Madness, Revenge and the Metaphor of the Theatre in Shakespeare's Hamlet and Pirandello's Henry IV." *Modern Drama* 24, no. 3(1981):338–53. Proser compares the metatheatrical dimension of the plays and their self-reflexivity. He classifies both plays as revenge tragedies. Would be interesting to look at revenge tragedies from a feminist perspective.

Quigley, Austin. E. *The Pinter Problem*. Princeton: Princeton University Press, 1975. Quigley traces the patterns of Pinter criticism and comments on the blockages that have arisen because of the psychologically and linguistically opaque elements of Pinter's work.

Rabey, David Ian. "Earning a Place in the Story: David Hare, David Edgar." In *British and Irish Political Drama in the Twentieth Century: Implicating the Audience*, 166–87. Houndmills: Macmillan, 1986. Rabey discusses the strategies the playwrights use to place human beings within historical contexts.

Rabillard, Sheila. "Destabilising Plot, Displacing the Status of Narrative: Local Order in the Plays of Pinter and Shepard." *Theatre Journal* 43(1991):41–58. A theoretical essay on how Pinter's *Old Times* and Shepard's *A Lie of the Mind* may sidestep traditional plot structures and replace them by a number of other minute patterns.

Ragusa, Olga. *Luigi Pirandello: An Approach to His Theatre*. Edinburgh: Edinburgh University Press, 1980. Ragusa views Pirandello's characters as masks or personae for the dramatist.

Reed, Robert. *Bedlam on the Jacobean Stage*. Cambridge: Harvard University Press, 1952. Reed sees madness as a dramatic convention whose popularity lies in its spectacular visual and theatrical qualities. He maintains that the Jacobean conception of madness corresponded to the dark world vision of Jacobeans, who were shaken by the political, social, and intellectual revolutions of the day.

Reno, Robert P. "Science and Prophets in Dürrenmatt's *The Physicists*." *Renascence: Essays on Values in Literature* 37, no. 2(1985):70–79. Reno argues that religion and silence are both bodies of knowledge that have to be shared. He insists that Dürrenmatt's play decries Möbius's intellectual arrogance.

Rich, B. Ruby. "In the Name of Feminist Film Criticism." In *Issues in Feminist Film Criticism*, ed. Patricia Erens, 268–88. Bloomington: Indiana University Press, 1990. Primarily of use to film students. The essay does show how mainstream film is inimical to women.

Richards, David. *Georg Büchner and the Birth of Modern Drama.* Albany: State University of New York Press, 1977. Transhistorical and universalizing approach to Büchner's work.

Rigney, Barbara. *Madness and Sexual Politics in the Feminist Novel.* Madison: University of Wisconsin Press, 1978. Portrait of the female artist as divided. Studies the trope in twentieth century women's novels, including Virginia Woolf.

Ritter, Alexander. *Erläuterungen und Dokumente Friedrich Dürrenmatt Die Physiker.* Stuttgart: Phillip Reclam GMBH, 1991. Ritter includes the journalistic reception, scientific contextualization, and comparison with plays of the same genre. Useful nucleus of information on science/ethics/drama.

Robbins, Leonard. "Madness in Modern Drama." Ph.D. Diss., State University of New York at Binghamton, 1984. Robbins investigates the mad subject's relationship with the world in terms of moral and psychological criteria. He insists that the mad subject is not really wiser than the rest of the world; he is complicit with the folly of the world. His interpretations revolve around the connections between the role-playing of madman and the role-playing of the actor.

Rogoff, Gordon. "To a Hare." In *Theatre Is Not Safe,* 235–37. Evanston: Northwestern Universty Press, 1987. Positive 1983 review of Hare's *Plenty.* Rogoff suggests that the play is about hypocrisy.

Rosen, Carol. *Plays of Impasse.* Princeton: Princeton University Press, 1983. Rosen claims that the contemporary theatre's images of madness are presented in a manner without precedent in the history of drama. Her study locates the central importance of the institution. Using sociologist Irving Goffman's theory on the dehumanization of the subject in the institution, she proposes that these plays show the self controlled by a stricturing mise-en-scène and depict the world as a total institution. Impasse underpins the dramatic movement. Among these works are plays by Weiss, Dürrenmatt and Storey set in insane asylums.

Rosenthal, Erwin. "Aspekte der dramatischen Struktur der beiden Tragödien Büchner." *German Quarterly* 3(1965):273–85. Rosenthal discusses Büchner's rejection of the closed form of drama. He pays attention to the innovativeness of Büchner's scene breaks.

Sakellaridou, Elizabeth. *Pinter's Female Portraits: A Study of the Female Characters in the Plays of Harold Pinter.* Totowa: Barnes and Noble, 1988. An exhaustive full-length study, unique in Pinter criticism, of the development of Pinter's representation of women from the archetypical to the androgynous.

Schechner, Richard, ed. "The *Marat/Sade* Forum." Peter Brook, Leslie Fiedler, et al. *Tulane Drama Review* 10, no. 4(1966):214–39. Stimulating discussion of the play's revolutionary potential and its impact on viewers. Conveys the sense of excitement that theatre people felt about the play.

Schlunk, Jürgen. "Auschwitz and Its Function in Peter Weiss' Search for Identity." *German Studies Review* 10, no. 1(1987):11–30. Schlunk goes through the life and work and shows that Weiss's journey was based on the search for identity. He attributes the need to Weiss's Jewishness and homelessness.

Schmidt, Henry. *Satire, Caricature and Perspectivism in the Works of Georg Büchner.* The Hague: Mouton, 1970. Schmidt discusses the use of the grotesque in Büchner's work and the impact such a technique has on the world of the play and the characters in the play.

Schoeps, Karl. *Bertolt Brecht.* New York: F. Ungar, 1977. Schoeps suggests that Brecht believed that humanity would be essentially good in a socialist society and believes that this is the predominant theme of *The Good Person of Szechwan.*

Schroll, Herman T. *Harold Pinter: A Study of His Reputation (1958–1969) and a Checklist.* Metuchen, N.J.: Scarecrow, 1971. Valuable information on production reviews of Pinter's work.

Schwarz, Alfred. *From Büchner to Beckett.* Athens: Ohio University Press, 1978. Schwarz discusses Büchner's world view as nihilistic.

Scull, Andrew, ed. *Madhouses, Mad Doctors, and Madmen.* Philadelphia: University of Pennsylvania Press, 1981.

Shenk, Robert. *The Sinner's Progress: A Study of Madness in English Renaissance Drama.* Salzburg: Institut für Englische Sprache & Literatur., Univ. of Salzburg, 1978. Shenk brings intellectual history to bear on his analyses of madness in the Renaissance theatre. He argues that the moral philosophers of the Scholastic tradition—Aristotle, Aquinas, Hooker—influenced the dramatists' rendition of madness. Sin was considered the cause of insanity, but no simple one-to-one correspondence between sin and insanity as punishment is posited. The scholastic discourse definitively images the insane as the Other, the sinner who degenerates into less than a human being.

Showalter, Elaine. *The Female Malady.* New York: Pantheon, 1986. As much about the innovations of Victorian psychiatric theory and practice as it is about the history of madness and asylums in England between 1830 and 1960. Showalter's concern is also to argue for a greater number of women in the mental health profession to protect the rights of women. She suggests that madness is an extreme form of withdrawal for the woman who finds that there was no consonance between her aspirations and society's expectations of her. Sexuality is a key factor in her analysis. Since women were mothers par excellence and were denied a body for sexual pleasure, this added to their distress. Women who were more voluble were also put into asylums.

Siemers, Paul William. "The Fear of Intimacy: Sexual Alienation, Metaphysical Insecurity in *Plenty.*" In "Theatre of Constraint: Culture and Sexuality in Select Plays of David Hare, Snoo Wilson and Stephen Poliakoff." Ph.D. Diss., University of Minnesota, 1992. Siemers focuses on Susan's need for heterosexual intimacy.

Sinfield, Alan. "The Theatre and Its Audience." In *Society and Literature,* ed. Alan Sinfield, 174–95. New York: Holmes and Meier, 1983. Sinfield covers post–World War II drama from John Osborne and Terrence Rattigan. The essay contains an interesting debate on the relationship between financing and theatre. Sinfield asks if the left-wing dramatist influences the theatre companies or if large companies absorb progressive ideologies.

_____. "Who Was Afraid of Joe Orton?" In *Sexual Sameness: Textual Differences in Lesbian and Gay Writing,* ed. Joseph Bristow, 170–86. London: Routledge, Chapman, and Hill, 1992. A thought-provoking essay on Orton's relationship to his time. Sinfield suggests that his achievements were possible because of the 60s. He is convincing on Orton's fairly conservative attitude to gay issues in his plays. Enlightening on Orton's theatre audiences.

Smith, Iris. "Brecht and the Mothers of Epic Theatre." *Theatre Journal* 43(1991):491–505. Fascinating article on how "gestus" can be adapted to feminist ends and how Brecht can be appropriated by diverse contemporary groups.

Smith, Leslie. "Modern British Farce." In *A Selective Study of British Farce from Pinero to the Present Day,* 120–38. Houndmills: Macmillan, 1989. Smith brings out the dionysiac elements of Orton's farce without neglecting the darker undercurrents.

Sokel, Walter. "Brecht's Split Characters and His Sense of the Tragic." In *Brecht: A Collection of Critical Essays,* ed. Peter Demetz. Englewood Cliffs, Prentice-Hall, 1962. Sokel suggests that the theme of the split personality articulates Brecht's own uncertainty about whether reason or instinct prevails or should prevail.

Somerville, Henry. *Madness in Shakespearian Tragedy.* 1929. Reprint. London: Richards, 1976. A psychiatrist, Somerville emphasizes the deep disorders of the tragic characters. He contends that madness rather than death is the catastrophe in Shakespearian tragedy. According to Somerville, Othello is a paranoic, Hamlet gay, Lady Macbeth is megalomaniacal, etc. Somerville does bring madness from margin to center.

Sontag, Susan. "Marat/Sade/Artaud." In *Against Interpretation and Other Essays*. New York: Farrar, Straus and Giroux, 1966. Sontag takes issue with the reasons for the critical dislike for the play and writes a spirited and convincing defense of the Weiss text and his conception of theatre.

Stamm, Rudolf. "*The Hothouse*: Harold Pinter's Tribute to Anger." *English Studies: A Journal of English Language and Literature* 62, no. 3(1981):290–98. A sympathetic reading of the play which concentrates on the way in which power corrupts and perpetuates itself.

Stern, J. P. *Reinterpretations*. New York: Basic Books, 1964. Stern interprets *Woyzeck* in naturalistic terms.

Strunk, Volker. "Taking Care of August Strindberg." In *Harold Pinter: Towards a Poetics of His Plays*. New York: Lang, 1989. Strunk shows Strindberg's influence on *The Caretaker* but more interestingly suggests that their techniques of using references imply a "mad dramaturgy."

Strützel, Dieter. "Georg Lukács und Peter Weiss. Ideologie und Erfahrungbei der Entstehung proletarischer Kultur-Thesen." *Wissenschaftliche Zeitschrift der Friedrich Schiller Univ (Jena)* 36, Heft 3(1987):383–88. Strützel defines the different modes by which Lukács and Weiss deal with the problematics of developing socialist art through theatrical text.

Suvin, Darko. "Weiss's *Marat/Sade* and Its Three Main Performance Versions." *Modern Drama* 31, no. 3(1988):395–420. Suvin uses allegorical and ideological indices to evaluate the performances. He differentiates between parabolic theatre and illusionistic theatre and the way in which the two use metatheatrical devices. Suvin situates the performances historically and ideologically. Theoretically interesting essay on the limits of the theatrical text.

Swaffar, Janet. "The Ethics of Exploitation: Brecht's Der *Gute Mensch* von Szechwan." *University of Dayton Review* 13, no. 3(1979):65–69. Swaffer insists that Shen Teh is conscious of her alter ego. Her basic thesis is that Shen Teh is being critiqued for her goodness.

Szasz, Thomas. *The Myth of Mental Illness*. New York: Harper and Row, 1974. Szasz's work is still pervasive as an explanatory model of society's treatment of the mad; he emphazises the role of the institution.

Szondi, Peter. *Theorie des modernen Dramas*. Frankfurt am Main: Suhrkamp, 1963. Szondi theorizes on the structure of the modern play as non–Aristotelean and "open."

Taylor, John Russell. "Art and Commerce: The New Drama in the West End Marketplace." In *Contemporary English Drama*, C.W.E.Bigsby, associate editor, 177–89. London: Edward Arnold, 1981. Taylor compares the commercially successful playwrights' techniques to the strategies of the new dramatists during the time of the New Drama. He also differentiates between the styles of the New Dramatists and their predecessors.

_____. *The Second Wave: British Drama for the 70s*. New York: Hill and Wang, 1971. Standard text on the 70s by a highly influential critic. A sympathetic reading of Orton's linguistic use which creates humor. Taylor traces Orton's developments through his work but finds *What the Butler Saw* wanting because of the absence of the "straight guy" who makes farce as a genre work.

Ueding, Gert. *"Der gute Mensch von Sezuan."* In *Brechts Dramen: Neue Interpretationen*, ed. Walter Hinderer. Stuttgart: Reclam, 1984. Ueding finds that *The Good Person of Szechwan* is composed of heterogeneous elements. He compares it with *Faust* and also runs a long discussion on the gods and the epilogue. Interesting suggestion that the gods embody the false consciousness of Wang and Shen Teh, their awareness of their economic and social conditions.

Walcot, Peter. "An Acquired Taste: Joe Orton and the Greeks." In *Legacy of Thespis: Drama Past and Present,* vol. 4, ed. Karelisa Hartigan, 99–123. Comparative Drama Conference Papers. Lanham, Md.: University Press of America, 1984. Walcot discusses how Orton's relationship with Halliwell could be "Greek." He also studies Orton's borrowings from the Greeks and his knowledge of them.

Wandor, Micheline. *Look Back in Gender: Sexuality and the Family in Post-war British Drama.* London: Methuen, 1987. Important historical look at gender relationships in postwar British plays, including the works of Pinter, Orton, Hare, Osborne, etc. Schematic conclusions on causes drawn in a chart at the end.

Weimar, Karl. "The Scientist and Society: A Study of Three Modern Plays." *Modern Language Quarterly* (Dec. 1966):431–48. A discussion of Brecht's *Galileo,* Zuckmayer's *Das kalte Licht,* Dürrenmatt's *Die Physiker.* Weimar shows the difference in each dramatist's approach.

Wetzel, Heinz. "Weibliches, Männliches, Menschliches in den Dramen Georg Büchners." *Zeitschrift für Deutsche Philologie* 3, no. 2(1992):232–46. A survey of the relationship between the sexes in Büchner's oeuvre. Wetzel sees Marie of *Woyzeck* as the most completely realized woman character in Büchner's work.

Whitton, Kenneth. *Dürrenmatt: Reinterpretation in Retrospect.* New York: Oswald Wolff, 1990. A book of considerable scope that divides the artist's work along generic lines. Excellent for an idea of the range of Dürrenmatt's projects. Useful for both novice and specialist. Fine annotated bibliography.

Williams, Raymond. "Social Environment and Theatrical Environment: The Case of English Naturalism." In *Problems in Materialism and Culture.* London: Verso, 1980.

______. "Strindberg and Modern Tragedy." In *Essays on Strindberg,* ed. Carl Smedmark. Stockholm: Strindberg Society, 1966. Naturalistic approach to Strindberg's work.

Wilson, Edwin. "Nelligan's Debut." *New York Theatre Critics Review* (1982):399. Wilson comments on Nelligan's impact.

Woods, Terry. "Starless and Black: Alienation in Gay Literature." In *Lesbian and Gay Writing,* ed. Mark Lully. Philadelphia: Temple University Press, 1990. Considers John Rechy, Andrew Holleran, Joe Orton, and Hart Crane and discusses gay "alienated desire" in each of them.

Worth, Katherine. "Form and Style in the Plays of Joe Orton." In *Modern British Dramatists (New Perspectives),* ed. John Russell Brown. Englewood Cliffs, N.J.: Prentice-Hall, 1984. Worth considers the relationship between what she regards as Orton's Victorian rhetoric and the more scandalizing elements of his farce. Also has a detailed comparison with Oscar Wilde.

Wright, Elizabeth. *Post-Modern Brecht: A Re-Presentation.* London: Routledge, 1989. A post-modern/materialist reading that concentrates on the more "unfinished" texts.

Zapf, Hubert. "Two Concepts of Society in Drama: Bertolt Brecht's *The Good Woman of Szechwan* and Edward Bond's *Lear.*" *Modern Drama* 31, no. 3(1988):352–65. Zapf suggests that Brecht's concept is materially grounded, Bond's super-real.

Index